FINDING YOUR FORCE

A Journey to Love

Sussy~
amor~ thwiar
you lights of love
as you continue
your journey
towards finding
your force ~ indeis
love
Alicia Anabel

Alicia Anabel Santos

Published by Alicia Anabel Santos

This edition was edited by Aurora Anaya-Cerda.

Library of Congress Cataloging-in-Publication Data
ISBN: 978-0-9837943-0-1
Library of Congress Control Number: 2011911418

Author: Alicia Anabel Santos
Email: Findingyourforce@gmail.com

Printed and distributed by CreateSpace

Courtniana, the reason I was born~
You're the reason I can fly~

Where there's the truth
You know I'll be there
Amongst the lies
You know I'll be there
I'll go anywhere
So I'll see you there
If you should fall
You know I'll be there
To catch the call
You know I'll be there
I'll go anywhere
So I'll see you there
I'll be there for you
~ Green Day

WHAT READERS ARE SAYING~

"I have so much respect for your spirit, strength and sincerity. Many people aren't able to survive the kind of trauma that you are writing about."

"You really put your all into your writing, I feel you. I really do when you write, which is like speaking. You inspire and I'm not just saying that. You inspire me and I'm sure others to BE, to be them, to be the person they need to be, you inspire them to have no excuses, you inspire them to get where they need to be by bringing them to where you are. And once we see you doing and acting in your moments how could I/one/we not do us?"

"The manner in which you release and share your soul is both raw and pure. A vulnerability we all wish we had."

"I am so proud of you for standing up for your words, for realizing your worth, over and over again. I'm happy that you show your humanness and allow your readers to see where you hurt and to see you revive and gain strength again. People respond because you initiate -dialogue, thoughts, and words! You also show what you won't tolerate, the non-negotiable. Part of that involves the space that no one is allowed to enter unless you give him or her access, which shows you are still in control. How do you stay strong? By staying true to all that you are now and all that you are growing to become!"

POPROCKS AND COKE~

As your birthday approaches I can't think of a better gift to give you than all of my love! As I sit on a train, heading home from Plattsburgh, NY. I'm thinking about how we love train rides, "Road trip!" We've gone from Florida to Virginia, from Providence to NYC, and from New York to Washington. I am looking at a picture of you on my computer staring at the intensity and strength behind your beautiful brown eyes. There's a story that I see. There's a story that is about to unfold. Who you're becoming and who you already are. I'm sitting here looking at everything that we've been through.

You are my most sacred blessing. You are my greatest gift and accomplishment. I sit here and think to myself, "WOW!!! Did I have something to do with that? Did I play a part in the person she is today?" When I look into your eyes I see my own reflection. I never could have imagined or dreamed of a better life. It's just you and me baby.

Sunday morning, September 16, 2007, I woke up from lying next to you. I kissed you as you slept peacefully and you just smiled. I rose to do my morning practice and meditated on the word, "Gratitude." Then I started to think about death and started writing: *When you take me lord this how I would like to be remembered*: I want to be remembered for how deeply I loved everyone. How my words touched maybe even hurt the ones I loved, but how deeply I love them. I want to be remembered for how I loved loving so many people so quickly. May the love I have shared with those met in this lifetime last them the rest of their days. But to the ONE I love most a love letter~

Dear Courtney: When I leave you know that I am still here. I am the wind, the rain, the snow, the hurricane, the tornado, and the sun. Especially remember me and see me in the sun. Think of me as your most beautiful sunset. As much as I'd like to promise you that I will be here forever. I cannot! I am with you for THIS lifetime and it has been amazing. Every single moment with you has been a gift. Life with you has been magical. Everyday that I get to be with you is like unwrapping a new experience. You bring me joy. You are a song. You have been my life. I am so honored to know you. Courtniana, thank you for choosing me as your mother I have learned so much from you.

Finding Your Force is my journey towards self-love and healing. It's a journey into the deepest parts of my soul. This is a journey towards understanding me for the first time. Here is where I pull off the Band-Aids and really look at my wounds. My wish is that you look at the scars that remain and understand why I no longer blame the world for my injuries. That's what I want to do with this memoir. It's time to clear the air and share my story with you. I want to not only prevent you from repeating my mistakes but also leave you with something that would serve as a roadmap into my soul. I want you to always have something to connect to me. Something that would keep me alive and remind you of how much I love you. I am so amazed by you. You are my best friend. Courtney, I had no idea what our life was going to be like. I had no idea how you would turn out. You have been my partner, my life and my world. You have given me so many gifts so this is my gift to you… the story of us. Happy Birthday~

I affirm: My intention is to allow all that needs to be revealed to come out… to not question my thoughts… to release the anxiety and tension in my chest. My intention is to surrender to my process. What will happen if I surrender… my story will be authentic, the lies will be erased, the self-doubt will turn to confidence, the truth will bring clarity (which is what I want most). What will happen is that I will learn some new things about me. YOU will

learn many things about me and I will learn about ALL that I am made of. I will learn from my past, especially from the people in my life who have used words to paralyze me. What I want most is to allow it all to unfold. My intention is to look at where I have been with fresh eyes and see myself differently. Looking at all I've been through and have new direction. With fresh eyes I no longer have to live in the past. As I move forward I am confident, a little scared, but confidant that I will complete the task at hand. I am excited about the possibilities of my potential to arrive and have all I desire and all that I deserve. I release fear. I release self-sabotage. I release toxic people. I release insecurities. I release other people's shit. Today will bring me one step closer to having everything I have ever desired. I am so grateful for all the people in my life who love me. I am grateful for this gift of writing. I am grateful for the love that surrounds me. I am ready to get this day started. Creator, thank you for your guidance, love and strength. I am ready to do this! And so it is.

So I'm home in our beautiful one bedroom apartment in Harlem. I was supposed to write you this love letter here in our house surrounded by everything we love. Staring at our paintings, red, orange and yellow walls, with music playing, photos that hang on every wall in a space that is filled with so much LOVE. I was supposed to write it here in our sacred space.

Today when I woke up to get ready to start my day I froze. I put on a movie and sat back down. I was fully dressed in my dressy black slacks, pretty black shoes, white button down blouse and favorite necklace. I was slowly putting on my hoop earrings, my rings and bracelets that are like my armor. My pen in hand serving as my sword but I am frozen. I am frozen in this moment. I was about to leave for work to do a job I really don't care about when I started thinking about all I've been through in my life. I know that right now isn't the time to really go there and write about all of it. But I am being called to GO THERE, to relive a moment, to really look at where I've been. How did I get to where I am today?

So much of my journey has already been documented in my blogs. But this time it feels different. I am not being called to write the same shit over and over again. I am being called to look at it with fresh perspective, new eyes and self-awareness. It's real easy for me to go back and read where I came from. It's harder to go back and relive it, open the wounds again, feel it all again, allow it to bleed again, revealing a different truth and this is what frightens me. The truth can be ugly!

It took me about a week to read all of my blog posts, over 1,068 pages and 66 journals of my writing over the past ten years. Who am I? What have I learned? What do I keep getting wrong? Who have I become in these 40 years? I'm thinking about my memoir and how people have told me that, *forty is way too young to write a memoir why would people read my story... I'm not famous;* none of that matters I understand that I have a beautiful story to share, a lifetime of stories.

I wanted to get to the source of what I've been feeling. I wrote this morning that I feel like I'm missing something like I'm searching for something. Is it meaning? Is it my purpose? Is it love? Is it money? Is it a sense of self? I was thinking this morning of the person I once was. I was thinking about the light that would just pour out of me. The light that complete strangers told me was like an aura around me when I walked into a room. The person I was then when I wasn't searching for anything yet *IT* found me. *IT* became LIFE through me. *IT* was in everything that I was doing, how I was dressing, how I was feeling. *IT* was all light, all through me and around me... all the time. Everything I read and wrote about was LOVE. I was light. I was weightless. There was nothing that the material world could give me that I didn't give myself. There wasn't a person that could give me all that I was getting in that moment. Rewind... there was nothing that the creator wasn't giving me. There was a time I just allowed God to live in me for God to work through me. And I was bathing in all of my blessings.

Everyday I would stop. I would see the messages in everyone and everything. I found messages in every song, every book and every ad. I would stop and listen to everyone. I would stop and write them all down. I was absorbing it, feeding off of it and sharing it. These teachings became my blogs. My blog became the responses to all of my most intimate thoughts. It became the place where I got all the answers for all the questions I was asking. It was a way to communicate my feelings and connect with people who were going through similar things. I was looking for *IT*. I was searching for *IT*. I was looking for the FORCE! The source where all the answers could be found and so I titled my blog FINDING YOUR FORCE~

That's what this journey has been for me all along, a journey towards Finding My Force. Force to me is just another word for inner strength. Force is my voice. Force is my spirit. Force is the place I go to for my self-confidence. Force is everything that I've been searching for and is still the place I turn to for what I need. To access my force I must be still, get quiet and really listen to what I've been called to do.

It's not about finishing things in the shortest amount of time. It's never been about getting there first. It's not about competition. It's not about ego. It was about *FINDING MY FORCE* and all that that means to me. There is no one who could give me what I need. I understand that all that I need — I already have and that *IT* lives inside of me. It's ok that I am not completely there yet. It's fine that I don't have it all together all the time. I'm good with not having everything that I desire right now. I am still searching for *IT* and know *IT* will find me. *IT* is my FORCE and for that I am incredibly grateful.

This is a new chapter in my life. I'm alone. Blank pages. Afraid the ink will run out maybe hoping it will so that I don't have to explore. I am the archeologist in my life and am being called to an expedition, my excavation into the great big dig. I am examining the ruins of my life and I'm sifting through my remains.

I affirm: This is a story of LOVE~ It's about loving where I came from with all the scrapes, all the bruises, all the pain, but in the end how love heals everything. And as long as I continue to breathe I know that LOVE got me. Love is my GOD. People pray to a God outside of them. I pray to the God that is my heart. Love is my spirit. Love is my guide. Love is my companion. Love is always at my side. Love is all I need. So today my intention is to be LOVE in everything that I do and say. And so it is~

When you were two years old I started seeing therapists. I went for a total of 14 years on and off. During one of my last therapy sessions my doctor asked, "Alicia, what are you afraid will happen? What is your biggest fear about moving forward? What holds you back? What keeps you from achieving success and having what you want?" She asked me to imagine myself standing in front of a door with my hand on the doorknob.

"Alicia, close your eyes. You're in a room. Can you describe it? Are there windows? Go to the door in the room and open it. I want you to walk through the door and tell me what's on the other side."

I started crying uncontrollably, "The room is white. There's a window. I see grass. The sun is out. It's beautiful. There's a beautiful garden. But I don't want to open the door!"

"What keeps you from opening that door Alicia? What do you think will be on the other side?"

I was petrified when I imagined that moment. My immediate response was, "NO ONE! My biggest fear is that NO ONE will be on the other side. That the people I love the most in the world would not be there and I would be all alone."

Writing this memoir for you did not come easy for me. There were so many fears that came up; fear of failure, fear that our family will disown me, this idea that I have no right to tell my story if it includes other people. Fear that the people closest to me will stop loving me. *Is my responsibility to write the TRUTH or filter it to suit others? Should I check in with society and my community?* I feel like I'd never get any writing done that way. The writers I know have shared with me that when they stop to consider how their writing will affect *their* family the fear alone is precisely what keeps them from coming to the page. What has paralyzed me is the fear that if I air the dirty laundry I will lose people along the way.

Then I turned to you. I remember calling you up at Syracuse and having a conversation with you about this book. "Courtney, you know that I'm about to write on some really dark shit. I'm really going deep. I'm writing about you in this book and I'm using your real name." It was important for me to get for your permission and blessing to write this story.

Your response was, "Mom, I love you. I trust you with my life. Write the story. Don't worry about what anyone else thinks."

So here we are about to journey together and look at our life through my eyes. We are about to explore my truth. I'm not afraid to speak, face or write the truth. I must remember who I am and why I do what I do and the place that I'm writing from. If people know me at all they will know that my writing comes from LOVE. I should never have to defend or sugarcoat it. What I must understand is that I have no control over how my words will be received. The only thing I have control over is what I put out into the world with my words and

deeds. And as long as I am good with it and YOU'RE good with it...
then *we're* good!

Fear is what had me frozen. It's scary to sit still and look closely at
my ruins, at all the chaos I've endured, how I've adapted, been
burned, have burned myself, been pillaged and then found a way to
build myself back up again. I'm sitting in the ruins, observing all the
beauty in it and continuing on this road to transformation. The room is
white and I'm looking out of the window, hand on the knob. I'm turning and walking out.

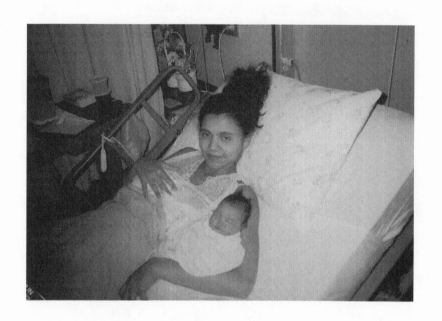

PART I ~ BIRTH

"You find out that you are not what you believe you are, because you never chose your beliefs. These beliefs were there when you were born. You find out that you are also not the body, because you start to function without your body. You start to notice that you are not the dream, that you are not the mind. If you go deeper, you start noticing that you are not the soul either. Then what you find out is so incredible. You find out that what you are is a force - a force that makes it possible for your body to live, a force that makes it possible for your whole mind to dream. Without you, without this force, your body would collapse on the floor. Without you, your whole dream just dissolves into nothing. What you really are is that force that is Life. The whole universe is a living being that is moved by that force, and that is what you are. You are Life. "

Quote from Don Miguel Ruiz's, Mastery of Love~

CHAPTER ONE ~ *Day of the Dead*

The first time I celebrated *Dia de los Muertos* (Day of the Dead) was when I was invited to *la Chicana's* house for *pan de muerto* and Mexican hot chocolate. Families gather to remember loved ones who have passed. This tradition dates back to the Aztecs. For *Dia de los Muertos,* a special alter is built and it is believed that the dead returns. When a child dies what is left for them might be their favorite toy or candy. When an adult dies they are offered tequila or cigarettes — whatever their favorite thing was. During this day we pray for the dead and it is believed that the family member will visit and hear our prayers — which is why we leave offerings.

La Chicana leaves paint for Frida Kahlo at her altar. Her altar was adorned beautifully, with candles, marigold flowers, *pan de muerto,* water, photos and anything that the deceased loved one might enjoy. There is artwork of skulls and skull candy left on the altar. Those who don't understand the tradition of *Dia de los Muertos* might consider it morbid. Day of the Dead is a beautiful way to remember ancestors and loved ones who have transitioned.

At Day of Dead parades peoples faces are painted with skull masks, which symbolizes the cycle of *death* and *rebirth*. Death can be difficult to deal with. Mexicans view *death* as a continuation of life and

1

embrace it. You and I aren't Mexican but this tradition feels like life to me. Over my lifetime I have worn many masks and have experienced *life, death,* and *rebirth* on many levels. When we wear masks our identity is hidden. Everyone around us believed that we were OK but the truth is I was dead. *Dia de los Muertos* was life for me everyday and I was walking around the world with a painted skull mask. Today we celebrate *Dia de los Muertos* and the birth of *Cielo.*

Cielo is little girl with dark eyes and no smile. She was my best friend. We met at daycare in Brooklyn, in 1976. She had beautiful brown hair that felt like silk. Her skin was the color of caramel. The first day we met she sat in front me speechless. I could tell she really wanted to play. But she's never played. *Cielo* had been in prison since the day she left the womb. Her eyes told me she was sad, that she was lonely, that something was missing, that someone had taken something very special from her.

No one talked to *Cielo.* No one looked at *Cielo.* No one saw *Cielo.* No one asked *Cielo* what her dreams were. No one ever told *Cielo* that she was special. No one ever told *Cielo* that she was beautiful. I wanted to tell her. So I kept visiting her. That's when she told me her secrets in silence.

One day, her eyes smiled at me when I said, "*Cielo,* I love you! If no one has ever told you allow me to be the first. Know that you are loved. *Cielo* you are magnificent. *Cielo* you can be anything you want be. *Cielo* I love playing with you. *Cielo* you are my best friend. *Cielo* your eyes are kind. *Cielo* you are special. *Cielo* you are beautiful. *Cielo* you were born for greatness. *Cielo* you are love and you are loved.

A tear fell down her face. "*Cielo* what did I do? What is it? Are you hurt? I can see the pain you carry. Don't cry *Cielo*."

"*Cielo*, what's that on your lap? What's in the box?"

She carried a beautiful black box decorated with gold and yellow flowers; hundred of butterflies all around it and it had a big lock on the front of it. She did not let go of that box and held onto it tight. She would not let me see it. She was protecting it. *Cielo* was afraid that if *he* found out what she carries in that box he would take it from her. I wondered if it was lonely for her walking in the world alone. A girl should never walk alone when she's only in the 4th grade and can't speak. A lot can happen to a little girl who walks alone in the world. Stripped of her core, her personality hidden, forced to be who she's not.

For adults riding the trains in New York City can be frustrating. There are so many things we must be alert to. Our eyes must be open to all that is happening around us. There are predators, homeless people, thieves, performers, poets, actors and singers. Everyone is looking for ways to make money. Then there are the children. I pay close attention the children who ride the train. This day I noticed this beautiful little girl. Her face was round, her eyes the color of onyx and beautiful long braids. She must have been 4 years old. She was just swinging around the pole smiling and laughing. She seemed happy. The D train was her playground and it didn't matter who was looking. Nothing could spoil her fun or take away her happiness.

As she played I couldn't help but think about all the kids I see daily and I often wonder if they're happy. I always wonder how children are able to hold onto their innocence.

On another occasion there was a little baby in a stroller who was with angry parents. As they were arguing and yelling at each other, the baby looked at me, I just smiled and she smiled back and in *that* moment I knew that nothing else mattered but the two of us smiling back and forth while the grown ups were pissed off at each other.

Other moments I'm recalling, are of the little boy who was walking with his father who one minute was happy and then got slapped in the face for speaking in a tone that his dad didn't like. Then there was a three-year-old boy walking with his mother, being yelled at in Spanish. As they approached a restaurant she said to him, *"abre esa puerta! Silve pa algo!* (Open that door! be worth something!)

All I kept thinking about was that little boy. *What will he grow up to believe about himself? Will he think that he's special? Will he know that he's gifted? Will he believe that he can be anything he wants to be? Where will he find his sense of worth when the people closest to him are stripping him of that?* These moments make me think of my own childhood. I envy happy children but it's the children who are NOT happy that remind me most of me.

If I had to pick one thing is this lifetime to fight for, its violence against women and children. On the train I couldn't help but think of all the little girls in the world who aren't happy, who don't know love and who don't know their worth. I often think about young boys and girls who don't know that they are beautiful and they don't know this because there aren't enough people around them who tell them so.

There is not a day I don't think about abuse towards children. It's not just these vicious attacks toward children that upset me. It's where the abuse actually begins that torments me. That comes from their homes. It's the parents, adults, and authority figures that I'm angry with. I kept recalling moments in my own life where children would be playing having a good time and an adult enters the room frustrated, annoyed, pissed off at life, angry at the cards that are dealt them and then they turn and bring that poison home to take it out on the kids.

I am guilty of this. I may never have put my hands on you but I know that you have been the target of a lot of my aggression, unhappiness and frustration. You've been on the receiving end of a lot of my pain. My broken childhood and my history of abuse have never had anything to do with you. I've had moments when I've hated the world, hated people, hated bosses and come home and punished you when you were never to blame. *Do you understand what that was about?* I was so fucking weak. I was so powerless. I felt so small. I was nothing. So like a jerk I looked to hurt someone who had less power than me (or so I thought) and for that I am sorry. I had no right. I knew better. What is it about being in that role of authority that gives people the right to hurt another human being, to put there hands on a child? I'm not just talking about physical abuse and sexual abuse. I include verbal, mental and emotional abuse. I include words that destroy children stripping them of their innocence. All those cases I hear about, every time I hear about a child who has been beaten, killed, drowned, burned, neglected, insulted, abandoned or punished in any way. It always felt like I was reliving my childhood.

For a long time *Cielo* felt like she was fighting for her life. Whatever it was she had been carrying was kept safe in that box. She wouldn't let anyone near it. It had been bottled up for such a long time. *Cielo* believed she had escaped the abuse. She was beaten, torn down and was filled with so much anger.

"*Cielo*, if it hurts so much why don't you leave?"

"I can't leave him. I want to do better. I want him to love me. I wanted him to be proud of me. But I am angry. There are days when I hate him. The anger consumes me and in many ways takes over me. It's not just him. I'm angry at the way people speak to me and how they address me. The beatings were terrible but it's the words that hurt me more."

CHAPTER TWO ~ *Summer 1991, Rhode Island*

I remember the first time your *abuela* and I found out. We went to see this bruja in Providence. The room was dark, candles were lit everywhere. *San Miguel* hanging on the wall, images of unfamiliar saints were on the floor, and an older woman entered wearing a red and yellow robe. Her hair was wrapped and covered with a silk scarf. She was pulling on a cigar in one hand and a glass of rum in the other. There were two chairs in front of her table. Squinting her right eye she looked at me and said, *"tu sabes quien soy yo? Di si o no si me entiendes?"* She crossed her arms in front of her body to shake my hand, spit in her cup and asked me if I knew who she was. She asked your *abuela* and I to take a seat. Just as I was getting ready to sit she said, "Felicidades! Congratulations!"

I was like, "For what?"

"Estas embarazada!!! You're pregnant!"

Abuela just looked at me and said, *"QUE… como fue?"*

7

FINDING YOUR FORCE

August 1991

We had only been dating three months. I was twenty years old and dating a guy who was so very different from the guys I was used to kicking it with back in the day when I would go dancing at Conquistador, Primera Clase, or International night clubs. Three of the IT spots in Providence back in the 80's and 90's. This guy was different.

I was warned by *abuela* about dating Latin men. "*No te case con un Dominicano.*" I was surrounded by the comments, "*Latin men are abusive, they're womanizers, don't marry a Dominican man they like to possess their women.*" Although my first love and most of my first boyfriends were Latino, I decided to date outside of *la raza*.

He didn't seem threatening, he wasn't a womanizer, he wouldn't dare put his hands on me, he would respect me, he was in college, and he was *civilized*.

Our courtship was beautiful. He wrote me love letters, we went for long walks and he took me to see the sunset. He was brilliant and had so much to say on various subjects. He took me on long drives and was attentive and kind. He pushed me on swings and we went on picnics. He even made me cassettes with the music he liked. Your father introduced me to The Doors and we almost named you James Douglas in honor of Jim Morrison. We spoke for hours. Our beginnings were wonderful. He was my best friend.

When I told him what the *bruja* said he didn't believe it.

"C'mon Lee, be serious! How can a *bruja* know you're pregnant? What is she some kind of doctor?" he said laughingly.

Then he looked at me and said, "We should buy a pregnancy test just in case."

8

It was about 97 degrees that day. I was wearing a pretty spring dress with flowers. We were at your grandmother's house. No one was home, thank God! I opened the box carefully, read the instructions, looked at your dad and said, "OK, here we go!"

I sat on the toilet holding the stick in my hand thinking to myself, *what if its true? What if I'm pregnant?*

I peed on the stick and we waited the required three minutes. When the time was up I walked into the bathroom, picked up the stick and saw the pink plus sign.

"What? What is it?" his voice was trembling.

"I'm pregnant!"

"What are we gonna do?"

"What are *we* gonna do? What *AM I* gonna do?

Court, I was terrified. I considered having an abortion. Ever since I was a little girl I never wanted to have a child. I never wanted to be a mother. I vowed that I would never bring a baby into this world. I always talked about how much I hated kids. Just the idea of being a mom scared the hell out of me.

Once *abuela* found out I was pregnant (thanks to that fucking *bruja* and her big mouth) suddenly, the catholic in her resurrected. Nervously she said, *"tu papa nos va matar!!!"*

Abuela was so scared that *abuelo* would kill us both.

"Mami, I don't know if I want to keep the baby. I'm thinking about having an abortion. I'm not ready to be a mother."

Abuela freaked out, *"mi hija, no hagas eso, te puede hacer mucho dano. Es un pecado.* You can't do that to yourself. Having an abortion is a sin and very dangerous. If you do that it will stay with you forever."

She was scaring the shit out of me. There was that and my own fears saying to myself, *God, I don't want to fuck up this child the way I was fucked up.* I didn't know what to do. I was terrified of bringing you into a world that was so fucking horrible. There was violence, pedophiles, pornography, evil people, war, racism, discrimination and hate. I didn't know what to do.

After praying on it for a few days I decided to keep you. I went forward with my pregnancy. Your father and I got married when I was two months pregnant with you.

You came to me in my dreams. I read and sang to you everyday. The idea of motherhood started to grow on me. While I was working at Hope High School you would kick me as I typed letting me know that you liked being around me.

I made a decision right then and there that if I was going to go through with *this* I would be ALL in.

I made you a promise. I promised you that I would never hurt you the way I had been hurt. I promised you that I would never beat you. I promised you that I would never hit you with a belt, radio cord, wet towel or throw objects at you. I promised you that I would never make you kneel in a corner on rice. I promised you that I would never lock you in a closet. I promised you that I would never raise my hand or fist to any part of your body. I promised you that I would always tell you the truth and I promised that I would be the greatest mother.

May 27, 1992

This was the day you arrived to save my life. I had no idea at the time that that would be the reason *you* were born—to save me. When you and I met I have to admit you were ugly… but you were mine. I was only twenty years old. The nurse came into the room and told me that I needed to breast feed you… that it was time for you to eat. I was like, "ewwww! You want me to do what?"

She came over to me and put you in my arms. I had no idea what the hell I was doing. She showed me how to get you to latch onto my nipple and that shit hurt. Thank God we didn't last long with the breast-feeding thing A) Because you were greedy and B) Thankfully, my breasts didn't produce enough milk. Five days later we went home together and that's when I knew it would be me and you forever~

I wanted you to grow up in a happy home. How the hell was I going pull that off? A happy home! Shit, the only time my home was happy was when music was playing, company was at the house, and alcohol and food were in abundance. When the music stopped and the company was gone my childhood was far from happy. The day-to-day life sucked… parents fighting about money and disorder. Marriage is fucking HARD. Raising four kids is difficult. Having a grandmother in the Dominican Republic with cancer was challenging.

My parents had huge responsibilities to the family *here* and the family across the ocean on the island. I didn't have the best examples of a happy home. There was a lot of fighting, yelling, disrespect and vulgarity. Yeah our family is beautiful and we love each other deeply

11

but there have been some moments that overshadow like a black cloud over my life.

When your dad and I were dating we went to a park in Governor Francis Farms near the old house on Dahlia Street. He was pushing me on a swing one night and we were talking about life and our future when he asked me, "What's the one thing you want in life?" He said that what he wanted most was to have a successful career and get his Ph.D.

I said, "I just want to be happy."

He looked at me and said, "That's idealistic!"

I felt like what he was saying to me was *keep dreaming! That shit is unattainable. Happiness que happiness ni happiness. Happiness doesn't pay the rent. Now a title, you're somebody if you have a title. You're of value if you have a title. You're owed respect with a title* and so I started questioning myself. Was he right? Was I being idealistic? Was my wanting to be happy unrealistic? I trusted your dad so much. I respected his opinion, his beliefs and his thoughts. So I wondered, *maybe I should grow up and focus my attention on titles.*

Those first years of your life were not happy times for me. I was so lost. I was exactly your age today when I had you twenty years ago. Twenty years old when I became an instant wife and mother. I hadn't even begun to live my life. I had dreams. I didn't know what those dreams were yet, but I had them. I was finally free of my father's regime, of being constantly punished and beat for the most insignificant things, like accidently flushing a towel down the toilet. I felt like *abuelo* and *abuela* were so unfair, your uncle had much more liberties than me simply because he was a boy. Because *las mujeres son pa la casa, y los varones pa la calle.*

Then I entered another form of incarceration. I was imprisoned in a marriage that was eating away at my soul and chipping away at my identity. I didn't know which way I was headed. I didn't know which way to go. So I went white.

When I married your father I didn't know who I was yet and he was molding me into the person he wanted me to be and that person was not Latina. I cut my hair really short and wore it straight the way he liked it. My curls were gone. No more red lipstick. The clothes I wore were all neutrals, tans and browns, nothing vibrant, nothing loud. My voice reflected the colors I wore, soft and weak. There is a photo that defined who I was in that moment in time. I was wearing these white spandex, stirrup pants that I tucked in my boots with the matching V-neck sweater. My style was a more, "academic/yuppie" look and anything ethnic was erased from my wardrobe.

Back then everyone called me Alicia, pronounced Al-ee-sha. I began to change. I conformed. I wanted so badly to be accepted into his world, a world that never wanted me to begin with.

Your father didn't want me to speak Spanish in our house because he felt like we were talking about him. And he was right. Sometimes we were, but the world didn't revolve around him. We tried to make it work but I am nobody's mold. I resisted his attempts and resented him for being so careless with me.

I started to notice things that I didn't like, like when we stopped holding hands when we were in the car. He stopped wearing his wedding band. Whenever I would see his ring on the bureau it always made me sad because it felt like he didn't want to wear me. It was like he didn't want to be married to me or maybe he was embarrassed of me. I believed that he didn't love me. I certainly didn't think he loved me as much as I was willing to love him for a lifetime. And that's when it happened, I realized that he was never going to show me love and I wasn't willing to show him how to love. I knew I deserved more than that.

September 1994

When your dad was studying for his bachelors degree in psychology I would make all his appointments for him. One day I called the psychology department and Luz answered the phone, "Good afternoon, may I help you?"

"Yes, this is Ms. Santos I'm calling on behalf of my husband. I would like to make an appt with Dr. Rubenstein?" I said rudely and dismissively.

"Absolutely, how does 3:30pm work?"

"That will be fine." I responded coldly without so much of a thank you.

I was so dismissive and she on the other hand was so sweet.

KARMA~ I registered for classes fall 1994 and enrolled in RIC's work study program for extra credit. I started a part time job in the psychology department only working Saturdays. When we met she was the staff person who would be training me. Luz gave me a tour of the floor. She showed me where the mail went and we just spent that first afternoon getting to know each other. I thought she was fascinating and incredibly interesting. She was looking at this magazine telling me how she wanted to take horseback riding lessons. I think I laughed my ass off on the inside. In my head I was like, *the black/brown people in my life are certainly not into that. The closest we ever got to horses was either on a carousel or at the OTB betting on those bad boys.*

She was always looking for ways to enrich her life and grow as a person. Luz had a full course load but was interested in learning about other languages, different cultures and music of the world. She wanted to travel and had hobbies. I had never met anyone like her. I was incredibly intrigued by her. She invited me to take a cigarette break with her and from that day we were inseparable.

When you met Luz you fell in love with her instantly. You crawled up on her lap and she quickly became our family. We did everything together. She invited me to go see a flamenco show at RIC and we loved it. The dancer came out on stage in this beautiful red dress, with a flower in her head and as soon as she stepped out onto the stage each tap of her heal echoed through my body.

We were so inspired and wanted more so we bought tickets to a show in Boston. Your dad went with me. He thought it was pretentious. I thought it was beautiful. Luz opened my eyes to a new world. There was a world that existed outside of my marriage, my family and my culture. What I discovered was that there was more outside of being Dominican. There was this entire world of different cultures and beliefs. There were other things to learn about and explore.

Luz and I were so inspired after the flamenco show that we decided to learn how to dance flamenco. *Pa que fue eso!* We bought castanets, special dancing shoes and these black flowing skirts. All we needed was that damn red flower in our hair. We were good to go. We went to our first flamenco lesson. We were both terrible at it and kept tripping over our feet. Uncoordinated doesn't even begin to describe us. I always prided myself on being a good dancer but I couldn't keep up. After just a few classes we stopped going, but we could always say that we at least tried and had so much fun.

Meeting Luz changed my life in such a positive way. Every time we saw each other I learned something new. She inspired me. She encouraged me. She was probably the first person who ever believed in me. She definitely is the first person who told me "that everything in life happens for a reason." She taught me that we may not always understand why things happen but that there is always a higher plan. With her I learned how to pay attention to all that was happening around me.

It's the conversations in her attic that I cherish the most. Some of the most important conversations and decisions of my life happened with her. She accepted me as I am and showed me by example how to access all my potential. She saw beauty in me that I didn't know existed. Whenever we would meet for coffee at our favorite spot on Federal Hill, *Dolce Vita*, I always left feeling so full of love. My life seemed to be a little bit better just from having her in it.

We would listen to jazz and talk about life, love and spirituality. Our friendship was unlike anything I had ever experienced. She became my best friend and to your dad his biggest threat.

On the days Luz went to the Equestrian Academy for her horseback-riding lessons I would join her. I liked to watch from the sidelines. One night this tall man entered, he was blond with blue eyes. He was *so not* my type. But he had this charisma and arrogance about him that I liked. Joseph walked in wearing a long, brown, leather riding coat, smoking a cigar like he was *the* celebrity of the barn. My immediate response to his entrance was damn he's full of himself. He's definitely full of something. After the riding lesson Luz, myself, Joseph, the riding instructor and some of the other riders would go out to the local tavern in Newport.

When Joseph and I met there was an immediate attraction, both of us tall, both cocky and both full of ourselves. We were like mismatched socks that may not go together but are oh so comfortable anyway. We flirted innocently for a few months. He was in a relationship for fifteen years and I was at the end of my marriage. But I *was* married.

I accepted the attention Joseph gave me. I could feel his eyes on me as I walked into any room. His hunger for me sent fire throughout my body. We were two caged animals ready to pounce. He flirted with me and I flirted right back. I knew it was wrong. I knew that I was already cheating in my mind but I was having fun and someone was showing me the attention I so desperately was seeking.

One night after Luz's riding lesson we all went out to eat and Joseph passed a Victoria Secret's catalog to all the women at the table asking each woman to pick out the style they would like. I picked this beautiful, sexy, red bra and panty set. It was hot! Weeks later Luz came to our house and said, "I have a gift for you in the trunk of my car"

"From who? What kind of gift?" I asked playing stupid.

"Yes girl! Joseph sent you something."

"Get the fuck outta here?" is all I could say.

We went to my office and opened it quietly and sure enough it was that little red number. I don't even know how he knew my breast size. Luz just looked at me and said, "Girl you know he didn't bring anyone else a gift!" I wore that red deliciousness every single time I thought I would run into Joseph. I fantasized about being alone with him but we never got the chance.

I went to a holiday party with Luz. When they ran out of alcohol Joseph and I went on a liquor run. We were driving in his BMW on this dark country road. There were beautiful tall trees everywhere it was pitch black and we did what we always did made fun of each other. We joked about how we were finally alone and now what? All his talk about what he wanted to do to me.

He stopped in the middle of the road and looked at me with those blue eyes that made me feel like I was swimming in the ocean. That shit would work if I knew how to swim. It was more like drowning in an abyss.

He asked me to look at the moon. It was full complete the perfect setting for a first kiss and I wanted him to kiss me. I hoped that he would kiss me. It was soft, endearing, passionate and loving. I pulled away telling him we should get back to the party but I would think about that kiss for many months later.

Winter 1994

Marc Anthony spoke to me! Yes the salsa singer. It had been months since your father and I had slept together. Forget about us having sex. I was slowly falling out of love and falling into deep dislike. We were

18

fighting all the time, mostly because I was never going to be the perfect wife. I was sleeping in the living room on the love seat when the TV woke me. It was Marc Anthony. He was giving an acceptance speech and back then his Spanish wasn't as good as it is now but the message he left me with was very clear. He talked about how proud he was to be Puerto Rican. How grateful he was to his father for raising him with music from his roots. I remember sitting there crying feeling like his message was directly for me, like he was just speaking to me and he was telling me to *come back home – to return to the place donde yo naci. Que soy Latina y por eso debo de sentirme orgullosa and that I should be proud to be Latina,* so I listened.

I felt empowered in that moment. I flashed back to the old me that didn't care what others thought. I missed the old Alicia who was strong and believed in things. I wanted the Alicia who believed in me. I saw you sleeping in your crib and whispered to you, *I want you to be proud of me. I want you to respect me. I don't want you to see me living a lie.*

I returned home to my roots with guns blazing. I re-entered my skin. I reconnected with my bloodline. I rejoined my family and returned as ALICIA pronounced Ah-lee-see-yah proud *Dominicana*! I was back and I was STRONG!

I was such a mess. I never thought I was until your father pointed it out to me every single day. "You're lazy! You're a slob! You don't pick up anything! You never finish anything! All you do is party! You're such a bitch! You're crazy!"

I'm not sure what my responses were to a lot of the verbal assaults but I'm sure most of it was filled with, "Fuck you's! Go fuck yourself! Shut the fuck up! How dare you?" something along those lines.

I began distancing myself from him. I started cooking our traditional food, making *arroz con pollo y habichuelas*. Our house was filled with the scent of *sazon Dominicano*. The more Latina I became, the emptier our marriage became. It was clear that your father didn't accept me for me and honestly, I didn't accept him either. We tried couples therapy. He went twice. I continued going alone. As I went to therapy I started to discover things about myself. I got stronger. I began to look at myself deeply. I began to see that *there were* things I needed to change about me for ME. Not because they were being pointed out to me as my flaws and imperfections. They now became the things that were important for me to change for YOU.

I realized during that horrible time that I needed to get my shit together for *you*. In therapy I spent most of that year talking about how unhappy I was and how I wanted to leave your father. Dr. R always said, "Alicia, you will know what to do when you're ready. You will leave when *you* are ready."

So I stayed. I would stay married. I would stay because your abuela said it's what we do, *"sobre jevalo mi hija! Don't break up your home. A child needs both parents. If you leave it will damage your daughter. Do you really want her growing up in a broking home?"*

The fear of possible breaking you destroyed me. Those words kept us together for a while. I couldn't live with the idea of ending my marriage and it damaging you in some way. I made you a promise. I was never going to fuck you up.

※

CHAPTER THREE ~ *New Years Eve, 1994*

I got all prettied up... we went to a party in Newport it was count down to midnight. 10, 9, 8, 7, 6, 5, 4, 3, 2, 1... HAPPY NEW YEAR!!! All of our friends were kissing and hugging their partners and your father was at the other end of the bar having a shot. I just looked over at him. In that moment I knew that it was over. That was THE defining moment of my life. I knew what I needed to do. I knew that *that* was exactly how I would start 1995... ALONE. So on January 5, 1995, I filed for divorce.

During the separation and preparations for our divorce I started to spiral. I never saw Joseph again. I became reckless. I drank every day. Anyone who came to our apartment at any moment could open the fridge and see that there was never any food but it was always fully stocked with wine.

When you were born you had a heart murmur an *irregular* heartbeat. The doctors told me you had a little hole in your heart. You were just three weeks old. I had a visiting nurse who would come to the house two times a week to see how I was doing with you. She checked your vitals, your weight, and your heart beat. There was something that concerned her. She said your heart rate was over 100. You weren't getting enough oxygen. You were having difficulty breathing. Your pulse was hard for her to count. You started to turn blue, so we called 911. The nurse went with you in the ambulance and I was so scared. I didn't know what was wrong with you. Once we arrived to Fatima Hospital they put you in ice to slow down your heart rate. I was freaking out. You looked so helpless. You were so tiny. After they worked on you for a little while they moved you to ICU. You were in a plastic bubble. I could only touch you by putting my hand through plastic holes. You looked so defenseless. I was so afraid that I might lose you. I never left your side. After a few days you came home with us and I watched you like a hawk.

You were in and out of the hospital a lot that first year of your life. We saw a pediatric cardiologist weekly and I learned how to use a stethoscope. I administered your medication and we used a ventilator at home. I carried a stethoscope everywhere. We had one in everyone's house. I slept with your baby monitor by my ears. I was so happy to learn that the little hole in your heart would eventually get smaller and close as you got older. But I still needed to be careful. I wrote you a letter while you were sleeping in the hospital that I put in your baby book:

What mom hopes for your future~

I only hope you lead a healthy and happy life. That any goals and dreams you may have you share them with me. And you can be sure that I will be there to give you all the love and support you will ever need to reach that goal. As I see you lying in your crib sleeping peacefully. I only want beautiful things for my wittle girl. Courtney, always be proud of any and all things you believe in, who you are, and especially where you come from. If you ever feel strongly about something always remember I am here to listen (good or bad). I am not just your mom I hope you can think of me as your best friend. I want you to feel you can tell me anything no matter what the topic or issue is. I won't judge you. As your father and I see how innocent you are right now, at this young age, we also see you growing up into a beautiful young woman and with that we plan on giving you the best education. All I'll ever ask of you is that you further your education. I want you to push yourself beyond your limits, because without an education you will get nowhere. Anything you want in life you can have if you put your mind to it. Believe you can be anything you want... because I already do. Just do your best, give it your all and if you tell me that that was the very best you can do I will be proud of you no matter what. Courtney, always be a lady and remember this; to be loved you must love yourself first and to be respected you must respect yourself. Know that no one should love you more than you and never be afraid to be confident. Love you now and always, your mommy.

1995

We lived on Hereford Street in Providence when I told your father it was over, that I couldn't do this anymore. "I can't live like this! I'm miserable. This is no good for the baby! We're not happy. I don't want her to see this. I don't want her to see us fighting. I can't do this anymore. I want you to leave. I want a divorce."

You were two years old when you realized something was wrong. You came walking into the bedroom in your little pink footsy pajamas and asked, "Mommy, where's daddy?"

You looked up at our bureau and noticed two of your father's drawers missing and said, "Mommy, where's daddy? Where's his drawer?"

As you stood there with two fingers in your mouth, twirling your hair looking at me I said, "Baby, your daddy is at grandma's house."

"I don't want daddy at grandma's house! I want him here!" as you pouted with sad eyes.

You were so upset. I just picked you up and gave you a hug. I kissed you and said, "Daddy's going to stay at grandmas for a little while."

You cried so much. Your heart was broken. You knew what was happening. How do I tell my two-year-old baby girl that my marriage to her father was over? How could I tell you that I was miserable, unhappy and that I felt empty married to him? I never wanted to break your heart. There were so many people who encouraged me to stay with him. But I knew I didn't have another choice. I wanted you to grow up in a home where you felt loved every single day. I wanted you to grow up knowing that no one was more important to me than you. I made you a new promise. When I left your father I vowed to be committed and dedicated myself to loving you with everything that I am. I vowed to tell you everyday how amazing and beautiful you are. I was dedicated to learning how to love *myself* as deeply as I love you.

When I asked your daddy to leave I started drinking heavily. I drank myself to lower forms of being. I was beyond unconscious. I couldn't go anywhere without getting completely wasted. Luz and I spent a lot of time in Newport. Mostly, I drank alone. We went to every bar, restaurant and nightclub across two states. I gave my number to every guy I met. One night we were dancing at Thames Street Station and I started to feel myself get dizzy, I was really warm. I had this horrible habit of disappearing when I was overly intoxicated. Whenever I felt myself unable to speak or walk I would disappear. I never wanted to be "the drunk girl" that people talk about. So I left the club and passed out on a park bench.

The men I've let have me. This part of my story really paralyzes me. There's a lot of shame here. Guilt! Embarrassment! I don't like to admit how I was. I'm ashamed of that person. I was a terrible mother to you during this moment in my life. I constantly disappointed you. I always left you waiting and never came to see you when I said I would.

The only guys who came to see me where the ones who came to fuck me. None of those men really liked me. None of them wanted to know me. They only wanted what they could get from me, what they could take from me. I made it easy for them to have me. They never took me out, yet they took me any way they wanted. We never went to dinner. I would meet them at bars and sleep with them immediately. There was a time I would have one guy come over at 11:00am and the next guy would arrive at 7:00pm for round two that same day. Two for the price of none zero was the value I placed on me.

I was barely taking care of you. On the nights you were with me we had our routine: 6pm we'd watch Barney, eat dinner and then it was bath time. At 7pm it was sleepy time. I loved your sleepy time because your sleepy time meant it was mommy time. As soon as you knocked out I opened up a bottle of wine. I often drank alone. This particular evening I was drinking to escape. I drank to fill the loneliness the emptiness.

When the music on one side of your cassette player ended, you would call out to me, "mommy fix da music." I drank so much that night that I passed out. I wasn't even thinking about your heart problem. I just wanted to be high. I wanted to be somewhere else. I wasn't just self-medicating I was self-mutilating. I was cutting myself down with my thoughts and actions. I was knocked out cold. Something woke me up in the middle of the night and I realized I wasn't hearing you breathing. I could always hear you breathing. I didn't hear anything coming out of your baby monitor. There was no inhale no exhale. I freaked out. I jumped up from the bed and ran to your room. I picked you up. You were so scared. You cried and I just held you saying, "Mommy is so sorry baby. I'm so sorry. I'm sorry to wake you. Forgive me baby."

I wonder… did you smell the alcohol on me? If anything happened to you I would have killed myself.

September 1995

He was yelling at me on the other side of the wall, "You piece of shit! *Asquerosa*! You disrespectful little bitch." It was like I was reliving a moment from my past. I was back in 1989.

"Don't let him in! PLEASE!!!!!! Don't let him in! Don't let him in the room! He will kill us both. Please hold the door shut!!!" I said pleading with Terrance.

Terrance was holding the door shut on one side and your *abuelo* trying to break it down on the other. I was terrified. Your grandfather did not want me seeing this guy and was furious when he found out that we were together. He wanted to control me. He wanted me to obey his wishes. He wanted me to be that little girl who lived under his rule. That's not even who I was anymore. The divorce was almost

26

final. I moved out of our apartment into a new space. And Terrance came along with us.

CHAPTER FOUR ~ *November 1995*

We moved to Ortoleva Drive, in North Providence. I didn't give anyone our new address. Not even your father. The space was dark. It was completely filled with dark wood paneling. There was no light coming into the house. It was closed in… hidden… and he lived with us… the new boyfriend. I really didn't want to live with a man but I allowed him to stay with us from time to time. He stayed whenever he wanted. You were three years old then. I was so not present. I was consumed by this relationship and my desperate need to be loved. At the same time I was yearning for freedom.

I allowed this complete stranger into our world. I don't know what the fuck I was thinking. There was a part of me that believed maybe being with a black man was just what I needed. Deep down I knew that Terrance would finally be someone I could relate to. He would be someone I had things in common with. He would accept me, he being black, me being Latina both of us minorities in this society. I believed, my family and culture wouldn't threaten him. Maybe he would lift me? Perhaps he would love me and be an active participant in my life?

I would go with him to his job most weekends. I left you in Rhode Island with your grandparents and father. One day I was working security for him. I'd check all the women. It was Latino night at some really grimy spot in downtown Boston. There were lots of questionable characters. There was one girl though, who stood out. She was really pretty. She definitely didn't look like she belonged in that spot. Her clothes were too nice. She looked like one those smart chicks. Something told me that Terrance and this girl had something—sure enough. I got up and walked to the door and noticed him pushing her away from the entrance I guess she wanted to get a good look at me. All I kept hearing was her asking him about me, "Who's that girl at the door?" and I was wondering the same thing. *Who was this girl?* I guess whatever it was they needed to resolve was handled because he came back into the spot trying to, "hey baby me..." I was like... *Hey baby — who the fuck was that?*

"Oh that was nothing. She's just some girl I was seeing. She won't leave me alone. Don't sweat that. She's just a groupie you know you're my girl!"

I was such a stupid bitch then. Yeah I fell for that shit. Weeks later, I was at the apartment he lived at in MA. I was taking care of his three kids (from three different women) and you were there. The four of you were sleeping in a bed together. That girl from the club came to the house. He was at work. She knocked on the door and I came down. We sat on the steps and talked. She told me that she was pre-med attending a school in Boston. She told me that she had been with him for two years. She told me that she was his girlfriend. I was stunned. *You're his what?*

"I'm his girlfriend." she replied.

Then I did something so stupid. I told her that I would prove to her that he and I were together. We got in his black Saab convertible (a car that he didn't own) and I decided to take her to our apartment in Providence. I showed her all of his things, but there was one thing that was all the proof she needed. There was a drawing of Martin Luther King hanging above our TV. It was a drawing of Martin Luther King's face with the words from his famous "I Have a Dream" speech written all around him. She just looked at it and said, "I gave him that piece of art."

Weeks later I came home and noticed my personal things had been touched. Terrance went through all of my personal belongings. A private box I had at the top of my closet. I was looking for my old phone book. That's how I noticed something wasn't right. This phone book was special. It was my little black book. It had numbers of people from my past, my life in New York, people I met while I was married. He went through all of it. He went through it and decided that I no longer needed those pages. He decided that I no longer needed to keep in contact with people from my past. *He* decided that he was all I needed. *He* decided that he was enough for me and *he* decided that he would decide who it was or wasn't ok for me to speak with.

All my numbers were gone. My history erased. He got rid of information for professors that I had met, relationships that I had formed… everything was gone. All the pages were torn out. I was so angry. How dare HE? Who the fuck did he think he was? It was just the ammunition I needed to get rid of him and ask him to leave once and for all. And I would… that very night!

"Did you go through my personal things?" I asked, standing tall and firmly furious.

"Yes I did!" said Terrance, arrogantly and quite smugly.

"Did you rip out pages from my book?"

"Yeah, and so what if I did! You didn't need them!"

"How dare you! Who the fuck do you think you are? That was an invasion of my privacy. Those were my personal things. You had NO RIGHT!"

"I have NO RIGHT! You're *MY* woman! I can look at whatever the fuck I want!"

"Oh you're confused! I don't belong to anyone! How fucking dare you! Those are my things. You have NO RIGHT to go through my things. You know what, I can't do this! I'm going through a divorce right now and I can't do this. I don't need this in my life. I want you to leave. Get the fuck out of my house! Go back home! Go back to Boston!"

He lunged at me and grabbed me by my neck. He threw me on the bed. He kept me pinned down. I could barely breathe. His face would be imprinted in my pupils. I was trying to pull his fingers off my throat. But he didn't let go. He held me down. His hand gripped tightly around my neck.

"You think you can fuck with people? You think you can fuck with people's emotions? You think you can kick me out of your life? You think you can put me out on to the street? You think you're tough? You feel stronger than me? I'm not going anywhere! You're mine!"

That's when I stopped. I stopped moving. I stopped kicking my legs. I stopped fighting. I just froze. I couldn't breathe. He looked me straight in my eyes as the tears fell down my face. I would remember his eyes, the yellow, the red, and the closeness of death... forever. I remember lying there thinking *God, please let me get out of this alive… I beg you.* That night I slept in your bed and cried all night.

I couldn't believe this was happening to me. I can't believe I let a man put his hands on me. That's what I always used to say in my teenage New York City girl days that I would never let a man hit me. *The day a man hits me! That would be the fucking day! I wish a man would try and hit me!*

I was so thankful you were with your father that night and didn't hear or see any of it. It was like I was watching a movie. *Was this really happening to me? Did this shit really just happen to me?* I never thought I would ever allow a man to hurt me? Not like this? I cried and cried endlessly that night. Then another thought entered my mind. I wanted to kill him. I was terrified, horrified. I was so scared. I went to see my cousin who I knew could get me a gun. I wanted him dead. But Diamondz wouldn't get me one. He kept talking to me about my daughter saying, "What about her? Alicia, you don't want to do something crazy!"

I gave you up informally to your father. I met your dad at a cemetery and told him everything that was happening in my life. I cried to him. I begged him not to fight me for sole custody. He could have won during that time. I told him about all the shit that I was going through in this relationship with Terrance. How I left you alone in that house in Boston. *What if that house had burned down?* I could have lost you.

During that time your father was building a case against me. I was being followed. I told your dad all about the hell I was living with Terrance and that I feared for my life. I shared with him that I feared that I was about to do something horrible in order to protect you and myself. He promised me that he would not take you from me and that he would be there for me, and he was. He took such good care of you. We

We both tried to protect you from the shit I was dealing with. Your father became the only person aside from Luz who knew all that I was going through.

The months that followed were torture. I was living in HELL. I was working at John Street Elementary School in Providence taking attendance when Terrance walked in. He asked me if I would go outside for a moment to speak with him. I accepted. I told a coworker to check outside the window and call 911 if he got stupid. Once we were alone he said he wanted to give me something.

"Open your hand!" he said.

"Why?"

"I have something for you."

"Terrance, please stop bothering me, leave me alone!"

"I just want to give you something. Give me your hand!"

He opened my hand and put two bullets in my palm, "this one is for your daughter's father and this one is for Luz." He said he would kill everyone I loved if I left him. I was living a Stephen King novel.

His threats continued for a while until the day he promised that he would leave. He said he just wanted to come over and get the rest of his things. So I allowed him back into the apartment. We were in my bedroom. We were in the apartment alone. He pretended to gather his things. He started to get angry. He was just being nice so he could get me alone. Once in the apartment he kept telling me that this was so easy for me. Who the hell did I think I was?

"You don't give a fuck about anyone but yourself. This is so fucking easy for you. You don't care about what happens to me. You're a fucking whore. I knew you were getting back with your husband."

He pushed me on the bed. Held my face down. He tied my wrists. I cried begging him to please stop. He tore off my pants and ripped my panties. He lifted my hips as he held me down. He put his hands underneath my waist to lift me. He took me from behind. I remember crying. As tears rolled down my face in disbelief all I could think was *why was this happening to me?*

I don't remember what he said as he was raping me. I don't remember the words that came out of his mouth as he was ramming his penis inside me anally. All I remember is what he said when he finished.

"I told you I'd get that ass!"

He said that shit with such a smirk. He was smiling. He was so proud. He was pleased with himself. He conquered me. He took me. He left me powerless. He took what he wanted. When he untied me I put my pants back on and was trembling. I got up slowly and asked him to please leave.

"Now I can leave! Now I WILL leave! One more thing, you're a whore!" as he spit phlegm at my face and left.

I locked the door and just sat there for hours crying in disbelief. Was I just raped? Had I been violated? I felt so empty, so alone and so dirty. What did I do in my life to deserve that?

So he left
not without leaving
ME
tainted
Broken
Dirty
Stained
He left me feeling like
trash
the lowest form
of a human being
like I deserved
all of it
like I was due
it
like
that's just
what I get!!!

CHAPTER FIVE ~ *Fast-forward to 2007*

Moment of Revelation

If you've got a question you can't solve on your own seek help. There are traditional ways to do this. You can go to counseling, a support group, call a friend or relative, buy a book, call an (800) number, have your palm read or like any true Dominican *buscate una bruja*.

I went to an event being hosted by a spiritual advisor in New York City. I had never gone to one before. It was beautiful. There were about fifty people in this apartment and *Revelation* would be giving each of us a personal message for the year. She guessed my favorite number so I was sold on her gifts.

I remember calling you during your visit with your father in Virginia for the summer. I was telling you about all the messages she gave me. How she told me that 2007 WAS GOING TO BE MY YEAR!!!

I told you about all the amazing things she saw coming for me and all the beautiful things she saw in me. The message Revelation shared was about me not knowing how powerful I really am. She told me that I would be tremendously successful and that my future looked bright. That once I knew *who I really was* there would be no stopping me.

When I finished you just said, "Mommy, did you pay her? Tell me you didn't pay her?"

"NO! Of course not!

"Mommy, you don't need to go to any spiritual guides or *brujas*. You don't need anyone to tell you those things because I tell you all the time. *Besides, God sent me to protect you.* I will never let anyone hurt you."

I started crying. I didn't want you to know I was crying but when you said that, I understood how powerful *you* really were.

I continued meeting with Revelation to discuss the issues that I didn't want to deal with. There were things about my life I didn't know if I wanted you or anyone to know. There was something that was keeping me stuck. There was something that I refused to face. She kept bringing up my past. A past that had been filled with the kind of pain suited for a Lifetime Network television special than to be the person living the nightmare up close and personal. My past was not something I cared to admit, face or share with anyone.

I was sailing in my sea of denial, quite comfortably telling myself that I was good. I tried to convince myself that it was ALL GOOD. It felt better to not dwell – to not live in the fire that was cooking my insides alive. On the outside I wore this mask. But something was happening to me that I could no longer run from. I was being exposed. My insides were now my outsides. *Will they leave me? Will they love me? Will they hate me? What will happen when they discover the truth? Can you forgive me? WILL YOU STILL LOVE ME? Will you still be proud of me?*

The moment I put pen to paper to write, *"The Letters"* came after I went to see Revelation. We spent a lot of time talking about a past I didn't care to face. I kept telling her that I didn't know what to do

She quite frankly and assertively said, "You know what the fuck you need to do!"

She's the most real spiritual being you will ever come face to face with. I love that she curses. She doesn't hold anything back. She doesn't take money for the gifts that she shares. She speaks the truth and you gotta be a big girl. You gotta shut the fuck up and take it!

She said, "Look bitch! You know what you need to do. You've got to look at your past. You have no choice. You are being called to go inwards. Here's what I want you to do. I want you to write letters to those people in your past who have affected you. Write a letter to someone you need to forgive. Write a letter to someone who has fucked you up. Write a letter to someone who has impacted your life. Write a letter to someone you need forgiveness from. Write a letter to specific moments and people from your past."

I didn't see what the significance of this exercise was. I thought it was a waste of my time. I RESISTED. I actually got incredibly angry. I thought it was crap. Why did I have to deal with my childhood now? I hated it while I lived it why relive it now? Just the thought of writing *him* a letter about how I felt about him, made me incredibly uncomfortable. What would writing letters prove? What would it solve? How would writing these letters fix things? Was this supposed to instantly heal me?

"I want you to sit down and write a letter. Once you have written them I want you to seal them. Don't look at it! Don't read it! Just write it and then put it away. Once you're done with that homework I want you to bring them back to me and we'll look at the letters together."

I looked her in the eyes and said, "OK! I'll write the fucking letters!"

Six months later I could no longer resist. All the signs were pointing inwards. Everything I heard and read that day had to do with looking at my past. I was getting these messages every single day. *Until you look at your past you will not be able to move forward.* I was hearing the same messages in everything. *Look at your past. Until you deal with an issue from the past it will remain unresolved.* I was seeing messages in the books I was reading, in my horoscope, my goddess cards, and my affirmations. All of the messages pointed inwards. I was being called to look into my heart. I was being called to enter that dark space that I was afraid of revisiting, reliving or unleashing. Darkness can be scary. The idea of what will be found out if I start unlocking shit scared the hell out of me.

My heart was racing I knew what I had to do. I got up from the floor, rolled up my yoga mat and grabbed my journal and pen. I began to write the first letter. As the pen moved across the page it was as if I went back to those moments I had locked in that box so long ago. It wasn't even me writing. I was writing so urgently. I couldn't keep up with my thoughts. It was life or death. It was like I needed to get it out and fast. It was eating me up alive. Fighting its way out of me. It was poisoning me. It felt like cigarette burns on my arm, the screech of chalk on the board, internal bleeding, exiting my pours. The blood was coming out of my eyes and fingers. I was exposed... raw... the truth was coming out of me... all of it.

I was releasing on those pages the truth about that time in my life and all that I believed to be the truth about me for over 30 years. I could no longer hold it in. The weight of it was too much. I was in captivity far too long, incarcerated, suffocating and lost in all of it. There was a voice screaming to be heard, a force greater than me that wanted to be released. I wrote that day from 10:00am until the evening. I did not stop. When I finished writing I had twelve letters. I cried and cried and cried. That first letter was to my father.

I read one day that the father-daughter relationship is the most important relationship with a man that a girl will EVER have. *What did the first man in my life think about me when he held me in his arms? What was the first thing he said to me? Was he happy I was born? What were his wishes for my future?*

"A daughter's relationship with her father is usually her first male-female relationship. This is where little girls gain their first reflection of themselves as a female. They develop a sense of acceptance or non-acceptance; they feel valued or discounted. Self-respect is initially based upon respect received from others. Their self-concept as a female person is largely shaped by this early relationship. In short, children regard themselves as they think others regard them and Dad is an important person in her life. This is where they learn how to negotiate fairly and compromise appropriately. When fathers exercise absolute authority, and rigidly set rules, daughters quickly learn to rebel. If a father is overly critical and all-powerful, men become the enemy. If a father is fair and listens to his daughter's thoughts, she will gain self-confidence and pride in her own opinion." [1]

Whatever it is I've been carrying I have kept it bottled up for such a long time and it comes out in spurts. I hate to admit it but I know that you've been the one on the receiving end of my anger issues. I'm sad and embarrassed to admit that I have taken out my rage on you. I thought I had escaped this. I thought I was free of abusing you. I promised myself and I promised you that I would never hurt you the way I was hurt. I really believed that I was doing a good job at keep-

---

[1]   Source: http://www.dr-jane.com/chapters/Jane125.htm

ing you safe. I have prided myself on believing that I have never put my hands on you. But I *have* beaten you, haven't I? I always wanted to build you up. There are moments I lift you with empowering words and with those same words I tear you down. Maybe not everyday but even one day is too many.

I called you one day to ask you to tell me what my rage and anger looks like through your eyes, "You look like a mad woman. Like you just want to smash somebody's face in. When you come home, the house is messy and there's food on my bed. Sometimes it's a big deal and sometimes you let it go."

I asked you if I've ever been out of control, "OMG YES! For the smallest things you just start screaming at the top of your lungs and your face is red. It makes me get up and pick things up. I feel like crap it and it makes me cry."

How could you love someone who beats you? You tend to love them anyway. You tend to love them more. You forgive them easily because you will do just about anything to gain their love even if that means taking their abuse. You want them to love you and you want them to stop beating you. I hoped that I was breaking the cycle, but I guess I have slowly been releasing my past on you - UNTIL TODAY! *Anger for me has appeared in my life as hate. It has been an anger that fills me. It has consumed me. In some ways it has taken over me. If I allowed love to be my guiding force I would never act that way.*

Where did I learn this? What triggers my rage? *It's when I'm feeling threatened. It's when I feel like I'm being attacked. It's when I feel disrespected.* How did rage show up in my life? In the way people spoke to me. The condescending way people addressed me. In the things that people said about me and in the names I was called? It was in the constant criticisms. Then I picked up the book, *Angry All the Time, An*

Emergency Guide to Anger Control. I had to put the book down it was making me angry. *I am ready to face my anger and rage and release it once and for all.*

Letter: Dear Papi,

Bendicion pa! I have been dreading writing you this letter because I've been afraid - - afraid of the things I need to say to you and afraid of what my words would do to you. Afraid of how my words would make you feel. The last thing I ever want to do is hurt you. Papi you hurt me so very much through out my life. The beatings were terrible but I believe the WORDS you said to me and about me, hurt me the most. I was an innocent child. I needed you to build me up. I needed you to strengthen me not beat me down. I stayed down for such a long time!

You were GOD in my eyes. What you thought of me meant everything to me. You hurt me so much. I don't know that I've ever fully recovered. But I try like hell. I think I've spent the better part of my adult life undoing all of the terrible things I went through and heard as a child. All the words I heard that, "I was a piece of shit / un pedaso de mierda, and that I would never amount to anything." I really didn't believe I was loved. Yes there were moments of good times - - family gatherings, parties, dinners where there was always music, food and laughter... but what I felt on the inside was this overwhelming feeling of worthlessness, of nothingness. MAN how I wish you had created me to be a FORCE full of love and light instead of wanting to put my fire out. I was left filled with anger and rage and nowhere to release it. And believe me I wanted to punish everyone... it was probably why I got into fights in school because I wanted to hit someone.

Oh and the men I chose as partners. They were all so very wrong for me. The drug dealer/addict that you hated because he wasn't good enough to be in our family because he was from the ghetto and you didn't raise NO ghetto rat! But the thing is dad he was exactly what I deserved. He was a piece of shit and so was I. We were perfect for one another. That's the place I was living in during that time in my life...my teen years. I was living in hell and that's how I felt in that moment like crap. I got the mirror image of me. Crap attracts crap!

You wanted to beat strength into me but what you did was the complete opposite. You beat the life out of me. You beat the love out of me. I got to a

*point in my life where I stopped caring about others or myself and all I want-
ed was to get out. I wanted to escape the hell I was living in. I didn't believe
that anyone cared about me.*

*My God dad, do you remember the last beating? I was 18 years old, naked
in the shower and because the drug dealer boyfriend called. He had the audacity to call our home after you specifically ordered me to never see him again.
You felt such disregard, and disrespect. You were filled with so much rage
that you came down to where I was. I was washing my hair when the bathroom door opened and I felt the first jab to my stomach.*

*Then I felt a blow to my chest. I kneeled protecting my face like I always
did. "You disrespectful little bitch. Tu eres basura te voy ensenar a respetar.
You're nothing but a piece of shit."*

*You beat the living hell out of me throwing blows with such venom as if I
was the enemy. You fought me like I was a man. You were going to show me
respect. Daddy that devastated me and I didn't even fight back. So it makes
sense that the men that would follow I'd take their crap too. I would take their
beatings (even if they were just words). Daddy you belittled me, degraded me,
violated me, scarred me, and broke my heart. I don't think I ever fully understood why that was.*

*Why did you hit me? What was the lesson that you were hoping to beat
into me or teach me? There were so many other ways that could have been
more effective. I was defenseless. I couldn't fight you back you were too big...
you were stronger. I really only wanted you to love me. I only wanted to make
you proud. So many times I thought I was going to die. I really thought you
were going to kill me. I was already dead on the inside. I finally got to a point
where I didn't care about getting hit.*

*It was like I had a resistance to it...to all the beatings. It wasn't even
phasing me anymore... yes I became the rebel. I did things just to spite you. I
decided that if I was going to get hit for NO reason anyway I should have fun
while doing it. My motto became, "I'm gonna get hit anyway...but did I have
a good time?"*

*I got to a place where I preferred the beatings than the verbal as-
saults...the words seemed to hurt me more. I remember that day a few months
ago when we were on the phone and talking about how I stopped looking,
wanting and waiting for my ex-husband's respect and validation of how far
I've come and all that I've accomplished. I told you that I no longer gave a
fuck what he thought because I was very proud of me. I was proud of who I
am and all I've accomplished and that I was extremely proud of the way I've
raised Courtney. And during that conversation you told me you were proud
of me. That was the first time I ever recall you saying that to me and I was so
happy to hear it.*

*That is ALL I ever wanted to hear from you. With those words you re-
stored my faith, trust, belief in me and erased all the hurtful things that I*

have ever heard... you are that powerful in my mind. I am not mad at you anymore daddy. I don't hate you anymore. I stopped hating you so many years ago. I don't want to punish you anymore. I don't want to punish me anymore. I don't want to punish Courtney for a past she has nothing to do with. I think I started to forgive you after Courtney was born but I never really healed from my childhood. All that stuff I suffered through was just swept under the rug so I could raise her. I didn't face any of that stuff then.

I love you Papi. I forgive you. I understand now that when I told you I wanted to be a singer why it was you shot my dream down telling me to get my head out of the clouds and out of my ass. You were probably trying to protect me from disappointment. I understand NOW that the only reason you said that to me is because it was done and said to you by your father. Your words stopped me from dreaming. The words I heard taught me that dreams CAN'T come true. So I never even tried. I went on to live the rest of my life just doing mediocre work. Doing whatever just to get by. I never wanted more than what I had because I believed that what I received was what I deserved. I know your dreams were shot down and I am so sorry daddy. You would've made a great cameraman and when I start doing famous political interviews and when my novel becomes a movie I want you to work on the film. I want you by my side as my camera guy. I want your dreams to come true.

Papi I forgive you for hurting me... please forgive me for my hateful thoughts. I know that you did the best you could with the tools you had and I know that I wasn't easy to deal with. I thank you for trying so hard to keep my head right. Thank you for always keeping it real. Thank you for being the ONE person I can talk to for hours about corruption, history, religion, terrorism and everything that is taboo... you are the shit. You are my boy. Thank you for teaching me that I should ALWAYS be proud of where I come from, my language, my traditions and my culture-DOMINICANA SOY hasta la muerte.

Dad, I love and respect you very much. You are one of the greatest men I've ever known. You are brilliant and kind and I thank you for being my father. I would not have wanted another man to be my dad... you are my ace, my partner in crime. Thank you for all the help you've provided me with raising Courtney. You are a great grandfather. Where you made some mistakes with me you sure have done right by her. We have raised an incredible human being who's going to raise hell someday. You better save some bail money for her ass. She's the next Lebron, Minerva, Mother Theresa and Peron. I thank you for the role you have played in both our lives. Papi I love you. Tu hija querida, Alicia Anabel

When Revelation read *"The Letters"* she said, "You're playing it safe. There's something you're not saying here. What's the truth about what happened to you? What's the truth about how you felt? What did that experience do to you? How has it changed you? How has it marked you? You don't say anything about that in these letters. This isn't the truth."

I realized that I was protecting Papi. I was more concerned about how he would feel then how he made me feel. I was the victim. I was the one abused. I was one left broken. I talked about being the kind of writer who just wrote on the surface. I never went too deep so I wouldn't have to feel shit. The person I am today takes more risks I'm not afraid to go deep. There was always this fear that if I got too deep I would not make it out alive and if I did fall in that hole who would be there to pull me out?

The woman who wrote the letters in 2007 ripped off the band-aid too quickly. In writing those letters I only wrote what I wanted you to know. I wrote a cleaner version. I would describe what the surface wound looked like but I never let you see it or touch it. It's like saying a 3rd degree burn doesn't hurt. I wasn't ready to face what it looked like under my skin. I wasn't ready to look at the color of the scabs. I would peel them off but they just kept coming back. The wound kept getting larger and deeper.

I wasn't able to face myself. I didn't want to look at my life, my mistakes and poor choices. I didn't want to believe what my life had become. I didn't want to accept the choices that I had made. I wasn't ready. I wasn't strong enough. I didn't want to face the truth.

The person I am today is better equipped. I can now look at the wounds and peel away at the layers of my skin. I can look at the

45

wounds and dissect them. I am ready to really go deep down into all of it and pull the skin up and look at the truth of each experience.

I don't remember being a child… something changed in my life. I can't pin point the exact date. All of it is a complete blur. It's as if the clock stopped. I'm frozen in time. All the beatings felt like one beating. I was little, 6 or 7 years old. My book bag was lying on the floor in my bedroom. It made your abuelo so angry. I was in bed when he started yelling, "How many times have I told you to pick up your shit?" For every word he yelled he hit me over the head with the bag. I started screaming and crying. My head was bleeding. The buckle on the bag had a hook like one from a belt… the hook went through my scalp.

How do you heal from all that abuse? Where do you put it? I have very strong feelings about parents who put their hands on their children it fills me with rage. It is a fury that is indescribable. Parents have no fucking idea what they do to these defenseless / innocent children. They have no idea what they have done to us! How they have damaged us!

There is residue that is left behind when a parent raises their hands to a child. A child left broken and scarred will become the child who is either shy and never learns to speak up for themselves and might grow up to take abuse from bosses, husbands, wives, lovers, bullies, and any other figure of authority. Or they might become the abuser themselves taking out their frustrations on others. Doing what was done to them. Or they will turn out like me be a scarred, frightened, beautifully broken child in a grown woman's body. A woman who works tirelessly everyday to break the cycle of abuse and leave a mark – A DIFFERENT MARK - not from beatings - - but from LOVE.

I was finally let out of this cage. My self imposed prison that I didn't event know I was living in. I had everyone fooled including me.

I had convinced myself that my past had no affect on my future. Ignoring it didn't make it go away. It takes a tremendous amount of strength to not only look at the events of my past but also to relive all of it. Allowing it all to rise to the surface in the name of exploration and expansion. I was ready to look at each letter closely. I was ready to look at the lies. I was ready to look at the truth and learn what the gifts were from those moments. I wanted to acknowledge their arrival so that I could release all of it.

Returning to 1995~

When I met Terrance I was at the end of my marriage to your father and looking for anyone to love me. My judgment was off. I settled for the first guy who would have me. A man I thought shared a common experience with me. A man I thought would love me, protect me and stand with me. SHIT was I wrong! We dated for a second and he moved in immediately. I wasn't aware at the time that this would be his MO. He'd get with women, use them and try to live off of them and I was usable material.

Letter: Dear Terrance,

WOW! You are the biggest mistake of my life! I was your cesspool! Your garbage can! You entered me in ways that on a good day I would have never allowed you in my space. But I realize that you were also my lesson for that moment. After my marriage ended I was an easy target. You took advantage of a vulnerable woman and I allowed you to take advantage of me because I was lonely, desperate for love and looking for it in all the wrong places.

There was something sexy, alluring about you and now in time I realize that what I was attracted to and found in YOU was danger. A danger I wanted in my life because I didn't care about my life. You were just another way for me to punish myself because I didn't believe I deserved to be happy. I certainly didn't deserve to be loved and YOU were what the universe sent me, a WEAK man for a weaker woman a LONELY man for an even lonelier woman.

You tried to possess me, to keep me, to have me as your prize. Then I started to see you for who you REALLY were and my best friend threatened to no longer stand by me if I was rocking with you. She could see what my eyes couldn't. But when I woke up that infuriated you. When I packed your shit and tried to kick you out you weren't having it. When I took my power back you tried to intimidate and control me. You wanted to scare me. You threatened to kill the people I love and came to my job with bullets that you placed in my hand telling me the names that were on them.

You threatened my life; you used words to hurt me, to belittle me, to demean me and to disrespect me. You manipulated me, you tied me, you strangled me, you spit at me and you raped me! You gave me what you thought I deserved and I stayed quiet not fighting back for two reasons ONE was that I wanted to get out of the situation alive so that I too could get a gun and kill you and TWO deep down inside of me I believed I deserved it. I believed I was nothing!

Thank you for coming into my life and teaching me what I would NEVER put up with again. I AM a different woman today! I forgive you for hurting me and I forgive myself because I know that what I saw in the mirror was the ugliest version of me and that's NO LONGER the case! ALICIA IS LOVE! ALICIA IS BEAUTY! ALICIA IS LIGHT! ALICIA IS MAGNIFICENT!

Sending you peace! Goodbye forever~ Alicia Anabel

CHAPTER SIX ~ *1996*

You were three years old with chubby cheeks and little hands. We used to call you mitts. Your uncle Tony gave you that nickname. He and your father called you mitts because you could grip a beer bottle and a basketball with one hand. I used to call you my little cookie monster hands. I think you knew all along what was happening to me. I think you could feel me. I know you felt me. I look at the picture of you on your third birthday and it's the first time I didn't see you smiling.

At six years old you asked me about the man with the kids, "Mama, what happened to them? What about the little girls?"

I pretended like you were crazy. I didn't want to acknowledge that question. I wanted to erase that moment from your life. I wanted to give you your third birthday back. 1995, that year was completely robbed from you. It was robbed from me. I punished myself so much for not being there for you. I hated myself for making the worst mistake of our lives. When you asked me about Terrance I wanted to die. I couldn't believe how much of the details you still remembered from way back then.

You told me, "Mama, I didn't like that guy. One day when you were at work and he was watching us. He made me eat tuna fish right out of the can. He wouldn't let me get up from the table until I was done." I had no idea how he treated you when I wasn't around.

Whenever we referred to 1995 I always asked the same thing, "Baby, did he ever put his hands on you?" you always told me no.

I have carried that moment your entire life. I would spend everyday after that experience trying to make it up to you. I desperately wanted you to forgive me. I wanted to fix it. I needed to erase it. But that moment did happen and I can't run from it. After he raped me, he continued to harass me and threaten me so I went to file a restraining order.

When I approached the counter at the courthouse I saw a familiar face and started crying. The clerk who was at the counter was someone I was in a beauty pageant with years ago. I was so embarrassed. I was crying hysterically and couldn't get the words out. She handed me the forms and pointed to a room where I could have some privacy. I sat there and relived the nightmare. The forms were filled out. I left them with the clerk and walked out. That was only part one... now the task would be to have him served in another state.

February 14, 1996

I was sitting at my desk at John Street School when the phone rang. It was a familiar voice. But I was unsure. All that he said was, "Hey YOU!" I just smiled. Joseph's smile came through over the phone. I laughed and said, "What's up Billy O?" We had lots of nicknames for each other. I was his girl Friday. He was Nick I was Nora. He was Cary Grant and I, well I was whoever the leading lady was for the hour.

He loved to call me "AL", saying, "It's such a masculine name for such a feminine woman."

So many months had passed. He called to invite me to grab some coffee and catch up with him. I accepted immediately. I had been looking forward to that moment for like two years. We had never been alone except for that time in the car. I was so nervous about seeing him. This time around I was divorced and single. He was the one that needed to be nervous. But I can't lie I was filled with butterflies.

I picked out the perfect outfit. I made sure that my hair looked amazing. My makeup was flawless. I looked FIERCE!!! I arrived to Dolce Vita and there he was with his cigar in hand looking so handsome. We spent three hours just catching up. We stayed until the café closed. He asked me if I wanted to go for a walk. I accepted.

It was our first date. We walked around the river at Water Place Park, hugging each other in the rain. Our first *real* kiss was near a bridge. The attraction was immediate. The conversation was light, fun and easy. We laughed all night and cracked jokes on each other. We had so much fun. It was exactly what I needed. I was finally in a good place in my life. We were about to move into the most amazing apartment on Hope Street, near Brown University. Later it would be known as your FAVORITE APARTMENT EVER!!! You and I were finally happy. Our life was looking up. It took us a while to get there but we were happy. Things between Joseph and I were moving along beautifully.

We dated for a while before I told Joseph about all that I had been through with Terrance and the divorce. Why I wasn't around as much. He just listened. I told Joseph about the restraining order that I had just filed. He asked me how he could help. I told him that I wanted

Terrance to be served in Boston at his job. The hard part was that the paperwork would have to be handled in Massachusetts.

Joseph was from Boston, so he took care of it for me. I was so grateful. He even helped us move into our new apartment. You and I were starting over. We had a fresh start. But there was one more thing I needed to do. I planned it perfectly. I booked a 10-day trip to Margarita Island scheduled departure was the day I knew Terrance would be served. I figured if he came looking for me I would be out of town.

Joseph picked me up at 3:00am and drove me to Logan Airport. Of course, I almost missed my flight. Once we were there he asked me if I wanted him to check on our house. I left him the keys and asked him to water my plants and I was off. I needed to get away (more like runaway). I left you with your *abuelo, abuela* and your dad. They would take care of you while I was gone. I knew you were safe. Once I arrived to Venezuela I was a mess. For the first five days I was homesick. I missed you so much. I had never been apart from you for that long.

Recently I found a picture of me holding you in that apartment. You were 3 years old and I had just returned from Santa Marta. Those 10 days must have felt like years for you. I didn't think for a moment how my leaving town so suddenly would affect you. I didn't stop to wonder how you would feel.

When I look at you in that photo now I see so much happiness. You were filled with joy. *Mama's home* your smile was wide, eyes bright. You didn't want to leave my side. We were inseparable from that moment on. So I'm left feeling like shit – thinking about how beautiful and innocent you were. How happy you were to have me home. But I'm left wondering how scared you must have felt. Did you wonder if

I had abandoned you? Did you fear that I'd never come back? Has that moment marked you?

Joseph and I saw each other for seven months before he made any moves. Not that I didn't want him to. One evening when we were alone he was helping me put my bed together and he wrestled me onto the bed. He held my wrist down, straddled me and I just looked at him above me. He went to put his hand around my neck in a joking fashion. He was trying to be all sexy. It wasn't working! It only brought up fucked up memories. I started crying. He jumped up and asked me what was wrong. He apologized a million times. He said he was only playing. I told him that that was exactly what Terrance had done to me the first time he put his hands on me.

Spring, 1997

"There's a somebody...I'm longing to see...I hope that he...turns out to be...someone to watch over me." By Gershwin

There was a song left on our answering machine, "There's a saying ol' says that love is blind... There's a somebody I'm longing to see." It drove me crazy for days. It was so beautiful. I called every radio station I knew that played jazz and played it for them and not one DJ could tell me who was singing that version of the Gershwin classic.

I received fresh flowers weekly from him. I recently found the card I saved from a bouquet of flowers that he sent. They were roses and the note simply read, "You are loved."

We fell madly in love we each other. We joked about how we weren't serious. But what I was feeling was very serious and foreign to me. I had never had a man treat me with as much respect as Joseph had. He respected my mind and body.

We went to the nicest restaurants in Rhode Island and Boston. We stayed at the nicest hotels. Dinner cruises in Boston, parasailing in Key West, strip joint in Palm Beach, drinking and making jokes near Hemingway's house, running around the mansions of Newport and touching everything. We were like two kids. Everywhere we went was a good time. We had music, dancing and lots of laughs. We had a code word for making love that we called, "playing patty cakes." One day at work I got a box with a doll called "Chatty Katty" and the first thing out of her mouth was, "lets play patty cakes." That's what our relationship was like days and nights filled with love and laughter.

You adored him. He spoiled you. You owned every single Disney movie thanks to him. You were always on his lap. We had good times. We went to Revere Beach and you and him built a sand castle. He was gentle and careful with you. For years you always said to me that no one would ever be like Joseph. "Mama, he's the man for you!" Every photo from that time in my life captured what I was feeling. I had the most genuine smiles. *"There's a somebody I'm longing to see~ I hope that he~ turns out to be~ someone who'll watch over me."* The entire relationship was a blast. It was a walking living Broadway Musical every single day. Everything we did was based on a song. There was so much singing, so much dancing, so many laughs, so many happy times. There are so many wonderful memories and the love that was shared even with strangers. We brought the party everywhere we went. The greatest love I've ever known. He was my knight in shining armor. He came to rescue me in his white Saturn. Joseph brought me laughter, fun, spontaneity, love, romance, love, love, love. I fell deeply. He was the first man to treat me like a QUEEN a GODDESS. He brought a mature immaturity to the relationship and treated you like the most delicate flower. He was always careful not to overstep his boundaries and respected our space. He loved me. He was sent to take care of me. He was sent to watch over me and for that reason, *"our love is here to stay."*

When we first met, we were both in relationships. If I was ever going to cheat on your dad it might have been with him. But I didn't cheat. Much later I would become the other woman. I was well aware that he with someone but that didn't stop me from allowing things to get serious. I believed that it was ok and that I knew what I was doing. It was OK because I didn't take him seriously. I didn't take us seriously. I thought I had it all under control. I believed that I wouldn't get hurt because I was the one who was single in this equation and had nothing to lose. Never for a moment did I take his girlfriends feelings into consideration.

I was happy for the first time in a long time. I felt like I could finally breathe again. You and I were doing great. We had our freedom. Mommy was getting her shit together. I looked the most beautiful I had ever looked. Scratch that… I looked fucking hot. It was as if all the joy, all the life, all the love, all the peace, all the tranquility and all the happiness were restored into my body. So much so, that I decided to throw a house warming/birthday party in our new apartment (it was March) it wasn't even my birthday. But it certainly felt like I was reborn. My relationship with Joseph was beautiful, but it wasn't enough. I wanted more for you and I. After everything we had been through. I wanted a fresh start. I told Joseph that we were moving to Florida. He couldn't believe I was leaving just like that.

CHAPTER SEVEN ~ *1997 Move to Florida*

On the road again... we were off on another adventure. Your father was accepted into graduate school in Florida and I needed a change. I wanted a new start. We needed new surroundings. Besides part of our divorce decree was that I was not allowed to move you out of the state without giving your father and the court system 30 days notice. Your father's biggest fear was that I would move us back to my hometown New York and that he would never see you again. So Florida was the next best thing.

I wanted to be in a place where we could make new memories. Your father and I may not have liked each other so much but there was certainly a lot of love for you. I didn't want you to be so far away from your dad so I decided we would go to Florida also. I wasn't completely insane. Before we left I made sure to take a leave of absence so I wouldn't lose my job at the Providence School Department. We packed our Penske truck and headed on 95 South to a new address. This was a brand new chapter where we would leave Rhode Island behind us.

We moved into our one bedroom apartment in Ft. Lauderdale. I gave you the bedroom and kept my bed in the living room. Even though you had your own bedroom you still slept with me a lot of the time. You were so excited that we had a pool. You couldn't wait to learn how to swim. And you learned so quickly. Joseph was visiting us for a weekend and before he left you were diving in the deep end. Your dad and I took you to see your new school. You were starting kindergarten. We had a routine. We got up together, you brushed your teeth, washed your face, and I'd make your cereal. We got dressed together side by side. Sometimes we were color coordinated. You were always in the bathroom with me.

Life in Florida was peaceful for us. Your *abuelo* came to Florida and stayed with us for a few weeks. He drove me crazy with all his criticisms. But I loved having him around. *Abuelo* loved Florida so much that the entire family moved six months later. Your *abuela, tia* Josie, *tia* Fabiana, and uncle Fabio all came to Fort Lauderdale.

It was nice having the family close by. I landed an incredible job at a major telecommunications company. Joseph was still hanging around. He'd come visit us once a month and send us packages and cards every other day. He had me convinced that he was serious about making it work between us. That he was going to make changes in his life. Joseph actually left his girlfriend of fifteen years and moved out. It sounded good. He started making plans to move to Florida to be with me. So I started looking for a two-bedroom apartment for the three of us. Our new apartment would be in Plantation, Florida. Yes girl they named it plantation—fucked up but true!!!

Your father and I started building a solid friendship and there was a part of Joseph that felt there was no room for him in my life. Joseph was right. He understood early on that he wasn't at the top of my list. He always told me that he felt lucky to even be considered in the top ten and that he respected me for not allowing a man to go before you.

Joseph could accept being 2nd to Luz, 3rd to my parents and siblings, 4th to the long list of cousins but to go after your dad — not so much.

Joseph started to resent that and it put a strain on our relationship. Whenever your dad wanted to see you I allowed it. I never went by the whole, "I'm the custodial parent" thing. We shared you. I never made it difficult for your father to see you.

One weekend Joseph was visiting for his birthday and he made it clear to me that *this* weekend was going to be about *us* with no distractions. He made it a point to tell me that he did not want to share me this weekend. Your father called me early one Saturday morning telling me that he had been in a car accident and that he needed my help.

Needless to say the weekend was fucked up and we didn't get to do any of the things Joseph had planned for us. After that visit our relationship started to breakdown. Joseph was pulling away from me. I didn't want to lose him so I decided that we should move back to Rhode Island. I wanted to show him how much I loved him. I wanted to prove to him how dedicated I was to our relationship. I decided that we would move back to Providence so that we could begin our life together.

January 1998

I pulled you out of your kindergarten class mid-year. We were back in Rhode Island. I enrolled you into St. Annes Elementary School. You made friends fast. Your best friend Alan was a student there. You adjusted quickly. You were happy that you would be able to see your cousins in Cranston. People love to say how resilient children are. But deep down, I knew that this shit was fucked up. Our moving so quickly like that. The change was harsh and abrupt. It was irresponsible of me. You needed stability and I was trying so hard to give you that. I rented a beautiful two-bedroom apartment near Mt. Pleasant Avenue. There were trees everywhere. The apartment had a double parlor with sliding French doors that separated the rooms. After your father and I divorced, I never lived with another man. So I was just learning how to share space and create a life for us.

Joseph was back to his weekend visits. I expected him to move in with us immediately. In my mind, the next step was marriage. I certainly didn't want to be that woman who allows men to just come to the house to fuck me and leave me. That's not the kind of example I wanted to be for you. So I started to put A LOT of pressure on him to show me that he was in this with me. I needed to know that this was real... that we were in fact doing this. After being back in RI just a few weeks I realized I'd made a huge mistake coming back to this state. I was kicking myself for retuning to this place where I had had the worst experiences of my life. I was fooling myself that he was real. I started to see the truth. He was only telling me what I wanted to hear. He was only telling me the shit that he knew would keep me here. Like the day he brought this book home about how to raise a daughter. I felt led on. Joseph knew that the way to my heart was through you.

I booked a flight for you and I to Florida. I needed to clear my head. I needed to decide what I was going to do. I had to figure out what my next step was... what the best thing for US would be. You were at your grandparent's house for the weekend. I made dinner for him. He showed up close to midnight. As soon as he took off his coat and boots I began to speak, "Joseph, we need to talk. Look! I booked a flight to Florida. I need to clear my head. I need to figure out some shit. I didn't come back to RI for this. I thought we were going to be together. I thought we were going to be a family. I need some space."

He just looked up at me—grabbed his boots and sat down in a chair and said, "You know what Alicia! You can have your space... you can have your space starting RIGHT NOW!"

As he laced up the first boot I was horrified. I could not watch the man I love walk out on me. After all I had done to prove to him how much I love him. After everything I was willing to give up in order for us to be together. Didn't he know that I returned to this dreadful place to be with him? I was like, *oh hell no! I can't stand here and watch him leave me!*

I'm the one who left. I grabbed my keys and ran out of the house. It was after midnight, snow was on the ground. The windows of my Nissan Sentra were iced. I was crying like a baby barely able to see out the windows and drove to a friend's house. The slamming on her front door woke her. I told her the entire story and she just held me. And that was it. The story of us was over. The song ended. We barely spoke after that day. We might have seen each other twice and then communication completely stopped. I couldn't afford the rent payment alone so we had to give up that beautiful apartment and moved AGAIN.

I stayed single for a long time. When Joseph and I broke up I didn't have another relationship for six years. I was stuck in that place and lost in our love. I was trying to go back to a place where I felt wonderful, spiritually connected to a source larger, wiser, experienced and more beautiful than me. I was looking for this someone to give me something that I believed I couldn't give me. I held onto every good memory about Joseph and I and our moment together.

While I lived my life and continued marching on I still never let him go for many years. I believed that when he left he took all that was beautiful in our relationship. I never realized that I was an active participant in the beauty that was us. In fact I was a major player in that relationship. The happiness I believed he gave me I finally understood that it was in ME all along.

During a writing session with a friend I was complaining about being reprimanded for not following protocol at work. I was almost going to stay in that funky angry mood and write about it. Then I sat at the table and something changed my mind. We both got our venting on! She was in the middle of writing out her frustrations when I interrupted her. So instead of writing we ended up talking. After we let it all out the conversation moved to LOVE. Rather than staying angry at the events of the day we decided to talk about the greatest loves of our lives. It was an amazing conversation. That's when I told her about THE MAN WHO GAVE BIRTH TO ME.

One of the most beautiful ideas about seeing the significance of Joseph in my life came from my therapist when we lived in Florida. We spent a lot of time talking about my last long term relationship. She referenced a book titled *SHE: Understanding Feminine Psychology*, by Robert A. Johnson. The story was about the love affair between Psyche & Eros. About a king and queen who have three daughters, Psyche is the most beautiful of three. Eros the God of love, son of Aphrodite, was out flying on his horse when he pricks himself with one of his arrows and in that moment notices Psyche and falls madly in love with her. Aphrodite agrees to let him have her, but warns him that she must never know that he's a God.

Once in the castle Eros informs Psyche that he will only come to her at night and she can NEVER ask to see him. If she tries to see what he looks like he will leave her and never come back. Eros gave Psyche everything she ever wanted. Yet she doesn't even know what her husband looks like.

Her jealous sisters come for a visit one day and warn her, "What do you mean you've never seen your husband? That's crazy! What if he's some sort of monster," They advised her to have an oil lamp ready by her bed and a knife under her pillow just in case. They told her that the next time he comes to visit her while he's sleeping she should turn the lamp on.

That evening Eros flew into her window in pitch-blackness and lay next to her. When he went to sleep she lit her lamp. When she looked over at him she noticed that he was the most BEAUTIFUL man she had ever seen. She was married to a God. She could barely breathe. Psyche got so nervous that she tilted the lamp and oil dropped on his chest. Eros jumped up angry as hell, and told her, "I warned you to never ask to see me. Now I must leave you and never return."

Joseph was my Eros. He warned me to never try to see him. To never question him. He was happy with what we had. But I wanted more. The lighting of the lamp was very symbolic for me. When I lit the lamp I saw Joseph for who he truly was. Of course he had to leave me. I might not have liked the truth being revealed to me. That's when my therapist looked at me and said, "WOW! All this time whenever you spoke of a man, I assumed you were speaking of your ex-husband."

Then she called Joseph, "The Man Who Gave Birth to Me." She explained that he was the man who gave birth to me as a woman. I loved the thought of Joseph being the man who gave birth to me. It had never occurred to me to see it in such a beautiful way.

As we continued speaking I shared with her a story about a revelation I had while I was with him. We were making love. We were in the hallway of our apartment on Hope Street. He wanted to make love in front of the mirror. So I obliged. I was incredibly shy. I never enjoyed having sex with the lights on. I despised looking at my body. I didn't want to see what we were doing. He told me to look in the mirror. I said no! He asked me again, "Alicia, look at yourself! Look in the mirror! Look at how beautiful you are! This is what I see when I look at you."

It was a moment that would transform me forever. It was as if he was no longer with me in that moment. I felt and saw this light all around me. I saw into my soul for the first time and she was amazing. I saw a beauty that I didn't know existed in me. I kept looking and looking at myself. I'm not sure if he was still speaking but I wasn't hearing his words. I was lost in this magical moment when all the love I was feeling for ME was pouring out of me. All the love that consumes me, all the love that I bring and all the beauty that is ME. It's a beauty I had often heard so many people say to me I possessed but that I could now see for the first time. I love him for that moment. I love him for taking such good care of me. I love him for the gifts he

63

tried to give me that were always inside of me. We'd always have music.

Letter: Dear Joseph,

The Nick to my Nora... Billy O... Your Girl Friday. Oh – we had some laughs. You and I met while I was married and yes we did steal a kiss under the moonlight. Man I had such a crush on you. Blond, blue eyes, charismatic, funny, you were the life of the party. You introduced me to so many BEAUTIFUL things food, music, passion and ME. We had so much fun together. GOOD TIMES! There was something inconsistent about you and I. There was missing information... unquestioning. I pretended everything was a joke. In the end what would be revealed to me is that you too took advantage of me. You were taken yes. I was the other woman. This is true. Initially I was ok with this. I never took you seriously or at least that's what I tried to convince myself. I wanted to believe that I wasn't falling for you. I had myself fooled that I somehow was in control of my heart. I never felt comfortable with the lying and sneaking around it weighed heavily on me. You and I were always out on the town having a blast and never for a moment did we worry about her heart.

"A bottle of whites... a bottle of red... perhaps a bottle of rose instead... I'll meet you anytime you want in our Italian restaurant." ~Billy Joel

We had so many songs – by so many artists. We had so many spots that were our spots. We even had entire states. Ours was a carefree love affair. Not some black and white movie. Ours was real. That thing that made us so great would be the very thing that would end our relationship. That idea of being free of cares concerned me. We were not living in this world. It was such an amazing fantastical affair. "If it ain't broke don't fix it." that's what you always used to say. We were just one version of what you wanted us to be. But that wasn't what I wanted for me. There was no room for real life issues and problems to resolve. What about Courtney? She deserved a home... a family. To you it was always supposed to be FUN. There was so much about you that I didn't know. There were unanswered questions, half-truths and deception. But when it was great - - it was fucking AMAZING. You filled me with love at a time when I didn't believe anyone loved me. You came at a time when I definitely wasn't loving me. We became each others welcomed distractions. We were each other's weekend escape from the lives that we knew.

At first I was cool with it... I believed your lies that you were unhappy and that you and her no longer had sex. So I would still enjoy you. I would take you up on all your invitations to go out on the town and have dinner just to be in each other's company. I felt like after all I had been through – I was owed this... I deserved this. It was my turn to have a man that would raise me up. I overlooked a lot of shit because we were having so much fun and I felt I deserved to be happy. But not at someone else's expense. I pretended to never take us seriously. I tried to let you go but it was so hard. There were things we shared like my sacred moment while we were making love. It was a moment of enlightenment for me. What it revealed to me was a beauty in me that I never saw before. And for that I thank you. Thank you for showing me ME - - thank you for giving birth to me. I will always love you. Goodbye – Love, "Al"

"Love lost gave me a new path to follow." ~Rumi

I finally needed to let him go to really understand that what I needed he could never give me. So I moved on. I learned the lesson that I needed to learn even though it took 10 years to release him. When I look back on those moments where I wanted to recall and bring into my present the fun that was Joseph and I. What I didn't realize was that I too was there. I was present. I was the source. The love, beauty, enlightenment, music, laughter that was shared was amazing but I am still that source. For such a long time I convinced myself that when Joseph walked out the door he took my heart with him. I credited him with everything. I forgot my role in it. I finally realized that I'm pretty fucking great. I can take credit for a lot of the laughter and love brought into our relationship. Just because we didn't work out doesn't mean I lose ME. Now I just needed to figure out how to put my life back together and get us back to Florida.

1999, Rhode Island

We got right back into the swing of things. Your grandmother was an amazing support for us. She picked you from school everyday. She had that routine on lock. You would come home from school and the first thing you did was take off your uniform and she would hang it up. You would eat a snack and do your homework. You and your grandma were very tight.

During that time I was working three jobs. I worked at the elementary school from 8am – 3pm, then I'd work at the Italian restaurant on Federal Hill as a hostess evenings and cocktail waitress at night, and a few nights a week I would work at one of the most prestigious strip clubs in Providence. I was working so hard to save money so that we could move back to Florida. This time I wanted to wait until you finished school. I wasn't going to pull you out mid-year again.

I worked my ass off. I was working all the time. I made so much money. I was making $300 bucks a night at the restaurant during their club nights. I averaged about $1,000 a week at the strip club and what ever pocket change I was making from the school department.

One night my car broke down while I was going to work. I called *abuela* to get the AAA number so I could call a tow truck. When your *abuelo* answered, he was freaked out, "*mi hija que tu hace llamando de allí? Muchacha, que tu hace en ese sitio?*"

He wanted to know what the hell I was doing in that club. Apparently the strip clubs name showed up on his caller ID — fucking caller ID. I didn't have enough time to even think of a lie. I just reacted, "Papi, it's not what you think. I swear to God I'm not taking off my clothes. I work here as a cocktail waitress. I swear I'm not dancing."

What I failed to mention was that as a cocktail waitress in the club to make extra cash I gave men massages (not that kind of massage... don't be DIRTY!!!) I would charge the guys $14.00 for ten minutes. Then on special nights, when I was brave I participated in a little something called wrestling night. I would jump in a ring with another girl and so began an evening of slipping and sliding on oils and whip cream for the viewing pleasure of all the male guests. There was a guy once who paid $200 bucks to each of us to wrestle him. The best hours to work were, "legs and eggs." They set up a buffet at 6:00am and men would come in for a lap dance to go along with their bacon and eggs. And right after that I would go to work at the school. Yup! And I call myself a feminist. I've always been against exploitation of women in any form and here I was exploiting myself.

Your grandma was my accountant she collected and saved all my money. She was my bank. That was your most FAVORITE Christmas. The gifts that surrounded your grandma's tree filled the entire living room. Everyone made out well that year. The joke in the family is that everyone got a t-shirt with the logo from the strip joint.

I saw a lot of shit in that club. I would walk in on girls doing all kinds of drugs before they went on stage. The lifestyle is dangerous. I never went home the same way. We lived fairly close to the club, but always took a longer route home so customers wouldn't follow me.

That business was dangerous baby. For a moment I was lost in all the money I was saving. I had saved $10,000 for our move. After the holidays when I went back to work the mood of the club was somber. I was told that the night before one of the girls turned up missing. One of her clients followed her home and wanted his money back. He pushed her into her apartment raped her, killed her, threw her in her bathtub and burned her body from the waist down. The girl's parents came from Maine to identify her body. They thought she was attending a college in Providence. That was the last day I ever worked in the club. What I noticed is that they don't give a fuck about anybody. There's no value on life. They didn't even shut the club for one day to pay respects to this girl. She was just a body and it was business as usual.

Man! Listen, you are my RIDE OR DIE! You have gone to hell and back with me. You're a trooper. As soon as you finished school that year we were out of there. All of our family came to see us off. YOU AND ME KID!!!

Determined. I was determined to get this right. We moved back to Sunrise, Florida. Things were looking up. You were enrolled in a Lutheran School that your *abuelo* worked at. You and your *abuelo* were inseparable. You know all his secrets. You guys went to work together and came home together. And me well I went to my new job working for the top rum company in the world.

CHAPTER EIGHT ~ *2001, Florida*

I was the assistant to a marketing manager. We headed the most amazing national campaigns. The brand would travel from state to state and throw parties at all the hottest clubs in Miami, NYC, California, Chicago, Dallas, Colorado, Georgia and Boston. It was the most amazing job. I had so much fun and made wonderful friends. I had a great working relationship with my boss. He trusted me with everything. I loved my job. I was happy there.

I was getting ready for work. It was the most beautiful sunny day. I dropped you off at your *abuelo's* and there was not a single cloud in the sky. My morning ritual phone conversation with Tia Josie as I drove into work. It was our daily check in and gossip about what was happening in the world, on the soaps or in the entertainment world. She was watching Good Morning America when there was interruption, "Yo! A plane just went into one the twin towers," she said.

"Get the fuck outta here!" We started to immediately come up with our own scenarios of what happened. I said, "Maybe one of the pilots had a seizure."

Your Tia was trying to make sense out of all of it. I was changing the radio station hoping that there would be something being reported describing what was happening in my beloved New York City. After a few more moments of our rambling, she said, "OH MY GOD!!! Another plane just crashed into the towers," all I remember saying was, "We're under attack!!!"

I arrived to the office and my boss hadn't heard the news yet. We all ran to a conference room and turned on the television. I said to my boss, "Look if one more thing happens I am going home to my daughter."

Only a few moments later did we hear that a third plane crashed into the Pentagon. The Pentagon! Are you fucking kidding me? This was not a TEST!!! I left work as quickly as I could. I called your *abuelo* and told him he needed to leave work. He said he couldn't. I told him that he needed to. "Does your job understand what is happening in New York? Leave work now!"

I'm not sure if he even spoke to you about what was happening. I rushed home and there you were sucking your little fingers. I just held you tight. *Abuelo* and *abuela* had the news on. And for that entire evening and the weeks that followed we watched the towers fall over and over and over again.

That beautiful Tuesday morning, in front of the backdrop of a magnificent blue sky, all we could see was thick dark gray clouds of smoke that extended for miles coming out of the side of the towers. Over 3,000 people died that day. They were mothers, fathers, grandparents, brothers, sisters, cousins, aunts, uncles, and friends. Black, white, Jewish, Hindu, Asian and Latino. Everyone in the world lost someone that day even if they didn't know someone personally.

The entire family sat and watched both towers collapse in two hours. We cried. We were frightened. We didn't know what to do. The house was silent. We knew that everyone on the flights that hit the towers died on impact. People were jumping out of the windows from the 90th floor. A dear friend called me franticly saying that her best friend, who was pregnant at the time worked in the towers. They never found her body.

That moment woke up an entire nation. That day changed the way New Yorkers treated each other. Hands were extended from unlikely places. Love was felt—at least for a little while. Until any person wearing a turban started being discriminated against.

9/11 changed the lives of many but would mark me forever.

CHAPTER NINE ~ *October 3, 2001*

It was two weeks after 9/11 happened and we were all still feeling the aftermath of that devastating day. While people lost loved ones the rest of the world seemed to get closer to those still here with us. You were eight years old when the towers came down. I'm not sure you understood what had just taken place in NYC. How that event didn't *just* happen to New York. The residue of that day was in the air and felt all over the world.

After September 11th happened, I felt this urgency to get my life together. I had turned 30 years old two months prior. When those planes came down I became desperate. I was experiencing this sense of urgency. It was a matter of life and death for me to get it together. I started questioning where I was in my life and who I am. I realized that my life felt insignificant and unimportant. I felt that I wasn't contributing anything to the world. I believed that my life was of no value.

I started to wonder about things like...*what would people say about me after I leave this place? How will I be remembered?* I started to get scared. I was questioning everything I had done and not done. *What have I contributed to the earth? What will I leave you with besides debt and rumors of promiscuity? "Que tu madre era una locita." What was I born to do? What is my legacy? Who am I? Where have I been? How would I want you to remember me?*

I decided that I would write you a memoir. That would be the legacy left for you a book filled with my life story — written for you. I had no intention on letting anyone read it. I decided that I would document where I was for ten years. I was going to write it from 1991-2001.

Since I had never written a book before I printed a calendar for ten years and started plugging in all the places I lived in, all the people I slept with, all the jobs I'd held. I wanted to give you a true account, an authentic story about where I've been. I wanted you to know all my dirt, the many mistakes and bad choices I've made. I wanted you to know where I came from. I didn't want someone else telling you their version of me. I wanted to tell you my story, my truth, so that you could form your own opinion about who your mother is.

One night we were lying in bed together reading. You were wrapped up in a Nancy drew story and I was reading a book on writing titled, *Writing from Personal Experience*. I was reading on how one goes about writing a book, when the most amazing thing happened. At 9:39pm as I was reading, I came across a line that talked about where one can find inspiration for writing and telling stories. This book was giving me all kinds of messages about material being found in everything in my life. In that exact moment I had an epiphany. I had one of those life altering Oprah AHA moments.

On October 3, 2001, what I read jumped out at me. It was about *how even in our own lives there's a story to be told*. In that exact moment I whispered to myself, *Oh my GOD!!! I'm a writer!!! I AM A WRITER!!!*

I knew that that moment was significant so I made sure to write down the date and time. I looked over to you and said, "Baby, mommy's a writer!"

73

You just looked at me with this glow in your eyes like you were looking at your sheroe and said, "I know mommy! I know! You're gonna write me a book."

"No honey, you don't understand – **I AM... A WRITER!!!**

"I know mommy... we're gonna be rich and you're gonna buy me a big house with a McDonalds and a Carvel inside."

I just laughed. You didn't get it. For me that moment would mark me. That moment would change the direction of my life forever. My heart was pounding. I finally understood my place in the world. I had spent so much of my time in the desert, without water and without a compass. I was simply flying with nowhere to land. I had no direction. I knew that after that moment I would never be the same. I finally paid attention to the signs. What seemed so crazy to me was that when I started my writer's journey it turned out that for several years I had been collecting books on writing without even realizing it.

I was born to write. I was collecting books on writing and on publishing that sat on our bookshelves moving with us from house to house. Sometimes the very thing you are meant to do with your life is staring you right in the face but you ignore all the signs believing everything the world tells you, *that dreams don't come true* and that writing... "Well who told you that's even a realistic job?"

Once I knew what my calling was there was NO STOPPING ME. The universe absolutely started to align. I shared my epiphany with a co-worker and she jumped for joy and was so emotional. She was so excited and told me that coincidently (we know I don't believe in coincidences) she read in the Miami Herald something about a writing competition. She wasn't sure if she'd thrown it away. She told me that she would go home and try and find it. The very next day she came to my desk with a bright smile with the paper circled and highlighted.

She understood that I was meant to have that clipping. It was one of those signs, a blessing, a miracle those things that happen as confirmations that everything happens RIGHT ON TIME!!!

When I read the article it was an announcement for the Miami Book Fair. It was a competition to submit 30 pages of unpublished work. The winners would have a one-on-one writing session with world renowned Latino Authors. The only catch was that the deadline was in three days and I literally only realized I was a writer yesterday.

I went for it. I took two vacation days and had four days to write 30 pages and had no idea where to even begin. I had a title and no story. That memoir was going to be called, *Becoming me: It's ok in my skin!* It was about me being born in Brooklyn, raised in Queens. I wrote about the love affair between *abuelo y abuela*. I wrote and wrote nonstop. I started at the year 1969 and kept writing. When I had what seemed like 30 pages I stopped. I was so proud. I had completed something. I was actually going to make the deadline for the competition. I emailed everyone in my life the news. I sent the story to someone I loved and trusted. When he read it I couldn't wait to hear his feedback.

He called me while I was driving. I remember that it was pouring. The first thing out of his mouth was, "No one cares how your mom and dad met. No one is going to read it. Latino's don't read! There are statistics that show..."

And on and on he went. When he finished, my eyes swelled up with tears, I became enraged. It felt like he just kicked my newborn child the moment she came out of my belly. He could have said that shit differently. He had a valid point although he went about it wrong. His criticisms could have come a little softer a little kinder. He wasn't completely wrong. Statistics do show that the numbers in publishing for Latinos and African American's buying books was low. *Pero cono!*

He didn't have to come at me like that. That shit destroyed me. I never trusted him again after that. My confidence level was on the ground.

I did get response back from the competition. My story was rejected. I felt so low. There was a weekend of events scheduled during the book festival a panel discussion with editors and major players in publishing. I was thinking about going but I wasn't sure. *Abuelo* called me at work and told me that you had a minor asthma attack at school so I wasn't sure if I should leave you. I wanted to do the right thing. I felt so much guilt about it... do I go to something that could help my writing career or do I go home and take care of you? After hours of me making myself sick over it I called your *abuelo* back and told him that I was going to be a little late because there was a conference I wanted to attend but to call me if your asthma got worse.

I was so glad I went. It was being held in this beautiful auditorium at the University of Miami. The room was filled with aspiring writers. I felt uncomfortable. I was so intimidated. I didn't feel worthy. The panel shared stories about authors who have had international success vs. those here in the states. There was one panelist that stood out to me. She was a fierce Ecuadorian from New York; she had been in publishing for seven years. Her talk was about finding *the* Latino Writer that was going to break barriers and change the way publishing views us. I was sold. Not only did I finally know what my life calling was but I wanted to be *that* Latino Writer she was looking for. I wanted to be a writer who would also be a leader in the publishing industry and in the Latino community. What I was looking for was in New York. And that's when I began planning the biggest move of our lives.

It was the summer of 2002. I had successfully pulled off an amazing event at the Four Seasons and decided to treat myself to some pampering. It was the kind of pampering that I could never have afforded on my own. There were private yoga sessions at sunrise, room service at night, a massage and manicure/pedicure before I left. I was living the life of luxury - - on my company's dime! It was my last hurrah! I figured it would be ok to treat myself after a job well done and I believed that no one would be upset about it.

Boy was I WRONG! A few weeks later I arrived to my office sat at my desk and noticed an eerie silence. No hustle... no bustle. There was nothing in my bosses outbox for me to handle. There was always stuff in his outbox for me to do. There were no forwarded voicemails with calls to return. There were no emails from him. Something was very wrong. Something bad was coming I could feel it.

I went about my business and did the work I had pending. I had this coin I carried for protection and tossed it around my hand hoping that this feeling would pass. Coincidently, that was the same week I had given my two weeks notice because we were starting our NEW LIFE in NYC. Then I got the call! "Alicia, can you step into my office?"

It did not sound good. I did not have a good feeling in the pit of my stomach. I was nervous and scared. I wasn't sure what they wanted to talk to me about. There were NO smiles on their faces. Everyone always smiled at me. They were not happy to see me! I was asked to sit down. They presented me with a document with the total of all my expenses accrued from the hotel. It was well over $3,000.00. My mouth dropped!

Letter: Dear Disappointed Boss,

I loved working with you. I wish I could take back the fact that I betrayed your trust and put your reputation on the line. At the time I did not realize what the consequences of my actions would be. I made a poor choice. I own that. I took advantage of a good situation. I see that. You could have been more understanding and compassionate. I made a mistake. I paid back every cent. I am truly sorry for what I did. I am here to ask for your forgiveness. I can't believe I did that. I tried to rationalize what I had done. I believed it wasn't a big deal. I didn't think I was hurting anyone. What I failed to realize or even consider was what the consequences would be for the choices I made and how those choices affected the group. At the time I didn't think about how what I had done would make you look to your bosses. I have tried to reach out to you over the years. You have never taken my calls. There is nothing I can do about that now. It's done! I've PAID my dues. I'm done punishing myself. Yes I made a mistake and I admit it. I forgive myself for that mistake. I forgive myself for taking advantage of that situation. With love, Alicia

After that meeting I was told I had until the end of the day to pack my personal belongings and leave. My boss walked me to my car, gave me a hug and wished me luck...and I was off. I was just glad security didn't escort me from the premises. I was so humiliated. I was filled with regret and remorse. I cried all the way home. I'm crying right now just thinking about that moment in my life.

I went home and told my family that the company had let me leave early and gave me two weeks paid. I looked at my parent's and told them how happy I was, "This is great news, now my time is freed up and I can continue to prepare for my trip." I lied right to their faces. I was so embarrassed, so humiliated, so disgusted and so disappointed in myself. I was in the shower crying and crying. I had to put a towel in my mouth so my parents wouldn't hear me. I could not believe I went out like that! What the fuck!!! That was so not me! They treated me like I was a thief.

A day later, I got a call at my house from the head of Human Resources she wanted to check in on me. She wanted to know how I was. I told her I was not good. I told her how sorry I was. I asked her to forgive me and thanked her for all the kindness she had shown me. She assured me that I had nothing to worry about that anyone who called for a reference would get a great review about me because my performance was always excellent and I was very well liked.

This was a woman who I had a personal relationship with and so much respect for. She was taking me under her wing. She had become my mentor. She offered me tickets to see Dr. Wayne Dyer live and constantly encouraged and supported my professional, spiritual and personal development. She took an interest in me and this was how I repaid her.

The last thing she asked me while we were on the phone was, "Alicia, now what are you going to do? What's your next step? What's your plan?"

I wiped my tears and as I sniffled I said, "I'm going to New York! I'm still moving forward with my plans!" I'm crying write now as I write this because this truly shows me who I am and where I was at in my life. I have come so far.

Her response, "EXCELLENT! It's so important that you follow through on your commitments."

I will always be grateful to her for those words. I have carried them everyday since our last day in Florida. I owe that woman so much. To her I say thank you.

I punished myself for such a long time after that mistake. It took me years to get passed that moment. When we moved to NYC I arrived with NOTHING. I no longer had a job waiting. The job that I had set up was taken from me because it came from a referral from the last job. All the money I had saved for our move was gone.

Ironically, the amount I had saved was exactly $3,000.00 and I had 24 hours to come up with the money to pay back the company or they would have taken legal action against me. That money was everything we had. EVERYTHING!!! After that incident took place in Miami I had nothing. WE had nothing. I was nothing.

CHAPTER TEN ~ *New York City, July 18, 2002*

After 9/11 I decided two things 1) I am a writer and New York was where I needed to be to make my dreams happen. 2) There is no other city in the world I'd rather live in than the one I was born in. Everything was moving so smoothly until my perfect little plan got all fucked up when I got myself into that financial mess in Miami. Everything I had saved not to mention the money I needed to borrow was used to get me out of that mess.

I tried like hell to keep it from you. I pretended that all was good. I had no money, no job, no phat apartment in Harlem. It was time to go. Our family was still so proud of me.

It was on your Tia Fabiana's birthday that I decided to leave. I was like, *fuck it I have to do this! New York City here we come*!!! I left you in Florida for the summer so that I could get things in order.

I remember feeling good when I arrived to NJ because I knew I was finally one state away from HOME! Once I got passed all the NYC traffic my mind kept going back to what happened in Florida. I carried this overwhelming feeling of failure. I was disappointed in myself. I allowed my mistake to define me. I was in a self-imprisonment, a self-torture and just kept punishing myself. I had to push it out when I arrived to New York… GAME ON!!!

When I arrived to NYC I had $100 bucks in my pocket, a carton of cigarettes, a suspended license and our car was uninsured. I was living off of soda and parliaments. I lost forty pounds. I allowed myself to be treated like shit by employers when I arrived to NYC and the men let's not forget them. I believed I deserved to be treated like shit. I was feeling so down. I was groveling. I needed every crap job I got. In my first week in NYC I sent out 70 resumes. I registered at every temp agency in the city. I was hungry and not just because I was hungry for a job. I mailed you a post card of the New York City skyline with an ocean liner cruising down the Hudson River with a note:

My beautiful daughter, I can't wait to see you. This is our new home. And it will be everything we ever hoped for. We will be sooo happy because we are together. We have so much to do. We are going to have so much fun. I will show you where your "new" school is. You will get to see and play with your cousins. It's going to great. I will see you Sunday. Be a good girl. Say your prayers – especially on the plane. I love you. Mommy xxoo

After only being in NYC two weeks, I started a temp gig at Tiffany's (thank you creator). However, don't get excited. Yes it was the famous Tiffany's on Fifth Avenue, which for some folks might sound fancy. But for those of you who don't know what Tiffany's is… it's not all that impressive. It's where they sell high priced shit, with the name Tiffany's on it and where they mark something up that was made for $1.00 to $100.00. I quit my first day on the job. When I was asked to take out the trash.

I didn't care how desperate I was for cash, you are not going to demean and disrespect me!

A few days later I landed the job of a lifetime. It was the job of my dreams. It was a temp gig working for one of top magazine publishing companies in the world. *I thought I arrived YO… for real*! Amen~

Two weeks before school started you arrived to be with me.

New York can be a tough place. It requires a resilient mind, strong spirit, confidence, courage, and a tremendous amount of patience riding the A train at rush hour. When things don't work out we get disappointed. It seems like we try and try and try and it never seems to happen for us. It's like we never seem to get there. Sometimes when we get to this place of defeat we want to give up, we throw our hands up and we don't believe we'll ever have IT.

At this point you and I had been living in New York now for about four months and those first two months were rough. We lived at Tia's, under her dictatorship. You and I slept together on a twin bed in her two-bedroom apartment in Harlem. I lit candles and prayed every night. *It's funny how when shit really gets rough all of sudden we turn to God in hopes that he/she will save the day.*

I prayed faithfully for a job. I prayed in the morning when I woke, in the shower and while I got dressed. I prayed before I ate and as I washed dishes. I prayed as I walked to the train. I prayed on the train. I prayed on the elevator up to my temp assignment and during the day while I worked. I prayed in bathrooms and during dinner while I ate. I prayed every night before I put my head on my pillow. I prayed that this new job would turn into something permanent because living in NYC wasn't cheap and I had catholic school tuition to pay.

We live in a world filled with people who wear masks. I'm thinking about all the people I will walk by on the streets today, the people I walk by daily, everyone in my life, those people I have just met, the people I will never get to meet, the girls last night who got into a fist fight on the bus right in front of you and I—who right before she started throwing blows with the other girl was smiling at us. We're all just people in survival mode, doing what we do, living how we live. Some of us are bordering breaking point... many of us though live at the MASQUERADE BALL.

The masks we wear day-to-day hoping to be noticed, that our potential will be recognized and acknowledged, we the undiscovered talent, wearing our false confidence mask. Those of us who demand to be respected yet at work get trampled on but once home stomp on those we love. These masks that would never raise voices to the bosses or people who we perceive are more superior or more powerful than us. We wear a mask pretending to be COMPLETE people. Yet we are totally broken inside with real problems and no idea how to fix them. So like everyone else I put on my mask of "super model, no problems in the world, I have it all under control, act like I got money in the bank and smile all the time." I wanted to convince you that I had it all under control. I wore my mask well—I had everyone fooled.

My temp assignment was about to end and there were no positions available. KB invited me to lunch one day (executives never eat with the help). I wanted to express my gratitude and passion for the job. I wanted him to know how eager I was to be apart of his team. He looked at me and said, "Don't worry, I think you're fabulous. You're not going anywhere. Even if you have to sit in the bathroom all day everyday until I find you a slot you're not going anywhere!" I just smiled because I knew he was a man of his word. And true to his word I did end up spending some time in the bathroom and hiding out in conference rooms. He always gave me these minor projects, like filling goodie bags and mailing things just to keep me around.

After proving myself for two months I got the job. *Ache!* God answered my prayers. I was so grateful. Once I was hired the days were long. I was working most nights until 8pm. It was a busy office. I was the assistant to two executives, a Vice President, a woman who was rising fast to CEO status, and KB, Creative Director in the Corporate Sales Department (which covered 30+ magazine titles). Name any magazine!!! They probably own it. When the VP hired me one of the things she stressed was that she understood that I was a mother, but that she hoped that it wouldn't get in the way of my job. She made it a point to express to me that she never wanted to hear excuses about me being late, taking days off or anything having to do with my responsibilities as a mother. Basically, what I understood was that my baby better never get sick or I would lose this job.

I was happy. I was grateful everyday and I never complained. I loved where I worked. Each day, I walked into this glamorous building where people dressed in Versace, Oscar de La Renta and wore Jimmy Choo heals. The cafeteria was the talk of NYC because it was the work of famous architect, Frank Gehry. The people who ate there were the "who's who" of fashion, entertainment and gossip. KB and the VP were a good balance for me. Where she was ALL BUSINESS all the time, KB was more creative, brilliant, vibrant, kind, caring and open. He wanted to know me not just work with me. He cared about you and asked for you everyday. He loved my stories about you. *Then I got the call I had been afraid of…*

That morning you told me you weren't feeling well. We were now living in Astoria, Queens so the commute was hell. Everyday we would take the M train to the L, the L to 14th Street, walk that long ass tunnel to the number 1 train, take the 1 uptown to 72nd and I would get off the train and take you to school. Then I would get back on the number 1 train and head downtown to 42nd where I had to be at work by 8:30AM. We would do the reverse to get home. Most nights we got in at 9:00PM. This day you were taking extra long to walk to the train. I carried your book bag for you. You complained all the way to school. I asked you if you thought you would be ok. You said yes. When we got off the train at 72nd you just looked at me and said, "Mommy, I'm going to be sick."

"Its ok baby, go ahead and throw up right here."

You were so embarrassed. You started crying. I tried to comfort you. I asked you again, "Baby, are you sure you want to go to school. Do you think you're gonna be ok?"

"Yes. I will be fine mommy. I don't want you to get fired for taking time off from work to take care of me."

I couldn't believe you said that to me. You were more worried about me being fired than how sick you were? I went to work feeling crazy guilty. I wasn't at work thirty minutes when I got the call from your school. "Ms. Santos, your daughter has a fever and has thrown up. Can you please come pick her up?" I was afraid to approach my boss and tell her, *LOOK I gotta bounce… my daughter is sick I don't care what you think… my daughter comes first.* I walked into her office and informed her submissively, that I had to leave but that I would make up the time. I ran out of that office to get you. I got on the cell phone to try to get you an appointment with a doctor. I picked you up and asked you if you would be able to ride the trains (we didn't have money to take a cab to Queens). You said you would be fine. Your face was yellow… you were flushed. You were so weak. You didn't look good. Once we arrived to Queens we jumped in a cab and you put your head on my lap.

I was rubbing your head, touching your hair. While I was watching you, I started crying. I felt so much guilt about what I had done to us with this move to NYC. Was I being selfish? I took you away from the life you knew. I started to doubt myself. I doubted my ability and questioned what I was doing here. *This* was just too hard and now you were sick and it was my fault. I didn't think I could do it. I was alone. I have aunts and uncles in New York but they didn't live close and couldn't take care of you because they all have jobs. You had never seen me cry like that before. I just looked at you and said, "Baby do you wanna go back to Florida? Do you wanna just leave NYC and go back to our life? This is just too hard! You could have your pool again and go swimming all the time. You would have your *abuelo* and *abuela*, your *Tia Josie, Tia Fabiana and Tio Fabin*… do you wanna just go home?"

You just looked up at me with those beautiful eyes and said, "NO MOMMY!!! This is your dream. I don't want to leave. You came here to be a writer. You can do this!"

It would have been so much easier for me to leave and go back home to be closer to my family. I know the life I would have there. I could have packed us up and headed south again and they would have welcomed us back with open arms. They would have made our life easier. We would have had our support system back. It would have been much easier to go back and do what I have always done. It's so much harder to stay and work my ass off for what I want. I didn't believe I could do it. I'm so thankful you encouraged me to stay. You believed in me when I didn't. What would I have taught you had I quit? This July 2011 we celebrate NINE years living in New York City. What I hope you see in me now is someone who follows through to the end.

"The closer one gets to realizing his personal legend -- the more that personal legend becomes his TRUE reason for being, thought the boy." The Alchemist by Paulo Coelho.

This shit has been hard. Moving towards my dream, developing my writing style, finding my writers voice, listening to the muse and creating a writing discipline. Making our dreams a reality has not been easy. It's not supposed to be. But the harder it gets, the more I work, the more I push myself. With you at my side I move quicker now towards it rather than running from it. When it gets tough and it will - we must press on no matter what comes our way.

I affirm: I know I am capable of achieving what I need and will have everything that I desire~ I remind myself that I've done this many times~ When I am scared I remind myself that I've been here before… I know how to do this… I know that I can do this… I know that I must do this~

Courtney, thank you for reminding me everyday of how proud you are of me.

PART II ~ DEATH

"The voices we need are so utterly absent, totally and completely missing anybody who writes anything is writing a fucking revolution!"

Quote by Junot Diaz

CHAPTER ELEVEN ~ *2003*

"Good morning beautiful!" KB said as he sashayed in to his office.

"Good morning KB! You look so handsome."

I was running around like a crazy woman... doing a million things. The VP of corporate sales had 14 sales people who reported to her. I was responsible for scheduling all of her meetings with them and outside clients. Her schedule was intense. My work for KB however, was always more fun... more creative. He gave me things to write about. I edited countless presentations and correspondence. I was finally using my brain and writing skills. He asked me for input quite regularly and we had lunch together all the time. One day he gave us two tickets to see Vanessa Williams on Broadway in the musical *Into the Woods*. That night you and I got all dressed up. We went to dinner on Theatre Row. We had Italian... meatballs and ravioli. We felt so important. We sat in the third row, center stage... we could touch Vanessa that's how great these seats were. It was such a magical night. He always did things like that.

FINDING YOUR FORCE

August 2003

It was the New York City blackout. We were scared that it was another September 11th situation. KB asked me if I had anywhere to go. I told him I didn't know what I was going to do.

"You're coming with me!" He invited me to go with him to his apartment and stay the night.

Thank God you were with your father for the summer! We walked from 42nd to 15th and Fifth. We went in search of water, food and flashlights. The man only had gold fish crackers, olives, nuts and vodka–no food (he ate out a lot). His best friend joined us and we stayed up all night sharing our dreams and goals. The entire apartment was lit by candlelight.

October 2003

He called me into his office, "Alicia, does this look normal?" His pace maker was protruding from his chest.

"KB I should call 911!" all I could see was this rectangular box lifted from his chest.

He was terrified, "No Alicia, that won't be necessary. I don't want to draw attention like that. Please order me a limo. Have them take me to the NYU Medical Center."

I stayed at the hospital with him until his friend arrived.

November 2003

KB is the definition of *fabulous*. Even after that scare. He was back to being joyful, happy, dancing around, just an incredibly positive human being. When he came into work it was like watching him walk the runway. He would show up with the fiercest outfits and his diva strut. Always well put together. He smiled every time he walked by me. His door was locked this particular day. He often locked his door so he could eat quietly without interruptions. The only exception was my buzzing him if he was running late for a meeting.

It was 3:30pm and it was time for him to go. He needed to be at a meeting outside of the building so I buzzed his line. No answer. I knocked on his door a few times and still nothing. I thought to myself, *great he left... he'll be on time*. When I didn't get a response I called out his name. I went to my desk to get my spare key. I knocked on the door one more time and then unlocked it. I opened the door slowly.

I walked in and there he was sitting at his desk with his head down. I thought he was sleeping. I called out for him, "KB, KB - wake up you have a meeting!" I thought maybe he had a headache and just needed to rest his head. His arms were folded and his head gently placed on them. It looked like he was sleeping. I went behind him to wake him. I touched his shoulder. Then I nudged him a little. "KB, wake up!" I shook him a little harder. No movement. I touched his neck. No pulse. I touched his face. He was ice cold.

93

I ran and ran as fast as I could for help. I interrupted a meeting and told them that KB wouldn't wake up. I told them that something was terribly wrong. They ran to his office to aid him. I just stood by my desk pacing. I was a mess, scared out of my mind, worried, crying, hoping that he would be ok and not understanding what had just happened. Someone called 911 because paramedics came to his office. I never left my cubicle.

When they finished doing whatever it was they were doing inside his office they opened the door. KB was dead! I couldn't watch them take him away on that stretcher, covered with that white sheet. I refused to leave my desk. I was so scared that I hid under it. This moment seemed so unbelievable to me. It's still unbelievable. It was the most horribly devastating, and incredibly traumatic experiences I had ever encountered. I went to work the very next day. I was extremely protective of KB and wanted to handle all of his personal belongings.

When his parents came into the office his mother just held me. She asked, "Alicia, were you the one who found him."

I shook my head yes and then I just started crying. She just kept holding me and whispered, "You were the person who was meant to find him. You loved him. That was the most intimate moment you and he shared."

This woman was amazing. She just lost her son. In that moment she turned what seemed like a horrible experience into the most beautiful act of love.

I continued to go to work after that. I didn't take anytime off. I never went to counseling. I did the same things every day for so many months. I never mourned his loss. I just kept going back to this building. I was forced to go back into KB's office every day when his new replacement started. I had to open that door again and again. Whenever I opened any door it sent chills up my spine. I dreaded waking up every day. But I did get up not because I wanted to. Not because I was happy to be alive. I got up because I had no choice but to go on living and do all the necessary things I was doing to get by in my empty life.

I was devastated. He died on your *abuelo's* birthday. I believe that it happened that way so that we would never forget him. You just don't forget people like him. But he too wore a mask pretending to be happy at a job that no longer was bringing him the joy it once had. He too had a story that no one knew. There were so many things that made him beautiful. I will never forget him.

The week before KB died he gave me a gift certificate. I was on the phone taking a message when he just shoved it in front of me and whispered, "Here, this is for you enjoy! You probably can only get a pair of earrings with this but enjoy it!" Then he walked away. I didn't open it until after he died. I had forgotten all about it. When I opened the envelope I found a $500 gift certificate to MaxMara.

I later received an email from a coworker who said to me, "You know KB told me he was giving you that gift certificate. He came up to me and asked, *can someone buy something really nice with this?* I told him of course. Then he told me that he was giving the gift certificate to you. I responded, wow that's really nice of you. He responded, *she's really nice to me."*

I was a zombie, a machine, the walking, talking, breathing, living dead. I walked into that office building for 12 months and did the same thing. I continued checking voice mail, responding to emails, mailing magazines, sending out media kits, scheduling appointments with top advertisers, processing expense reports, making travel arrangements and throwing little girls birthday parties?

No one knew how I spent the months that followed reliving that traumatic moment over and over again. It's funny how the simple act of opening a door can alter a person's life forever.

January 2004

I couldn't do it anymore. I went into the VP's office and told her that I needed a change. I asked her to please help me find something new. The company was really good to us when KB died. They paid for our flights to Grand Rapids, Michigan for his burial. They paid for our hotel and sent flowers. The Vice President of Human Resources always made time to meet with me. I think my boss kind of resented that I could get an appointment with the head of HR before her. The head of HR did her best to find me a new position.

SUCCESS!!! I received word that I was being considered for a position at one of the top fashion magazines in the company... on the editorial side. This was perfect. This would be the entrance into my writing career.

I've always been a strong interviewer so I got the job. I would be shadowing her assistant who was leaving in two weeks.

It's my first day on the job. The new boss was FIERCE!!! She was the Editor-in-Chief. I was in charge of organizing the stylebook that she would take on trips. The woman even had a clothing budget. Part of my job was to work with the style department and put together binders with images of all her outfits, the shoes that went with them, the color make up that complimented them, and the accessories. I LOVED IT!!!

My boss walked in wearing this white suit, these beautiful pumps and her hair was straight. This chick was bad!!!! We met for a few minutes. She told me she had some meetings but that we would catch up later. *I could finally breathe. It was a brand new day. I could begin again. I was alive again. I could move forward.*

She returned, asked me to step into the office and shut the door. Her office was beautiful. There were paintings everywhere, a couch and large bookshelves. There was a private bathroom. "Alicia, have a seat, what I'm about to share with you can not leave these walls." *I was like ok awesome, company secrets. I'm in.* "They just fucking fired me. I have until the end of the day to gather my things. After being here over ten years they just let me go. There's a lot I need you to do for me."

Did she just tell me that she was fired? ON MY FIRST DAY OF WORK! You're fucking kidding me right? This is a joke! This is a horrible joke! This can't be happening to me. Where are the hidden cameras?

I spent that day scheduling meetings with her direct reports. She asked for a meeting at the end of the day with the entire editorial team of over 30+ people to say goodbye. I wanted to die. This was so not happening to me. I was moving up. I was moving forward. And now I was moving all of her shit out of her office. I only stayed in that role until the new publisher came on board and then I would be out of a job because he was bringing his assistant with him.

WHAT???? The head of Human Resources told me not to worry about it that they would find me something. This was just all just so fucked up.

"Alicia, we have some great news. We are launching a new magazine. You would be supporting the Editor-in-Chief. Are you interested?"

HELLO!!!! Am I interested? Hell yeahhhhhhhh!!!

The interview went great. I met the EIC and we hit it off. This was her first magazine and role as Editor-in-Chief. She had no experience launching a magazine and was putting together a strong team to launch her baby. I was excited at the potential to write for this magazine. I couldn't wait to get to know her. I joined the editorial meetings. She shared concepts with me. It was so much fun learning the step-by-step making of a magazine. I was involved in ordering all of the office equipment and décor. I finally felt like I was part of a team.

Once KB died I never wrote again. I was uninspired. Our house was an absolute mess. There were piles and piles of clothes everywhere. We were living in an episode of hoarders. I was so unhappy. I hated my new job.

After working together for a few months I started asking for more responsibilities. I showed interest and initiative. My boss knew I wanted to write for the magazine. She didn't respect me. She was horrible to me. She was incredibly disrespectful and condescending. I believed she was a racist. I spent more time ordering shit for her private house parties than doing any real work.

Anytime I spoke out on anything it seemed like she had a problem with me. I really believe she had a problem with the fact that I had ideas and thoughts. I think she just wanted some young, fresh, right out of college, newbie, "white girl," as her assistant. Honestly, I think she picked me because she *had to*— not because she wanted to. And so as the months went on I continued to take her shit and downloaded all the photos from her camera of her travels, ordered the pizza and cupcakes for her daughter's birthday party, bought her makeup at Sephora and ordered her lunch everyday.

I was incredibly depressed. I saw Dr. Kate every week for therapy and Dr. Chan for my medications. I was on all kinds of medications for ADD, antidepressants, pills to help me sleep, pills to get me going. I was drinking a bottle of wine every night. One day you looked at me and said, "Mommy, you always have a glass of wine as soon as we walk in the door. Why?"

I don't even know what I said to you. I probably said something lame like, "I just like to unwind. I have glass once in a while to relax." When the reality was that I was self-medicating and numbing the pain. The job was completely draining me. I was dead on the inside. I felt the creativity being beat out of me.

Wednesday, October 6, 2004

Something woke in the middle of the night. It was 3:00am I believe it was KB waking me. He told me it was time to create. He told me that I had an important story to tell. He told me that I could do this. And I believed him. I jumped out of bed and got to work. I started to create again. I started to write again. It felt wonderful. I felt POWERFUL!!! I was strong, full of life, happy, ready to conquer the world. I was full of energy. I went back to working on the manuscript for *Becoming Me...Its OK in My Skin*. I felt fucking fantastic! I put on my nicest outfit, A-line skirt with the slit up my thigh, low cut sleeveless blouse, my tallest sexiest strappy heals the gold ones that tie up. And I started writing again. I wrote until about 6:00am. I was ready to go. I was back. I was in a great mood. It was on!

Rewind... just weeks before that POWERFUL AWAKENING.

I knew I needed to make some immediate changes. It felt like life or death. I was working with an Editor-in-Chief. Actually, let me rephrase that, I worked *for* her. Working *with* her would have meant that we were partners. Working *with* her meant that there was a mutual respect and understanding. Working *with* her meant that there was compassion present in the relationship. Working *with* her meant we worked *together* to reach a common goal.

So I worked *for* this Editor-in-Chief and she was preparing for a meeting with *her* boss. She needed assistance taking portfolios to her meeting (it was a total of 10 or so - - she was in the process of looking for a new art director). So we're walking

101

down this hallway side-by-side and right before we get to his office she said to me, "Walk behind me! I want to go in first!"

Walk behind me! Let me go in first! Did she actually just say that to me? Seriously, I can't remember what I said but I can only imagine my face in that moment and my mind saying something like *are you fucking serious? What did you just say to me? And what side of the world do we live in?* I was shocked! That shit was deep. I just sort of shrugged it off and pretended like it didn't bother me and went about my administrative duties of fetching her coffee and toasting her bagels just right.

There is nothing sadder than a person building his or her power by attempting to take someone else's.

That moment in my life was one of the darkest moments I had ever experienced and not just her ridiculous requests and demeaning, condescending ways. It was everything that I endured in one year. I didn't defend myself. I never spoke up to her. I was carrying *Cielo's* box when all I wanted to do was hit her over the head with it. I *let* her have my power!

There are so many catchy phrases, clichés and books about finding your power, tapping into your power, attaining power, owning your power! There are many people in the world all aspiring to reach a certain level of power, fighting wars for power, beating women for power and abusing the powerless in order to have more power. It's amazing the shit we tolerate to survive.

That week I shared *the walk behind me* story with Dr. Kate. She looked at me like I was making it up.

102

"NO! I am not that clever. Yes SHE did really just tell me to walk behind her!"

"Alicia, you do understand what that was about right?"

"No! Actually, I don't understand it! She's fucking crazy! I haven't analyzed her actions that deeply. I found her behavior to be incredibly rude. I mean really who says that? Who does that?"

She went on to say, "Wow, she's threatened by you! She's really insecure! Think about it for a moment Alicia! You and her walk into a room who looks like the Editor-in-Chief and who looks like the assistant?"

I didn't understand her point. I didn't quite comprehend. She was afraid I'd out shine her? She didn't like me WHY? Because I'm smart, well spoken, outgoing and have confidence? She intentionally wanted to break me down? What she wanted was for me to know my place and that place was under her foot. She wanted me beneath her and needed me to stay there. I can't imagine what it must have felt like for her to have to look up to me everyday *una amazona*??? She was "Power Trippin'!"

Returning back to the day of the "Powerful Awakening," KB woke me up and I was incredibly inspired. When you got up you couldn't believe I was already dressed. You were so excited to be coming to work with me that day. We had the best train ride. We sang we laughed. I looked fabulous and felt that way until we arrived to my office. Reality slapped me in the face in the form of an 8:00am phone call from HER!!!!

That morning my boss was extra rude, extra demeaning, extra disrespectful and extra demanding. She was just EXTRA! Now you remember how I woke up that morning right? POWERFUL! In a matter of 30 seconds flat I was completely deflated. When she arrived to the office she began her dictatorship. She made me feel like I was nothing. Powerful was replaced with INSIGNIFICANT. I felt burned and used. I was done. I couldn't do it anymore. She WON! I SURRENDERED! White flag up!!!

She wanted me to know my place and it was below her and I bowed down. I was severely depressed in that moment after starting my day so high – so grand. In a matter of moments I was completely destroyed. And you were there with me. You witnessed all of it. There is no worse feeling than having my child seeing me be disrespected and not even standing up for myself!

You and I went to lunch. We found a quiet place to sit but I couldn't eat! We sat in an empty cubical and I put my head down on the desk and surrendered. I gave up. I started crying like a baby and said to myself, "I can't do this. I can't do this. I can't do this."

You just looked over at me, slurping your noodles, with this look of pity and said, "Mommy, don't cry. Its ok! If you're so unhappy just quit! QUIT!" and you went right back to slurping.

It sounded easy enough - just quit! So I got up and walked over to my boss's office. I asked her to step outside for a mo-

104

ment. Once outside I told her I couldn't do this anymore and I walked away.

The days that followed were rough. I wasn't thinking straight. Did I seriously just walk away from the job of a lifetime? There was NO thinking about where the money was going to come from. NO rational thought. Logical and practical were certainly not in my vocabulary in that moment. I just thought fuck it... fuck her! But I was in so much PAIN. Internally I was destroyed. I spent those days that followed in bed. I didn't eat or shower for days. I didn't care about myself and I certainly was not taking care of you.

I went to my Saturday morning class at NYU and during the lecture I just broke down in tears and walked out. I went and sat near the fountain in Washington Square and called Dr. Kate and told her I was falling a part. I was having dark thoughts. I was a mess, crying in hysterics. I was talking crazy, telling her I wanted to quit school. I envisioned burning all of my journals. I wanted to burn everything I'd ever written and abandon my life. I wanted to run and never come back. I was going to leave you. I had gone through ENOUGH in my life. I was sick of being beat down. I've been beaten my whole life. When was it going to fucking END? Maybe when I ended it!

She said; "Alicia, GET UP! Get up and start moving. Just walk! Keep walking! Don't stop! Go for a walk. Clear your head. Just keep walking."

So I did, I kept moving. I walked all over the city that day and ended up in front of this spa and thought to myself *that's what I need a massage.* Bitch! You don't have a job but you need a massage. After the massage, I kept walking. I walked and walked and walked until I was exhausted. I walked to a dear friend's house. She had invited me to spend the night so she could take care of me. She ran a bath for me, lit candles, gave me a towel and a robe, had lovely music playing and told me to soak in the hot water for 20 minutes that she would order us some Thai for dinner.

I got out of the tub and moved to the living room and lay down on her bed. I was all snuggled up under her goose down comforter. It was wonderful. All of sudden, I felt my stomach doing summersaults. I was feeling a little dizzy, queasy, and incredibly nauseous. I ran to the bathroom and just started throwing up uncontrollably. It seemed as though there would be no end in sight. My friend came into the bathroom and started rubbing my back. She was holding my hair up. I just kept apologizing to her. She told me that it was ok and that she loved me... *to just keep letting it out... let it all go...*

She told me that what was happening to me was that I was releasing all of the poison and toxins that were inside of my body. The massage helped to move things around internally and everything shifted. She told me that this release was very neces-

106

sary for me to begin my healing. I was cleansing. I was finally getting rid of all of the crap that I no longer needed. I was releasing all the shit that was destroying me, killing me, hurting me and beating me down. I finally understood that I was releasing ALL of the terrible things that had ever been said to me or about me. I was licking the wounds internally of the years of abuse at the hands of men in my life and some women (physically, mentally or emotionally), especially at the hands of that terrible boss. I was releasing ALL OF IT! The process felt like it lasted a good 20 minutes of non-stop purging. I was completely empty. I lay back down and shortly after I went back into bathroom for round two.

I thought I was dying, but what I later understood was that that was exactly what needed to happen. I needed to be completely broken down. I needed to be completely empty so that I could build back up and fill myself with beautiful things. After that moment I have not stopped moving. There are still areas in my life that need attention and matters that need to be resolved but until I am ready to deal with them like my girl Margo used to say, "I just keep it movin!"

The real ME~

I don't always have the answers…
I don't always
know what to do…
Sometimes
I need help…
I'm feeling a little lost…
Trying to find
my way…
Trying to find
a way out…
Trying to find that place inside me that knows
that really knows…
how to pull me out of this - -
Searching for that place that strengthens me…
that place that guides me.
Creator,
help me…
I am so sad…
strengthen me.
I want all you have for me…
Clean my wounds…
Remove all the toxins from my body…
Remove all the poison that does not serve me…
Walk with me…
Fill me…
Strengthen me…
Please work through my words today…
guide me…
push myself harder than I've ever worked..
I need to work nonstop…
I need to get it done.
Help me be authentic…
I need your help…
Authenticity is based on truth…
The truth is I am weak…
The truth is
I am getting stronger…

The truth is
I am learning all that I need.
The truth is
I am getting ready~
The truth is
I am always growing…
The truth is
I wasn't always THIS way…
The truth is
I was completely torn down…
The truth is
I am re-building from scraps…
BUT I AM RE-BUILDING…
I am STRONGER WITH EVERY PASSING DAY…
The truth is
I am getting rid of the debris that was left in me…
The truth is
I am working with the parts that remain
I am starting over…
The truth is
I don't pretend to be perfect.
Or act like I have it all together.
The truth is
she told me she felt deceived…
I say she saw the truth
and didn't like it…
The truth is
she met MY AUTHENTIC SELF

CHAPTER TWELVE

Prayer: I know that there are NO OBTACLES~ that what you put in my path is for my learning... is for my greater good. Please help me to release the poison inside of me. I'm miserable, unhappy and feeing un-fulfilled in my life. Spiritually, I know what I need to nourish myself with. I know that I'm stronger than this. My writing is suffering. I haven't given it the time it deserves. I haven't given myself the time I deserve. I need to release this tension and anxiety. I know that no one can come in and fix it for me. All the work has to be done internally. I need to get to the core of me... all that is beautiful, loving, compassion-ate, tender and gentle.

Mostly, I want to be able to give ALL that I possess to myself. All that I give so freely and openly to everyone else but me~ I release all that causes me pain. I forgive myself. I surrender all my worries. I don't have to believe what others tell me about my life. I don't have to worry about security I have all I need. I know who I am! "YO SOY UNA AMAZONA!" No one can take my peace unless I give it to them. I know YOU got this! I know YOU got me! I am DIVINE! There's nothing in my way. Light shines all around me. I ask YOU to clear my heart of fear. I hold positive thoughts and intentions. I have a mission. I feel my strength. No wind can knock me off my path! I know that I am ready! I know that I am a leader! And when I forget YOU always hold my hand. And so it is~

I affirm: I call forth my strength and I move forward anyway! This journey to healing is not an easy task. Things will appear to knock me off my path. Things will come in to test where I am at and show ME where I still need work. And ITS ALL GOOD after crying I had to remember where to turn to for my strength and acknowledge... that I have been here before and my force reminds me everyday that I'm strong enough to continue~

When I walked out on my dream job I had a nervous breakdown. I didn't need a doctor to diagnose it as such. My nervous system broke down. My mind was a mess. Then ELLEN DEGENERES came in and saved my life.

We stayed at our friend's apartment for a few days after my purging. I was still incredibly depressed lying on her couch clicking through the channels and stopped on HBO. There was a special about to start called, *The Beginning*. I was getting ready to change the channel when I saw her walk out on stage. I hadn't really heard anything about Ellen for a few years since she "came out" on national television. I was curious to hear what she would open with so I continued watching.

Ellen walked on stage to an audience of over 2,000 people who came to see her at the Beacon Theater. I could feel from the television ALL the love for her in *that* space. I saw how humbled she was by the warm reception. I just watched her and thought to myself *Wow! Ellen is so brave after all of her private and professional life was plastered in every magazine on every talk show. After being the topic of discussion by everyone.* I just sat there and thought... she's gangsta! I don't know if I could do that. Then I thought *shit... she better be funny... there's a whole lot of people up in there.*

The first thing she talked about was how she had been planning the evening and wasn't sure if she was going to share where she had been over the past three years and all that she had been through. She decided that she was going to tell us the story through an INTERPRETIVE DANCE. When the music started playing, I almost fell off the couch. I could barely breathe. I laughed the entire time. I laughed and laughed. It was so hilarious. The combination of the music, lights and her movement had me on the floor. Her interpretation of "coming out" as a lesbian and how she dealt with darkness and found light all of it made me laugh.

I laughed and cried. They were tears of joy. I had not laughed like that in such a long time. I couldn't even remember the last time I had felt joy. I hadn't felt happy in years. I had forgotten how to laugh. Ellen gave me permission to laugh again. I could release all the pain. I could turn everything I had been through and laugh at all of it. I didn't have to live in this darkness. I didn't have to continue punishing myself for my past. I could laugh. I could be happy everyday that I am alive and know that at any moment I could start again. So I would tune in everyday to the Ellen show just to watch her dance.

Your Tia Josie surprised me with tickets to a live taping of the Ellen show in Burbank, California in 2005. I was so excited. I hoped I'd have an opportunity to tell her exactly how she had impacted my life. I wanted Ellen to know how grateful I was to her for pulling me out of my darkest hour. I wanted to thank her for being alive and spreading love and laughter. When we arrived to the studio we were really close to where she sat on stage. I was nervous and excited. What would I say to her if I got to meet her? I didn't know if I would be able to speak to her after her show so I wrote her a letter. I gave it to one of her producers. I don't know if she ever received it. The show was about to start. I heard them announce Ellen DeGeneres and when she walked out on stage I just started crying. I couldn't control myself. When you're in the presence of someone who changes your life like that it's incredibly profound. I just wanted to say to thank you to Ellen for being there during that moment. Laughter was the beginning of my healing process. There was still so much work to do... but there was even more work to undo!

I was cleansing. I was readying my self for a new chapter. I was allowing the old me to die so that I could make room for the new me. I was making changes. I read a book titled, *Succulent Wild Woman, Dancing With Your Wonderful Self,* by Sark. In one of the chapters she talked about marrying herself. She bought a ring, beautiful flowers, wrote vows to herself and picked a beautiful location for the wedding. This idea was a perfect way for me to begin again. This would be a way for me to express the love I was beginning to feel for myself. This was a way I could allow the old to die, transition and commune with the universe asking for the things that I wanted to attract for my future.

I was remembering the memorial service that was held for KB in NYC. Before I headed to the private reception at the W Hotel in Union Square, I went to a bookstore and bought a card. While I was waiting in line I noticed a book by Paulo Coelho, *The Alchemist*. I remembered a story my old boss from Florida told me about *The Alchemist* and how it reminded him of me in pursuit of my dreams. He thought I might find it interesting. I forgot all about that story until I saw the book sitting near the register. I took it as a sign that I was meant to read it. As if it were placed there for me. Timing is everything and everything happens right on time.

The Alchemist is about Santiago, a boy who has a dream about finding a treasure. It's a beautiful tale about his journey towards reaching his personal legend. Will he reach his destination? What will his tests be? Will he succeed or fail? Who will show up to aid him or betray him? It's an inspiring tale about finding and fulfilling ones purpose.

Whenever I get to a place of questioning my journey I turn to *The Alchemist* as a compass to find my way back home. Sometimes we all need a reminder that we *will* get there. All our lessons are part of the journey. We must build up strength. We learn that there are people we are meant to pick up along the way and those we are supposed to let go. Every person that you meet on this journey you are meant to meet. Everything that you experience on this journey you are meant to experience.

"It's the possibility of having a dream come true that makes life interesting, he thought, as he looked again at the position of the sun, and hurried his pace." The Alchemist

The Wedding~ 2005

The first time I got married (by law) I was too young. I wasn't ready. I was immature, too militant, too rigid and too angry. The first time I married myself (spiritually) I was only beginning to understand what being married to me meant and I wasn't really sure if I knew or liked Alicia well enough to make that kind of commitment, but I married her anyway and continued to get to know her. When I decided to go through with that wedding it was after the breakdown. Part of my healing process was to marry me, for better or worse... for drama and crazy. I wanted me even with every item of baggage I brought along. I still wanted me. I was married at sunset with you as my witness. We were on the roof of our apartment in Ridgewood, Queens. You were my ring bearer, priest, photographer and caterer. I had a ring and you at my side. It was a beautiful wedding. I realize now that it was WAY too much pressure to put on a marriage, my original vows were 8 pages filled with many promises, expectations, needs and desires. I needed to do something a little different this time for this marriage to work, something a little more realistic so I planned a simple wedding.

CHAPTER THIRTEEN ~ *2005 Finally Home*

It was freezing that December 31st. It would be my last day
EVER walking into that building. I would never have to walk
back into KB's office. I would never see those people again. After
everything that I had been through the head of HR was *still* so
supportive of me. She paid me for three months after the breakdown. One of the terms of my termination was that I would float
from department to department just to keep my benefits. I
would then receive a small severance package. She let me keep
my laptop and cell phone. She made it possible for me to have
the kind of termination where I could collect unemployment. I
was so incredibly grateful for that.

Then at 2:00PM I put on my coat, my hat and gloves, grabbed
my purse and walked out of the revolving door and never
looked back. The moment I stepped onto the streets of Times
Square it was as if I could breathe for the first time. I took a deep
breath and allowed the cold breeze to fill my lungs and in that
moment it was as if two tons were lifted from my shoulders and
I was floating. I just smiled. That chapter was finally closed.

This was going to be our greatest year yet!!! Big things were going to happen!!! We finally got the call that our number came up. We had been on a waiting list for three years for the apartment in Harlem. The building we were moving into was just remodeled. We would be the first people living in our space. Things were changing.

I decided that this time we would make our apartment HOME. I had never really cared to decorate our apartments before now because they always felt so temporary. None of the apartments we lived in felt like they fit. I didn't buy stuff to make it too comfortable because I always felt uncomfortable. Warwick, Providence, North Providence, Pawtucket, Davie, Plantation, Tamarac, Sunrise, Astoria, Far Rockaway, Ridgewood, *tia's* house, *tio's* house, *abuela's* house and grandma's house. GIRL WE MOVED THIRTEEN TIMES. You are a trooper!!! I have moved you everywhere. How do you do it? How is it that you are this amazing? You put up with so much shit. Thirteenth time is a charm and we finally got it right.

This time we were not moving again!!! I was so excited that we got this apartment. The management office had no idea I was unemployed. And I certainly wasn't telling them. I had to come up with a few thousand for us to move in. We bought paint for the first time. I didn't want us to move into the space until it was exactly the way we wanted. I wanted it to be perfect for us. I remember charting out exactly how I wanted the house to look. I drew a sketch of the entire apartment. The living room was painted red and orange, purposely so that we would feel warm

117

like we were in the Dominican Republic. The color of the entry hallway we decided on was special to us because it was called "brilliant" and it reminded us of KB. He always said, "That's brilliant!" We had our beautifully painted brilliant yellow hallway and your bedroom was painted lavender. I rented a truck and hired movers. It was moving day! This was the perfect month for our move, as you would be turning thirteen. We were finally home!

It was time for me to return the truck to the rental place in Queens. You and I were driving onto the bridge. There was a checkpoint at the tollbooth. Since 9/11 NYPD presence was everywhere. They pulled us over to check the truck. The police officer asked me for my driver's license, registration and the rental agreement. He came back to the truck and said, "Ma'am do you know your license is suspended?" I played stupid. Of course I knew it was suspended. Where was I going to have the time and money to reinstate my license? How was I going to pay that $300 speeding ticket that I got in Atlanta so many years ago? I considered falling apart in front of him and telling the officer about everything I'd been through from leaving Florida to the breakdown in New York City. "No officer, I had no idea my license was suspended?"

"You realize I can have the truck towed and arrest you for driving with a suspended license?"

My eyes started to swell up. All I could think about was how *my little girl,* was going to have to watch me be arrested. We were parked on the Triboro Bridge for a long time and you were just looking out of the window smiling. You were staring at the women's prison on the right. I'm sure you were thinking to yourself, *we're gonna be fine. Mommy gets us out of worse messes. He has no idea who he's dealing with!* You looked at me and said, "Don't cry mommy it's gonna be fine. It's like that movie I saw the other day. We're on an adventure!"

I started laughing hysterically because you had no idea how serious this shit really was. My ass was about to be thrown in jail. The cop was kind. He had me pull the car over and we called your *tio* to meet us on the bridge and drive the truck back. He let us off thank God. After that scare we were back in the game.

We lived off all the money I had saved in my pension, 401K, severance and unemployment. We were happy. Our rent was paid. You were finishing up the school year and I was taking full time classes at NYU. We loved our new apartment. That summer you went to Florida for one month and spent a month with your father in Virginia. For as long as I can remember there has been only one constant WANT for me. There's only one thing I've ever wanted for YOU. Since the time I was young I understood and believed that only one thing would make my life worth living. HAPPINESS. Not just the moments of happiness that pass us by. I wanted to live a joy-filled existence. The feeling of happiness for me is the sense that all things are possible. It's the undying

undying belief that all things are achievable. It's steadfast momentum toward all things attainable. I often think about what we ALL do for a living and how we live our lives. Most people are working to live and living to work. *But are they happy in their present jobs? Are they happy in their relationships? Are they happy with the way their lives have turned out? Are they happy with who they are and how they show up in the world? Are people happy? Are people doing things that bring them joy?*

I've been told that wanting to be happy is idealistic. I've been told that my ideas of attaining happiness, is an illusion that doesn't exist. I've been ridiculed that happiness is only found in fairytales where only pretend characters live happily ever after. I refuse to believe this. I think the key to happiness is removing those things from our lives that make us miserable and unhappy and moving towards a place of doing that which brings us joy. I think finding, having and holding onto happiness is just starting from a place of happiness. It's waking up everyday and feeling happy to be alive.

There are so many people living unfulfilled lives afraid to even begin living. Happiness is that treasure that Santiago in *The Alchemist* seeks. It's waiting for us. I think it's necessary to just START. Start where you are. Start anywhere. Start somewhere and once you get started keep it moving. Happiness is that *thing* we have been working so hard for. Happiness is found at the beginning, during and at the end of the journey. Happiness is starting that major project and following it through to its conclusion and knowing that once we get there we're not done YET.

Your father couldn't stand seeing me happy. It was so foreign to him. Your father and I were on the phone one day talking about your child support, "Lee, when are you going to find a job? You need to work."

I told him that I *was* working. I was writing. I told your father that I had no intention on getting a job anytime soon. After my last job I needed a break and all I wanted to do was focus on school and my writing. He asked me one day, "How is it that you're so happy? You have NO money. You have NO job. How are you paying the rent? How are you paying your bills? Why are you so happy?"

"I'm happy because I am doing what I love. I'm happy because Courtney's happy. I'm happy because even though I'm not working the money that I do receive is enough to survive. The rent is paid, we have electricity and my cell phone is taken care of. I can make $20 bucks last me weeks."

He resented me so much. It's almost like he wanted me to be miserable. He couldn't stand that I was happy. It didn't make sense to him. What made sense to him was having a job, getting up everyday and going to work, paying the bills on time, coming home to sleep and waking up tomorrow and doing the same thing all over again. My lifestyle got on his nerves.

While you were with him for the summer I reminded you to have him buy all of your hair products and anything you thought you might need because we didn't have any extra cash for fancy products and lotions. I was about to cross Amsterdam Avenue when you called me. There was such excitement in your voice. "Momma, daddy bought me so much stuff. I got my special mousse, shampoo, conditioner and face soap. I can't wait to show you." I was so happy for you. "Mommy daddy wants to speak to you."

"What's up? Thanks for buying her products you know I can't afford it."

He responded angrily, "That better be the last time you make me spend $60 dollars on your stuff. I know it was for you! I feel like I'm dealing with one of my drug addict patients who lie all the time to get what they want—lying to get drugs!"

"What did you just fucking say to me? What did you call me? YO! Put my daughter back on the phone! *Baby, I'm so happy you got your stuff. Mommy's gotta go I'll call you tonight. I love you.*"

That shit stopped me dead in my tracks. I literally froze right where I stood on the street. I looked at my phone and felt the rage rising inside of me. I was so mad that I cried from the fury. He was so lucky you were with him. I wanted to go off on him. Once I got into our apartment it was like a volcanic eruption. It came out of me full force. I punched the wall, cut open my knuckles. I really wanted to put my fist through that wall.

I threw my books off my bookshelves. I was throwing things around the house like a lunatic. I slammed everything against the wall. I wanted to break things. I wanted to break his face for saying such a fucked up thing to me. He assaulted me.

Your dad and I have had many arguments in the past but this insult went too far. He crossed the line. It was just far enough to be effective.

I called Tia Josie and exploded. I was yelling at the top of my lungs. She was trying to calm me down but I was far-gone. I wanted to hurt him. After several hours of carrying on like this I received a call from a friend who said, "Why are you so angry? Alicia, are you a drug addict?"

"NO!"

"Alicia, are you a liar?"

"NO!"

"Alicia, out of everything he called you what part of it was true?"

"None of it was true. None of the fucked up shit he said was the truth about me. What made me angry is that he sees me as such a low form of a human being. What hurts me is that he never respected me. The thing that hurts me the most is that I even care what he thinks of me."

She calmed me down a little bit and then added, "Alicia, don't ever let anyone take your PEACE! Alicia, you gave him your PEACE."

I sat with that for many days later. *Don't let anyone take your peace!* Never let them take my PEACE!!! After my meditation I realized that I LET GO of my PEACE. I gave him my power. I realized that I needed to get my peace back.

FINDING YOUR FORCE

Letter: To the man I chose as my husband,

I don't remember the last time I wrote you a letter. You and I have been through a whole lot together. We once had an incredible bond but it was severed with the words you used to hurt me with. You were a terrible husband and I was not such a great wife.

We weren't ready. We just jumped right into the roles. You happily jumped into the role of husband and I into the submissive role of wanting to answer to your every need. I began the preparations of being a mother, a wife, a homemaker (ok maybe not the greatest homemaker), as well as holding down a job all at the same time.

We were both two incomplete people and completely damaged with a tremendous amount of baggage. You came up in a house where you received NO love and verbal abuse on a regular and me I came up in a house with a ton of love and beatings.

You hurt me. I gave myself to you and I trusted you. I had faith in you. I believed in you. I held you in such high regard. But you never treated me the same way. I was never your equal. And I definitely wasn't your partner. The words you said were hateful, hurtful and tore me down. Your jokes about my family were not funny. You were offensive and it finally got to a point where I didn't like you as a person at all. There was a time where I hated you.

I know that I have said some pretty terrible things and for my words I am sorry. You didn't see what you had in me - a partner for life because you see that's how I was programmed to serve my man and stick by him no matter what. But you know what? I stopped buying into that shit when you didn't love me as much as I was willing to love you for a lifetime. When you stopped wearing your wedding ring and stopped holding my hand you sent me messages without words.

You didn't lift me. You didn't encourage me. You were distant. You were cold and unemotional. I didn't fit into your plan. I was an accident in your perfectly planned world. When we had our daughter something changed. I knew I could not allow her to watch me taking shit from a man. I didn't want her to see me being spoken down to, belittled or disrespected. I didn't want my daughter to be raised in an unhappy household like her mom and dad. It didn't matter that there were those occasions when it might have been a loving home. It wasn't enough. I wanted more for her. I wanted more for me.

The dissolve of our marriage was a life-changing event in my life. With my filing for divorce I took back my power in a HUGE way. I finally got my freedom but our problems didn't end there. For the years that followed you would continue to hurt me, to punish me for leaving. You knew exactly how to get under my skin and destroy me with the put downs and insults. I couldn't escape the words. I didn't know how to release them. I continued to believe all the things you told me.

YOU were a man of significance in my life. You had no faith in me. You saw no beauty in me and to tell you the truth I didn't either because when you said it I took it as truth. Boy was I wrong. 13 years of therapy, self help books; empowerment seminars, affirmations and mediations have fed me a different truth.

First, I don't care what you think. I am no longer interested in being accepted in your world. It's a farce. It is a web of misery. You can have it. I only want love and happiness in my life.

I wish for you much success in your career, a lifetime of happiness and an abundance of love. I thank you for the gift of Courtney she is my biggest accomplishment. You SEE, I actually followed through on something. I'm not just a good mother - I AM A GREAT mother with a brilliant child so thank you for stepping aside and letting me do my thing. I forgive you for the hurtful things you have said to me and I forgive myself for hurting you. I love you, Alicia Anabel

CHAPTER FOURTEEN ~ *Fall, 2005*

I found love on an online dating service. I hadn't been in a relationship since 1998. I had no idea how to date. After my relationship ended with Joseph, I believed that there was no one else who could replace him. This time around I would not settle. I was very comfortable in my skin. After marrying myself twice I was pretty INLOVE with me at that point in my life. I knew what I wanted. I knew who I was. I was no longer that Alicia who went along with things just to have them. I decided that I would measure my next relationship based on Joseph's standards.

I found a match. His name was *Gabriel*, Puerto Rican, 6'3, dark hair, dark eyes, average build, never been married, no children and from New York. So I winked. We emailed, talked on the phone all the time and sent pictures of ourselves (with clothes on—thank you). We sent our *real pictures*. We scheduled our first date.

I admit I was impressed. He went all out. I told him I don't do dressy and he said that was fine. I put on my trademark look tight blue jeans, nice blouse, high-heel Carlos Santana boots, makeup was on point and my hair looked beautiful. When he picked me up he was wearing a suit.

"You cheated!" I scolded. I let him slide because he picked me up at my front door and gave me the best hug. He opened the car door and I got in.

"You look beautiful," he said.

"Thank you. You look handsome yourself."

"Can you do me a favor? Will you go in the glove compartment and grab my gloves for me?"

As soon as I opened the glove compartment a present fell out. I was blushing and he was WINNING!!! When I opened the gift it was a beautiful journal dedicated to me along with this amazing brown marble colored pen. I kissed him on the cheek. He certainly knew how to impress a girl. We joked like we'd known each other our entire lives... *que confianza*. I felt so at ease with him. It was comfortable.

We went to this very swanky Spanish restaurant on the Upper East Side and were immediately seated. He had made reservations. In fact, he preordered our entire dinner, oysters, mussels, seafood, *arroz con pollo*. Gabriel asked me if I noticed anything.

"Yeah I do. Why is our table the only one with flowers on it?

He smiled and said, "I had them delivered for you."

Oh yes girl! He was in there. He passed with flying colors. So I did what I always do. I began asking the *real questions*. "Gabriel, do you want to have children?" Yes I asked on the first date. There was no need to beat around the bush. Let's jump right into the tough shit.

"Yes Alicia, I absolutely want children. I can't wait to be a father. I love children. All I've ever wanted was to be a father. I can't wait to give my mother grandchildren."

Yo! The screeching sound of breaks sounded off in my head. My reply to him was made with one of those deep sucking air through my teeth type noises that said, *damn really? Good luck with that!*

127

I let him know immediately that I had no intention of having another child. It was never in my plan to have a second child. I couldn't imagine myself changing diapers again, waking up in the middle of night and putting my life on hold. I vowed to dedicate my life to you. I was very happy with how our life was. I had a plan. Once you were in college that's when I'd do all those things that I had dreamed of. So having a little baby was *never* a part of my plan. *The date was going so well until that moment.*

He drove me home. We hugged. We talked on the phone that night until like 3:00am about our dilemma. We decided that we wanted to continue dating and see where it went. We had so much fun together. After seeing each other only a month Gabriel brought me to meet the woman in his life—his mother. I fell in love with her. She was an older version of me. *Bella* was a spiritually strong woman. She showed me all of her personal artifacts, her goddess cards. She welcomed me into her sacred space. Bella was so cool. I was absolutely looking forward to forming a tight bond with her. Oh! And his father... we shared a love of Greek Mythology. I was incredibly tight with his family.

"What are you doing the rest of your life, north and south and east and west of your life~ I have only one request of your life~ That you spend it all with me." by Barbra Streisand

That December Gabriel and I went to Florida for Christmas. He asked *abuelo* and *abuela* for my hand in marriage. Things were moving really fast. At the time I wasn't concerned about the pacing of our relationship because like I said I knew who I was and I was all about LOVE. We moved quickly into the preparations of living together.

I had never allowed anyone in our space. For me to even consider him meant that I was pretty confidant that this relationship would last. I just knew that *he* was the ONE!

2006

So amazing to be loved I'd follow you to the moon and the sky above ~ by Luther Vandross

I was watching Oprah and she was interviewing Senator Barack Obama. I spent the day watching autobiographies of celebrities. There was story about Lionel Richie's daughter Nicole using drugs as a teenager. I had an amazing idea for a children's book. I wanted to write a book about how famous people have achieved greatness through adversity. I wanted to show young kids how much shit people have to go through to finally make it. This book wasn't going to be pretty. I was going to tell the truth about what it takes. I wanted to write a book that displayed all the hard work, perseverance, determination, resiliency, endurance and faith necessary to achieve greatness.

Gabriel came home from work with an advertisement that Senator Barack Obama would be speaking at a conference in Washington, DC promoting his new book, *Audacity of Hope,* on May 20, 2006. He knew how happy that would make me. This was my opportunity to get my interview with Obama. So I began getting ready for it. At that point no one was really talking about Obama. On her show, Oprah asked him if he would run for president one day, and he said NO. But I saw something in his eyes. I knew I wanted to meet him and have him be my first interview for the book. Only problem was that my cousin Diamondz was getting married that very same day in Rhode Island. I had a decision to make. Do I take one step toward my writing dream or be with my family?

The week before Easter Gabriel and I had dinner at his best friend's house. It was a beautiful Italian feast. She had an announcement to make. She looked at her husband and went on to say, "Guess what everyone? I'm pregnant with twins!!! Now we're going to have four kids!"

My immediate response was, "Oh my god! Don't drink the water!" Yeah! He didn't find my joke even remotely funny. When we went to bed he didn't even speak to me. He was devastated.

Easter Sunday we went to church and it was like "attack of the babies". There were newborns everywhere. This was the worse possible place for us to be. I could feel how badly he wanted to be a father and having all these babies around us was not helping. The church was standing room only and there was this little baby making eye contact with him. At one point I saw a tear fall from his eye. It was horrible.

A few days later we would be celebrating our anniversary. We ordered Chinese food, had Luther playing in the background. He asked me to dance. It was a quiet night. During dinner he asked me if I was happy when I was pregnant with you. He wanted to know what I thought about carrying you.

"At first, I was scared. I didn't want to have the baby. I never wanted to be a mother. But something in me changed. I knew I was having a girl. I dreamt of her. I wanted her. I fell madly in love with her in my belly. I told how much I loved her everyday."

"You really don't think you will have another baby? You don't think you'll ever change your mind?"

"No Gabriel, I will not change my mind. I'm done. I love you but I never want to get pregnant again. I'm sorry."

"I'm sorry too. I can't imagine my life without a child. That's all I've ever wanted. I need to be a father."

That night we cried in each other's arms. It was over.

That moment when we had to say goodbye to each other was a rainy day in April. It was cold and the sky was dark. His decision was very difficult for me to accept. Our entire relationship was perfect. Everything felt right. Why did it have to end?

That last morning together he got a call that there was a death in his family. I felt like there was a death before the phone even rang. It was the death of us. He dropped me off at our house and we said goodbye.

The pain was too much to take. I continued to hold on to the idea that he would come around that he would come back to me. I really believed that he would realize what he had in me. I was prolonging the inevitable. I got so desperate with my phone calls and texts.

One Saturday afternoon, I was sitting in Central Park after doing the Revlon walk. I was on the lawn watching all the families, happy couples in love, the many strollers and babies, these perfect pictures. I saw a dad giving his baby boy a piggyback ride and during a weak Alicia moment I actually sent him a text telling him that I would have his child. I wrote him *that I would give him a baby*. For a moment I thought I could do it. I was fooling myself into believing that it wouldn't be so bad that I could start over. What the fuck was I thinking? HOW DESPARATE AM I? How far was I willing to go to be LOVED?

Once the insanity subsided... that and he totally called me on it. I needed to get it together. You and I were at church. We were standing side by side when I started to get dizzy, my stomach was sick, I was going to faint. You looked at me frightened and asked me if I was OK. You took such good care of me that day. You went all out. You had all our favorite snacks laid out on the bed, our favorite movies, Drop Dead Fred, Notting Hill, Sliding Doors, Romy and Michelle's High School Reunion.

I told you that I was OK. That I was going to be fine. I wasn't OK! I was allowing the end of this relationship to break me down. I was falling apart over a man. I was allowing myself to internally punish myself for the failed relationship. I *knew* in that moment what I needed to do. I needed to let him go. I needed to release all of the ideas I had of ever getting him back. I needed to LEARN TO LOVE ME. What a scary thought! How do I even begin to do that?

Letter: Dear Gabriel,

It was instant for us. Love at first sight. Actually, I think we were both so blinded. We wanted to believe that the love reserved for us had finally arrived. WE were the perfect MATCH. On our first date I said, "I don't want any more children!" And you so desperately wanted to be a father! We ignored the truth and stayed together despite what we heard. We both wanted so badly to believe that the other would change their mind. You thought I would see how wonderful you treated me and I'd reconsider. I thought you would take me as I am. I BELIEVED that I would be enough. Was I supposed to reward you with a child because you treated me like a queen? What was I supposed to say, "Thank you. Thank you for loving me. Here you go here's your baby?" In the end we discovered the truth that we loved ourselves too much to give up something that was so innate for us. We both deserved more. So much of what we shared was AMAZING. It was a beautiful relationship. You surpassed even Joseph in the way you expressed your love for me. So many beautiful moments our first date, Valentines Day and the countless conversations. Even with all of that we deserved so much more. I forgive you for not accepting me as I AM and I forgive myself for expecting you to give up something that you deserve to experience. You will be an amazing father. I hope you have ten kids. I wish you happiness. Love, Alicia

CHAPTER FIFTEEN ~ *2006*

That's when I overdosed. I needed an intervention. I OD'd on all kinds of books I thought might help me out of all the pain I was feeling. I read Iyanla Vanzant's, *In the Meantime: Finding Yourself and the Love You Want,* Don Miguel Ruiz's, *Mastery of Love: A Practical Guide to the Art of Relationship: A Toltec Wisdom Book,* Paulo Coelho's, *The Alchemist,* Leo F. Buscaglia's, *Love: What Life is All About,* and M. Scott Peck's, *The Road Less Traveled* in one week.

I was looking for something. I wanted to fill myself with beautiful words. I wanted to lick my wounds and move on. I wanted my strength back. I had to accept what IS. The truth *is* that on our first date we told each other exactly what we wanted and exactly who we are yet somewhere along the road we tried to convince ourselves that one of us would change their minds. What I was going through was killing me. I didn't understand why it was over. We respected each other. Things were good. I needed to STOP! I was walking around devastated. I didn't want to be sad anymore. I needed to find something that would pull me out of this state. Two weeks of this torture was too long. I wanted to get back to being happy and full of life.

I affirm: Today I am able to accept that I am flawed. Today I accept that I still need to work on acceptance and being more accepting of others. Today I accept you for you and I release all judgment. Today I accept all the gifts in my life. Today I accept people the way they are with everything they bring. Acceptance means I can take the good and bad realizing that your drama is not about me so I will not take it personal. Acceptance means that my drama is not about YOU so don't take it personal. I am now willing to accept that there may be people who will never forgive me. I am now willing to accept that we may never get back what we once had. Today I accept what is. Today I accept myself just the way I am. And so it is~

What I wanted most was to feel LOVE for myself. I wanted to love myself through all the hurt. I thought I had found it when I started going to 12 step programs and just sitting in on meetings. I felt like I needed support. I wanted to be surrounded by people. I felt like I needed help pulling myself out of this. It started to work. Just making the simple change of feeding myself positive thoughts helped me to slowly release Gabriel. When I released him I began a new relationship with me. And what I learned was that something better was coming.

I was returning home from a dinner and got on the 1 train at 72nd Street. A few of us from the party were on the platform talking when a homeless man pointed to me and addressed the women I was with. *"See that lady right there? She is powerful. I can see her light."* I said thank you to the man and he left. The women just shrugged it off as, *just some drunk* homeless guy talking crazy. I kept smiling. Internally I thought, *WOW! He can see me?* In that moment I realized that the presence of God shows up in all kinds of people. I finally understood that God showed up as the people I saw everyday.

What I believed was that the people I was meeting all brought with them amazing messages for me. All I needed to do was pay attention. What that homeless man was telling me was that I was getting there. I was healing and that *he* could see me. He arrived to reveal to me that God was pleased. I never felt more grounded. I never felt more loved. I was standing tall. In that moment I was the strongest I had ever been in my entire life. I was OPEN! I was open to all the good that existed in the world. I was feeding myself with so many positive things. I was filling myself with love.

No more breakdowns! My life was now filled with all kinds of *breakthroughs*. After taking a year and a half off from working to heal it was time to reenter the world. Momma needed to get a job. We had a good run for a while but the money finally ran out. I had done so much spirit work but I wasn't doing anything to bring in money.

May 2006

I got the job at *Businessweek*. I started out as a temp and was not interested in anything permanent. When I met the publisher I made it clear to him that I did not want a fulltime job. I told him that I was pursuing my writing career and that I was not looking to be married to a job. When he interviewed me he just laughed at me and said, "I felt like you were interviewing me and not the other way around." He hired me on the spot.

Financially, things were going well for us. You and I had money in the bank. We were able to go out to dinner, movies every weekend and shop for new clothes.

Things were going great except I couldn't handle all the goodness that I was receiving. I didn't feel like I deserved it. It was too powerful for me. I felt unworthy of all of it. It was overwhelming.

I went back to all those thoughts of my past that told me that I was a piece of shit. I believed I deserved a lifetime of unhappiness. And that's when I started to push away all the gifts I was receiving and attracting things that were not so good for me.

Summer 2006

I was moving through men pretty quickly. When ever I came
into work Margo and Patricia got such a kick out of my latest
stories. They tried to keep up with me. I had a different guy every week and they would just laugh. They knew each guy by
profession and instrument they played. Everyday I had a new
tale. I was averaging about two weeks with each guy. In two
weeks I knew if we were going anywhere. I was a busy girl.

I met piano man at Summerstage in Central Park. His band
was headlining that day. When we met, I thought he was so arrogant. I really wasn't interested but I kept telling myself, *stay
open Alicia!*

There were things about him that didn't align. His story was
sort of all over the place. He was incredibly unstable. However, I
overlooked some things because I loved that he was an artist and
we would have some really deep conversations about spirituality and the universe.

He was a *leo* like me so we were bound to clash. There was
something about him I didn't trust but I moved forward anyway. At that point I was looking for inspiration and wanted
companionship. But it wasn't working.

One night he invited me to see his friend's performance at a
club downtown. That very evening I was going to tell him that I
didn't want to see him anymore.

Letter: Dear Piano Man,

So what was our story? I think there was an animalistic chemistry between us. Last summer when we met I was looking for inspiration and male energy in my life. You were in the right place at the right time and so was I. We were in sync. But there were inconsistencies in your story. I wasn't really buying it. While I didn't fully trust you I still went forward with getting to know you. I wasn't really hearing you what you were saying.

I wasn't listening to the truth. I chose to ignore my internal sensors, my intuition and betrayed my self. I gave you the benefit of the doubt. Before we met I had only been out of a relationship for three months. It was too soon for me to date. You have your own shit to deal with. You caught me while I was doing intensive house cleaning. I was in a process of unfolding and doing that inner work which is why I was at a high frequency when you met me.

I was feeling truly powerful, creative, full of love, full of light. My life seemed perfect. This was the best I had felt in such a long time. You would have never known that just a few weeks before we met I was unemployed and just lifted myself out of a year of depression.

So here I was feeling strong, powerful and you believed that you could match that. You too were filling me with what you thought I wanted to hear.

People lie… people can be so full of shit about who they are and where they're at!!! How could you take me to your ex-girlfriend's house to play the piano for me? Did you think that would impress me?

We were never a good fit from the beginning. I forgive you for coming into my life with your negativity and darkness. I understand that I attracted you which mean's I still had work to do. I had my own darkness to release. I forgive myself for dishonoring me and not listening to my spirit. Thank you for your presence in my life.

Peace~ Alicia Anabel

August 2006

On the train ride downtown to meet Piano Man I was writing in my journal. I was releasing all that I was feeling on the page. I was having a private conversation with myself when I caught the glimpse of this young man staring at me. I smiled at him. He smiled back. He asked me if I was writer. I said yes. It was hard to understand him because he was hearing impaired.

The Dancer was deaf in one ear and had an implant in the other. When he spoke it required me to really pay attention to the movement of his lips. When he told me that he was dancer I immediately thought he was gay. He was ten years younger than me. He wrote poetry. We exchanged numbers. And spoke a week after I broke up with Piano Man.

As Piano man was on his way out this new guy was on his way in. It's like I wear some kind of magnet that reads, "I pick up strays."

The Dancer and I went out a few times. I learned that he *wasn't* gay. In fact, he was actually married and had a young daughter. He shared stories about how horrible his wife was. He told me stories about how she disrespected him because he was hearing impaired and she was the one who made all the money. He wanted to impress me. He knew what to say to me and I fell for it. He manipulated me. He used his handicap to blind me. He wrote me beautiful love letters and eloquent prose. He was a storyteller. He was gifted and blessed. He knew that I was a lover of words and that was how he trapped me in his web. He

139

wanted *me to love him* because his wife didn't. I felt sorry for him. I enjoyed his company. I slept with him.

It was like anytime I'd feel progress and great things were happening in my life I would self-sabotage and retreat to those moments where I believed I was not worthy. Here I go again.

This was such a familiar place. I'd been here before in the other woman's space just like with the pianist. How would *I* feel if the man I loved brought a strange woman home and slept with her in *their* bed? This is what kept playing in my mind. *I* didn't want to violate his wife in that way. I never accepted his invitations to go to his house. That was a line I would not dare cross.

What kind of man asks a woman to meet him at his house to defecate on the sheets he shares with her? Did he hate her *that* much? Did he wonder what that would do to his wife to come home and find me in *her* bed? Maybe he didn't care. I felt like I was violating her. I felt like a home wrecker who hadn't gone *that* far YET. I was playing with fire! But maybe accepting any invitation was *too* far.

He invited us to go to church and then brunch with him and his daughter. I asked him what church he wanted to take me to. He gave me the name. Then I asked him when the last time it was that he'd attended that church?

He responded, "The day I was married!"

Letter: Dear Dancer,

Look at what I attract now! A married man claiming to be unhappy with a small child at home. How did I let this happen? How did I get to this place? I was on a healing journey. My life was good.

Let's see! I just came to the realization of how you came into my life... the very day I was removing (the pianist) from my life. That day (to the exact second) I was ending things with him and there you were... sitting next to me on the train. You were able to seep your way in because I was in a low point in that moment. You engaged me in conversation about writing and that's how so you were able to slip by me. I was in a vulnerable place and you were able to get in because I was low (and so were you). I was low because the piano man was dragging me down with him.

Perfect timing! I thought you were gay and a part of me must of known and believed that this was some how safe and that I could control the outcome. Then you told me you had a small baby at home. I was confused. Then you said you had a wife... more confusion. Then we slept together. I wanted to be wanted. But you belonged to someone else. I was on a healing journey. I guess when I was getting too close to actually loving myself I needed to show myself that I don't deserve to be happy. I wanted to prove to myself that I don't deserve love. So I attracted YOU. You were a way for me to punish and dishonor myself. Yet again!

You who were never worthy of me! You who were disrespectful when I tried to end things! You who knew I was conflicted. You didn't want to release me so you punished me for choosing ME over you. You were disrespectful and ugly in the end. Another liar I attracted. Like attracts like - - so I guess I too was a liar when I chose you. That mistake that I made while I was with you is NOT who I am.

I forgive you for weaseling your way into my life and throwing back in my face my intimacies. I forgive myself for believing I deserved less than what I am worthy of. Thank you for showing up in my life - - now I am BACK on track. I'm back to LOVING me the way I deserve to be loved. Peace! Alicia

CHAPTER SIXTEEN ~ *September 10, 2006*

There are consequences for every choice we make. After that intense summer finally ended I was in desperate need of healing. I needed to correct things. I needed to find my way back to me. I returned to my practice, yoga, morning pages, and daily meditations. I purchased more self-help books. The Dancer was harassing me every single day. He would not stop calling me. I wanted to crawl into a shell and die. Karma's a bitch! Karma implies that your actions determine your destiny. You reap what you sow. You will pay for it either in this life or in reincarnation. So for every fucked up thing I had done I believed I was being punished.

It was your freshman year of high school. I had been working at *Businessweek* only a few months. We were just getting back into our groove. You and I were at the hair salon when my cell phone rang. I was in the middle of getting my hair washed. It was your Tia Fabiana, "Alicia, Diamondz died."

"Diamondz who?" I asked confused...like I knew twenty people with that same name.

"Our cousin Diamondz!!!"

"whose cousin? What are you talking about?"

"Our cousin Diamondz died! What the fuck Alicia!!! Our cousin Diamondz died!"

She was a mess. I couldn't understand what she was saying to me. She was screaming in hysteria. Did she just tell me that our cousin is no longer with us? I couldn't believe it. I was in a state of shock. I got up and don't remember how we even got home. I couldn't see. I remember walking out onto St. Nicholas Avenue and I told you to hail a cab. I couldn't see anything. I remember being in this cab not knowing where we were headed. He was three days away from his 33rd birthday and I was filled with so much regret.

Four months earlier~ May 20, 2006

Diamondz was getting married. I was so conflicted. Do I go to his wedding or go meet Senator Barack Obama? I still went through with my plans. We only had $500.00 to our name. I used every cent to get us to DC. I paid for our Amtrak tickets, we stayed at the Marriott Hotel, and we even had dinner at Ruth's Chris. We went all out. We arrived to DC and immediately I took you to the pool. When we got back to our room I told you that I needed to prepare for my interview with Obama. I didn't actually have an interview with him but I was going to try and get one.

The family was so upset at me for choosing to go to DC than attend Diamondz wedding. It was not an easy decision for me to make. I wanted to be at his wedding. I also wanted to make my dreams come true. We were so excited about this trip.

The next day we would be attending a private "breakfast with the authors," in a banquet hall at the convention center. Our tickets were $96.00 each. Once there, we took our seats and waited with the hundreds of other people in attendance. My plan was simple, at the end of the book reading I would get in line and hand Obama an envelope with a formal request for an interview, as well as, a copy of the questions I would be asking. I was ready.

The event began. The applause stopped. They announce Senator Barack Obama to the podium to deliver the keynote address. He spoke for a few minutes and read an excerpt from his new book, *Audacity of Hope*. Once he was done, he said, "Thank you everyone. Enjoy the rest of your day." Then he exited stage left.

My mouth dropped, we weren't sure if he left or just stepped outside to go to the bathroom. I looked at you in complete shock, "Baby, I think he left." Even you said, "WHAT?"

I sat there for a minute; my mind was going all over the place. I was racing through everything I had done to prepare for this moment and did he just leave? I didn't know what to do. My eyes got watery. I was visibly upset. I had NO interest in listening to any of the other authors that were there. I sat there in complete panic and disbelief. Then a voice whispered to me, *GET UP! Get up right now! Get up and walk out that door!*

I gathered our things. All the free books, even our breakfast and said to you, "Lets go."

You were mortified. You knew that exiting like that would be completely disruptive and everyone would look at us. You were so embarrassed. "Mommy, we can't leave. We have to stay. It would be rude."

"I don't give a shit. We did not come all the way here for nothing. I used every cent we had even if we have to run up and down the streets of Washington we are not leaving without speaking to Barack Obama!"

We headed to the front of the banquet hall and exited from the same door Obama walked out of. As soon as we opened the door... *there he was.*

He was standing right there, Barack Obama and only a few other people. I just froze.

You looked at me, smiled and said, "Alright momma, this is the moment you've been waiting for. Here's your chance! Are you ready?"

I looked at you, smiled, and said, "Hell yeah, I'm ready!"

We waited patiently for him to finish speaking to people and then it was our turn. I introduced myself and then introduced you. He came down to your eye level to speak with you. He asked you questions about school and your favorite subject. He was incredibly generous with his time. I told him who I was and

145

about the children's book. He thought it was a wonderful idea and had his assistant give me his card. He accepted my letter and asked me to contact his office.

MISSION ACCOMPLISHED!

I was determined. I believed that I was going to meet Barack Obama and we did. It felt great. I was so happy. While we were back on a train heading back home all I could think about was how I wished we had money so we could just take the train all the way to Rhode Island and still make Diamondz wedding.

I chose Obama and I will have to live with that choice for the rest of my life. I got what I deserved. I believed that his death was my fault. I believed that I somehow caused his death by all the darkness I was attracting. That I deserved to lose someone I loved because of the choices I made. I believed that his death was my punishment. I missed his wedding to meet Barack Obama in DC and then he died four months later.

If I could get back one moment in time it would be his wedding day.

CHAPTER SEVENTEEN ~ *2006*

After our cousin died the entire family was destroyed. It was the biggest blow. We didn't just lose someone we loved. We lost a great father, friend, brother and son. It was a huge loss in the family and we all dealt with our grief in our own way. My way was through writing. I wrote a piece that was dedicated to him that I read at his burial.

In my dedication I described Diamondz as the most beautiful butterfly. After that day I only see butterflies as a confirmation that I am on the right path. He is always flying with me.

When we lost him I tried to fill my time with many things. I was so angry at the universe for taking him from us. I was so mad at God and the Goddesses. I didn't understand why it was his time to leave us. I got back into my practice and returned to my prayers for understanding.

When he died we went to a 12-step meeting because I wanted to be in a sacred space of sharing. There was a woman crying who shared that her daughter beats her. She told the group that she snuck out of the house to attend the meeting. Other people talked about their addiction. I shared our story about LOSS.

That was the first time I cried over him. I was so angry that Diamondz came to me in my dreams and asked me not to cry. Telling me that I needed to be strong for his mother. I cried so much that night. When we left the church you said to me, "Momma, that better be the last time you go to one of those meetings. It made me so depressed."

You didn't understand that some people feel so alone. That sometimes there is comfort in being around people who understand how you're feeling. I'm sure the stories seemed horrible. But to me it felt like a safe place where I could be vulnerable and where there would be no judgments.

October 2006

After we lost our cousin my new mantra became; *every ending is a new beginning. The end of anything brings something new, something beautiful and I'm excited at its arrival.*

I attended a writing workshop about Latinos breaking into publishing. As the facilitator spoke she talked about stereotypes and breaking barriers. She talked about the publishing world. There was something she said that stayed with me, *we need to stop allowing for media to portray us as the drug dealer, sexy secretary, cocinera in the novella and write our own stories. What we need is a revolution!*

As soon as she said the word *revolution* my mind drifted. I was no longer in that space. I went to a far away land and started writing *The Daughters of the Revolution.*

A week later we went to Bryant Park for an author discussion. One of the questions the moderator asked the writers on the panel was what they thought of the label, "Latino Writer." They each responded differently. One of the women responded with fury, "Don't call me a Latino Writer! I don't want to be put in a box. I want to be labeled — *Writer!*"

I took huge offense to the *way* she reacted — to how she said it. It made me feel like she wasn't proud to be Latina. What I heard was *don't call me Latina I want to be in the category with Hemingway, Poe, Cummings, Austen, Twain and Woolf* which I don't have a problem with.

However, her self-hatred came through in her comment, which to me had less to do with being recognized as a *good writer.* Perhaps if she had said *that* I wouldn't have been so mad at her statement. I can understand some one wanting be seen as *one of the greatest writers of our time.* But most of *those* writers come from somewhere and when we read *their* bios it states the country they're from. She didn't say that though. She said she didn't want to be seen as a *Latina* Writer.

And I totally get the other side of that discussion, where we don't want to be "typecast" as being a writer who writes only *one kind* of story. That is not my debate. I am writing a story about women in the world who I am not. However, I take great pride in calling myself a Latina Writer because I am Latina... PERIOD. Of all the labels I've been called, that's one I'm proud of.

So when I left that discussion I was angry. I told *La Chicana* that I wish there were a Latina Writers group. I shared with her that I wanted so badly to have a space where I could develop my writing skills, finish my book and perhaps publish one day. She looked at me and said; "If you can't find it—create it."

The very next day, the New York City Latina Writers Group (NYCLWG) was born.

Initially, I started the group because I was furious with that writer's statement. Then I realized that it would open the door to women who wanted support in finding their voices. It now became a platform to get our writing careers off the ground.

There were so many insecurities I needed to leave at the door when I began this journey with the NYCLWG. It took a long time but I finally let go of the self-defeating thought's that were telling me *who the fuck am I to start a Latina writers group? I'm not a serious writer? I've never been published. What do I know about running a group? Who's going to show up to write with me anyway?"*

I'm so glad I was wrong! I made a choice despite all my fears. I knew nothing about organizing a group of writers and providing guidance to women especially since I was so desperately searching for guidance myself. All I knew for sure was that I needed to spend more time honoring my craft and myself. I wanted a safe space to create! I could no longer wait for the right group to find me.

On this writing journey what I've realized is that I was born to create work that affects change. My intention is to create work that contributes to what our children are reading and learning. I want our Latino communities to have books that speak their language and speak to their experiences and struggles.

I want to write stories that elevate and expand. I want to be an example and a role model for that nine-year-old Dominican girl who gets beat all the time and is told by her parents to stop daydreaming, that writing isn't a real job.

I want her see my reflection when she looks in the mirror. I want her to know that *that* shit that they're trying to sell her just ain't true. She *can* be a writer. Latino's do in fact read. We do buy books and have something to say!

CHAPTER EIGHTEEN ~ *Fast Forward to 2011*

Today in church I understood why I was having such difficulty starting this chapter. I am about to explore the FEMININE SPIRIT. I am about to journey into my soul and unlock feelings that we as women have been taught to stuff deep down. We have been taught to lock the power within us and place it into the Holy Grail never to be found.

It's Mother's Day and the minister at Unity Church shared a story about Mary Magdalene and the reasons perhaps that the Catholic Church has kept her out of the bible.

As he spoke I wondered *were they afraid of her power? Would acknowledging Mary Magdalene for actually being significant to Jesus' really pose such a threat? Why were Peter and Paul so angry that Jesus appeared to her first? What if Jesus saw how powerful Mary Magdalene really was and decided that he must have her at his side?*

At the end of the service I was incredibly emotional; I called forth the strength of all the women who were present to help me write this section. I called on all the strength and pain of all the women in the world and when you ask the universe for something it arrives. After having a wonderful lunch with my cousin and her son I headed home and began writing. This part of my journey requires everything that I am made of and everything that I have learned.

After I was home and settled in *la Chicana* came by with groceries and we had a picnic on our living room floor. She stayed only a short while. Then it was time for me to begin writing. I went to turn on the computer and it wouldn't start. I was sitting on my bed and was like, *oh no! NOT my manuscript!!!* I kept restarting it and restarting it and nothing. The computer screen just stayed blue. I didn't understand what was wrong. I worried that all the pages I had written were gone. All of sudden I got so tired. I felt the spirit of every woman in my life inside of me. I was exhausted. I was completely drained.

My entire body started to shut down. I was falling asleep with the computer on my lap. I was thinking about all the women in my life, my mother, you, cousins, friends, spiritual sisters, aunts and our grandmothers. I was feeling all of the women of the world. I called forth today the pain and strength of the women of the world and one by one I could feel each of them. It got to a point where it felt like too much. I turned off the lights, took off my clothes and pulled the covers over my head. I slept for two in half hours and now I'm up. It's 8:40pm and my computer *finally* turned on. ACHE! My body was calling for stillness, quiet and sleep. This work requires that you take care of yourself and rest. Once I woke up I was ready, although I still felt a little

153

felt a little strange. The left side of my face was numb, almost paralyzed as if it was still asleep. With all that I've gone through the past few days writing this memoir I now feel ready to begin my journey into my spiritual awakening.

Writing for me is a revolutionary act! Part of our history as Latinas has been to NOT HAVE A VOICE, to remain in the shadows and to cry privately or withhold our tears. Women from our countries are constantly having rights violated. In most countries they are invisible. Many women lack the courage to speak up. For many women having a voice is a brave act.

Then there's the relationship amongst women. Why can't women give it to each other straight without worrying that they will hurt her feelings?

I think about the women in my life (myself included) who spend a lot of energy and time talking about other women. There are women who spend hours conversing about how other women should live *their* lives. Gossiping about what they don't like about certain women. That *JLO can't dance or act*, commenting and complaining about how they feel betrayed by women. Why are some of our female relationships healthy and others poisonous or toxic? Why are we threatened by the success of other women? Why are we insecure? Why are we Jealous? What are we competing for? Why aren't women happy for other women

women who reach a level of success? What would it take to stop the fighting? What would men say our problem is? One man in my life likes to call this CHURNING BUTTER but I will get back to that theory later.

I read somewhere that we learn how to have relationships with other women from our relationship with our mothers. Over the years I can relate to the idea that *whatever my relationship has been with my parents will be reflected in the types of relationships I have through out my life.* That the thoughts and feelings I've had for my dad will show up in the kinds of relationships I have with men. Same goes for mom, if I've had a rough relationship with *her* it might be hard for me to have good relationships with women. *How much of who I am today comes from who my mother is?*

Our relationships with our mothers can either be wonderful or it can be devastatingly painful. I think that you and I have built a beautiful relationship. Only time will tell what your relationships with men and women will be like. I am not sure what the mother son relationship is like. But as a daughter there are things we go through separately and together. It's like there is a tug of war... *abuela* wants to be right... and I want to gain her respect as a woman. There are things we as women inherit from our mothers—some good—some not so good—but all that we receive or don't receive IS what makes us—US.

There are mothers who have left this earth. There are mothers who have abandoned their daughters. There are mothers who feel children should fend for themselves. There are mothers who lift. There are mothers who put down. There are mothers who love deeply. There are

155

mothers with NO heart. There are mothers without mothers. There are mothers who have no business being mothers. Then there are mothers who are EVERYTHING these mothers are not!

Today I'm not talking about just anybody's mother. This is about your *abuela*. My mother has sacrificed everything for her children. All of her dreams have been about us. She was the first to teach me how to speak Spanish, she fed me (still does), clothed me (still does), loves me unconditionally and endlessly.

My mother taught me how to dance and I have been dancing from the moment I left her womb. She remembers everything about me. She knows me. She is ALWAYS there for me. She is the kind of mother who calls me everyday to see how I am feeling. If it were up to her I would still be living in her home because she loves to take care of me. My mom has taught me how to be a lady. She is definitely not responsible for my foul mouth and terrible temper. *Ella me enseno delicadesa* and most of my mannerisms and facial expressions come from her.

It has taken me a long time to appreciate how amazing my mother truly is. Becoming a mother myself has helped me understand all that my mother has done for us. I understand how incredibly hard it is to be a mother and the great responsibility that comes along with it.

As a child it was hard for me to see my life as great. It was hard for me to see that she was only trying to do her best. There were things I needed that I didn't feel I received from her. I am 100% positive that if she could take away my past pains and heal my wounds she would have.

156

But nonetheless, I was and am in some ways still wounded. What is it about our past pains that refuse to leave us? Why do we allow the pains to cloud us, to consume us, to paralyze us, to dictate what our relationships will be like in the future? I don't want to hurt my mother. Our relationship is really good right now. Our relationship is always good when we don't talk about the past. All is fine when we don't look at those things that bring up bad memories. I am sure she wishes I could just erase all those years of pain, hurt, beatings and trauma. I don't think she has any idea of how it has played out in my adult life. While I don't want to blame your *abuela* or my father I do blame them. I have never told her until now.

Letter: I AM My Mothers DAUGHTER~

Querida Madre Adorada,

Bendicion mami! I write you this love letter out of pain. Mami, I don't want to hurt you because I suspect that you are suffering through your own personal pain. I began a list of things I wanted to say: We are a walking contradiction. We constantly do for others. We have always been better friends to others than they are to us. We have bad luck in female friendships. Standing by your man. Self sacrifice. You let him hit me. You didn't protect me. You didn't stand up for me. You didn't demand I be respected and treated like a human being.

Mom, I suspect that your strength is a wall for the weakness you possess... a powerlessness you must be feeling or are suffering from. I feel this because I too suffer. I am suffering from the very same things. I AM your daughter. I feel what you feel and I know that you feel me.

On the outside we are both a force. We put on our masks, our makeup, our fiercest clothes and we saunter. Pa'lante, there's no stopping us. No one can tell us anything. No one in the room looks better. We definitely can walk in some heels baby. And can we work a crowd! We walk in ANY room with such confidence... it's so natural for us.

We were born with it. We truly own every place we enter. We enter like royalty. "We ARE the shit!" You're Princess Diana and me I'm Whitney Houston.

Unfortunately mami, its all a lie! We are weak women. We are scared and lonely. We know what it's like to feel like we're dying a little each day. We just get by hoping to never get found out. Hoping another day will pass us by where we're not discovered for the women we really are — two women in pain. We're two women who believe a bunch of crap. People will sell us anything. We buy into our own lie about having it together. We have put our faith in people who are unworthy of our trust. We constantly do for others saying we don't expect things in return. But we do expect things. We expect to be appreciated, cared for, showed we are loved and told often. We expect and demand respect. And we get our feelings hurt when those WE love don't tell us they love us back.

Our friendships with women... we have had some bad luck in this department. It could very well be that they're jealous or even envious of us. But who are we? Who am I? You've raised me to be strong. To believe I could be anything. To believe I could be everything. What you didn't teach me was how to focus on one thing. You didn't teach me how to be exceptional at any ONE thing. Mami, that really messed me up. Throughout my life it has been so difficult for me to stick to any one thing. I have started things that I don't finish and that will never make me a success. I hate that my ex was right about this.

You sent me out into the world in some ways unprepared and disarmed. I've had to teach myself all kinds of things to survive and undo some of the programming that I received in our home. You and daddy raised me so unfairly. I had so much responsibility at such an early age. I really don't feel like I had a childhood. Most days I resented you for that. I blamed you. I feel like my childhood was robbed from me. Anytime I was happy or playing... that moment would be the time to clean. During any fun it was always time to pick up the house for show of course because we were about to have company. I felt like you took away my happiness.

During the summer while I was recording a show, I was asked to recall the last time I had fun. I tried to remember the games I used to play. The exercise called for me to have fun to be carefree. I was being asked to be childlike. I just started crying. I could not for the life of me remember my childhood. I didn't know how to access those memories. I didn't know where that child was. I called Josie to ask her if I was a good sister if I played with her. I could not remember having fun as a child. I couldn't remember any of the games I played. Josie shared a wonderful story with me of how when daddy fell asleep I would take her and Fabiana outside and we would play under the streetlights until almost 1:00am right before you got home from work. She told me I was a fun sister but I couldn't remember the fun times. It was like they were erased. They were gone!

You didn't protect me mom! You allowed dad to put his hands on me. You hit me too. I felt demeaned in so many ways. You said some pretty horrible things to me. I was the punching bag for all of the problems you and daddy were dealing with. That's really messed up. I was your little girl - - your first girl. How could you stay with him? Why didn't you leave him? You saw beauty in me and put me in pageants but did you know how ugly I thought and believed I was. There was NO way the few times I heard a positive compliment compared to all the negative, ugly, and hurtful words I heard about being too skinny, my grades in school too low, that I would ever become anything. How was I ever going to believe I was beautiful? That's why I didn't take modeling seriously. I didn't believe it. I didn't believe in me. I didn't feel that the people I loved the most believed in me.

You should have stood up to daddy and told him, "NO! You will not beat ALICIA – not my daughter!" You allowed him to disrespect and demoralize me. You believed I deserved it. I believed I deserved it. I used to sit on my bed looking out of the window onto Woodhaven Boulevard just crying. As I watched the cars go over the bridge I wished I could be in one of those cars escaping. I hated you and daddy so much during those days. I wanted to leave and never come back. I wanted to runaway. I did run away but I came back. When daddy picked me up at that ladies house, when we got home he beat me again. After he hit me he said, "Go ahead call 911, I'll beat you in front of them. Tu me vas a respetar!"

Then I got pregnant. Remember when we went to that bruja and she told me "congratulations on your pregnancy." I think you almost fell off your chair. When I found out I was pregnant I told you I wasn't sure if I wanted to keep it. You made me. You said that I couldn't have an abortion. I am sure you were protecting me from the feelings that would come after that decision. That and you mentioned that if my father found out he would kill us both. Thank you for your counsel during that time. Courtney is the best thing that ever happened to me. I kept the baby and was married. That time in my life was one of the un-

happiest moments of my life to add to my already miserable existence. Your advice to me was to stay in the marriage and try to make it work. Basically what I got from you was stay miserable. "Mi hija, stick it out...sobre jevalo." I had to go through more fucked up shit to go along with the rest of the fucked up shit I had to put up with throughout my life. I will never forget that your advice to me was to stick it out and be unhappy, be miserable, almost as if that was just the way we women do things.

How dare I want and demand respect for myself? Why would I want a loving home free of abuse and beatings for my daughter? How dare I want a house full of fun, laughter and love served unconditionally? I still have much to learn on how to love unconditionally but what I wanted most was a loving home free of beatings. I wanted my daughter to grow up in a home where she could have her OWN opinions and be respected for her individuality. I wanted a home where it was encouraged to dream and believe in herself. I didn't want her to just trust blindly what her parents say or what the elders in the family say, but to trust and find out the truth about life on her own. I wanted to encourage my child to even question ME. I wanted to create the home I wish I had for me.

I think I'm hurt at what daddy did to me but furious with you. You were supposed to be the FORCE, the rock and the strength. You are who I looked up to. You are the woman I wanted to become. I wanted to be just like you. If you had dreams you should have went for them so that I could have had a role model and been taught how to achieve my own dreams. I needed someone to show me how it's done. I didn't need the traditional Latina recipe of "let's just make nice. Don't speak up. Deal with it. These are the cards that we are dealt so take it." We shouldn't just rock the boat we should tip that shit over.

Thank you for always telling me and reminding me that it's never too late to go after my dreams. These days I'm trying to teach myself how to ACHIEVE them.

I surrender mommy! I don't want to be angry with you anymore. I know that you love me. I know how hard you worked your entire life to give me everything... to give me clothes, a house and food. I know you love me. I truly believe in my heart that you only wanted the best for me. I know that if you could have done more for me when I was in pain you would have. But how could you help me with my pain? You've never dealt with your own. Mami, I hope you find ways to heal. I hope you have peace. I am so grateful to you and am indebted to you mom.

While I know I have inherited some traits that have stifled me. You have also given me many gifts. You have given me the gift of life, the gift of love, the gift of standing up for ME and standing up for the things I believe in. You have given me strength to endure. I AM A POWERHOUSE because of you. You have given me gifts that elevate others and myself. This is my greatest gift. I cherish this gift the most. We make people feel good. We love deeply. We know exactly what to say.

Because of you I have learned to lick my wounds quickly. Whenever I fall I get right back up. This I learned from you and I thank you. What ever I don't know I teach myself. This too I learned from you. Whatever I say I want I go get it and that's definitely you speaking to me, through me and walking with me on this journey. I THANK YOU! I honor you! I ADORE YOU. We are light for so many people. Thank you for teaching me loyalty and for giving me the love you have always shown me.

Thank you mom for everything you have given me, for all you symbolize to me, I AM your inheritance. I am proud of the woman you are. I love you with everything that I am. Thank you for always preparing my favorite foods when I come to visit. Thank you for calling me everyday just to let me know how much you love me. Thank you for worrying about me and Courtney. I'm so grateful you are my mother. I love you mami. Please forgive me for all the hateful names I have called you in the past. Please forgive me if my words in this letter hurt you. Please know that I love you and I forgive you. I know that you did the best you could with the tools you had. Con todo y todo... you did an amazing job with me. Despite the pain and suffering I endured I am a strong woman because of you. I am here because of you. Mira a Courtney she is the image of you and I - - A FORCE TO BE RECKONED WITH! Te adoro madre linda – te deseo todo lo mas lindo de este mundo. I AM My Mother's DAUGHTER! Soy hija de mi madre! La bendicion, Tu hija Alicia Anabel

CHAPTER NINETEEN ~ *January 2007*

For the longest time I defined myself by what men thought of me. I wanted to be liked by men. I wanted to be loved by men. I wanted to be valued by men. It was important for me to find *the guy* for me and *he* be the person to show me — ME. I believed that through men I would discover my purpose. Through men I would find self-love, self-worth and self-awareness. I started to move away from the *search* for a man and focused my energies on tapping into my femininity. I really began to do that inner work of accessing parts of me that I'd been ignoring. I started to establish stronger bonds with women.

I attended a book reading with a sister friend and was completely inspired. I was enamored. It was such a profound experience. The story was about being a Latina in the United States and all that we go through to prove that we are Latina. I could totally relate. This was a few weeks after I started the NYCLWG. When I launched the NYCLWG there were only six members who attended that first meeting in our apartment in Harlem. After the first month there were 30 members. After six months there were over 100 members. We were *all* looking for the same thing a place we could belong. At that point I was very aware of how powerful I really am and all of this knowing was without a man telling me so. There was nothing stopping me. After the reading I approached the author and asked if she would help me promote the writers group. I asked her if perhaps we could collaborate on something.

You and I met her for breakfast and she seemed very interested in working with me. She shared an idea she had about a show that she wanted to launch and offered me an opportunity to co-create it. I would be the host and head writer. This was a fantastic opportunity for me. During the show I would review a book and tie it into a personal life experience. The show was a combination of my writing, spiritual and personal journey. In one episode I talked about writers who risked everything to have their voices heard, who speak up for the weak; and speak up for what they believe in. I reviewed, *In the Time of the Butterflies*, by Julia Alvarez it was a story about the Mirabal Sisters. In another show, I reviewed a documentary on Lisa Lopes, from the girl group TLC.

Most of my inspiration for the show came from those women I admired and considered role models. The stories that affected me the most were about women who used their adversity to strengthen their soul, their spirits and the spirits of others. I love stories that teach us how to pull ourselves out of darkness. I've always been interested in learning about women who are constantly evolving, expanding, transforming and reinventing themselves while bringing other women forward with them. These are the stories that inspire me. While I was writing an episode I couldn't help but think of the many ways women have been abused and continue to be abused. The stories I wrote for the show were about brave women.

At the time I didn't realize that what I was writing about was starting to change me. That the women I was writing about in many ways were all me. The people who inspired me most were who I was becoming. I started to think about women who speak against those who try to oppress them and saw myself in them. I was inspired by these women who defeated odds and stood tall, those who gave or lost their lives in hopes of freeing others and themselves. This is where my writing was headed. I wanted to be a voice for these women. I wanted to write about the things that we as women have in common. I wanted to show the strength that could be found after abuse. I wanted to show that there was life after abuse. I wanted to show that I was *destined to heal.*

I wrote about what abuse did to me and how it wounded me for many years. I shared how I felt angry, bitter and hated my parents. I knew what abuse felt like. There's a mental incarceration abused women suffer through. We go through denial, self-hate, self-destruction and guilt. Being abused is a quick way to diminish a woman's sense of self. Stripping her of her self-worth. When I watched the documentary, *"Last Days of Left Eye,"* I knew I needed to write about abuse and share her story. She was working on the documentary up until her final moments when she died on April 25, 2002 in a car accident. I understood what it was like to be hurt by someone you love.

I felt connected to her. I connected with Lisa's strength. I connected to the strength found in her pain. With all the ups and downs she endured both personally and professionally it was inspiring to see how she could still come out on top. What I saw was strength in her face, power in her words, self-assuredness, confidence, softness in her eyes and her innocence. What I saw was her spirit. *That was the last show I ever recorded with that partner. I never heard it. I never watched it. And it was the last time we worked together.*

2007 brought me many achievements. I have worked with some pretty amazing people and have formed some incredible relationships. The opportunity she offered me was amazing. It transformed my life. It pushed me in a direction I had no idea I was headed in. It was the first time I would be working with a partner. In the beginning things were really good between us. Her and I had a great vibe. She had accomplished so much already and I had hoped to learn from her. I heard so many times about the importance of surrounding yourself with good people, surrounding yourself with people who want to help you, with people who will take you forward. I was all about finding and surrounding myself with like-minded people and I believed she was of that thinking. I thought that I found that in her.

But there was something missing. She taught me about INTENTION! What was her intention in this partnership? What was my intention? Did our intentions align? Were we on the same page? When you are unable to speak openly and honestly with a partner then chances are the intentions are not aligned. There should have been a clear understanding of what was expected from both parties. We didn't have this. In partnerships or any relationship communication is instrumental. In business one must be able to have difficult conversations and come to a compromise were all parties are satisfied with the outcome. The communication has to be open, honest, holding nothing back, with mutual understanding and respect.

Letter: Dear Perfect Partner,

There was something you said during the last recording of the show that has always stayed with me, "She's got it!!! She's finally got it!"

I wasn't completely honest at the end of our partnership. I didn't communicate exactly what it was I was feeling and why it was that I made the decision to walk away from our partnership. I wanted to talk to you about the project we were working on but I didn't know how to approach you.

What I wanted to say was "I feel like we're losing momentum." What I should have said is that "I feel like we have not had forward movement in a while and I am just wondering what's going on. I am curious to know what direction we are headed in."

From the few conversations we were having towards the end I was picking up ON something. But you never directly told me what was happening. You never told me what changed for you. You came at me in a round about way and I never spoke up about how I was feeling. I never asked you what was up.

What I should have asked was "Where's your head at in this partnership? Are you still down? Have you changed your mind about us working together?"

It seemed like you were more focused on other things. You were consumed with drama that didn't align with who I am. You were more concerned about what other people were doing. You were worried about what people were saying about you rather than creating good work.

Initially, there was excitement about us working together but something changed for you and you never told me what that was. I never got to see that last episode. Because you said you were having problems with the recording. All was fine up until that point. Weeks went by and nothing. I never got to see my work and I felt like it was holding my process up.

"She's got it!!! She's finally got it!" That's what you said under your breath as you watched me from behind your video camera. That was the last day we ever worked together. I've always thought about that moment. How I was transforming right before your eyes. There was something you saw that day that I wish you had given me. There was something that you saw happening that I wish you had told me. I felt like you withheld that moment from me. You stole that moment from me. I did feel like something shifted. I felt like we hit a wall. The creativity was halted. I felt like something out of my control was interfering and impeding my growth. Perhaps it was how fast I was growing that scared you. Something was keeping me from moving forward and I felt like it was stopping my growth and my writing. It felt like something was attempting to stop me from moving forward.

I had to listen to my heart. I had to be willing to be me. Something changed for ME too. I started to feel what it was you saw that day. It seemed like my growth threatened you. I prayed on it. I meditated on it. I needed to say what it was that I needed from this partnership without fear of how it was going to be taken. I could not be around anything that was threatening to impede my growth. It should have never been done in an email and I hope you will forgive me for that. I was afraid of having the necessary conversation… afraid of a confrontation because I have never known how to ask for what I wanted. I was afraid that I wouldn't get it. I was more concerned with your feelings and betraying you. I had to accept the consequences of the choices I made. I had to get comfortable with accepting that people may not like my decisions but I must move forward anyway. I didn't feel that my needs were being met. When you don't feel like your needs are being met it's important to be honest and honor where you are at. I should have said these things to you but I didn't know how. I was afraid to speak up. What I knew, believed and affirmed internally was that in order to salvage our rela-tionship I would have to end the business partnership.

I was your student. You were my teacher. I trusted you. A teacher nurtures. A teacher builds. Teachers should not destroy – they should encourage. There's a point though… a moment when the teacher sees that the student is about to surpass even them. The teacher can either push the student to go even further or stifle them. I was surpassing my teacher. She knew it… and I knew it. I felt it~ it was POWERFUL.

I was Santiago becoming the Alchemist. A good teacher allows the student to leave them to spread their wings and continue growing… But not this teacher… this teacher wanted to control me… to control my growth… to control my process… to control my writing. I needed to keep moving and continue to apply ALL I had learned. The point is to share my learning with the world. Sometimes the student needs to say goodbye to the teacher.

When I let you go I learned some new things about me. Things I needed to learn alone. What I learned is that I don't allow jealousy, competition, fear, envy, worry or doubt to paralyze me or drive me. I am a warrior. I am here to be great. In letting you go I found me. The end of anything brings something new.

It was time. It was time for me to move on, spread my wings and speak my truth. What I discovered was that my truth cannot be cen-sored. I am still learning. I am still growing. But I can't worry about the result of THIS ending. I must honor me.

I forgive you for not being clear about what you wanted and ex-pected from me and I forgive myself for not doing the same. I forgive you for not allowing me to know what you saw in me. But I felt it. It lives inside of me. It's a force that could never be kept from me. I forgive myself for taking this long to get here. I am awake. With love, Alicia

CHAPTER TWENTY ~ *Solidarity and this idea of Sisterhood*

I was thinking about the people in my life who are the closest to me. Who are the people in my inner circle? Who are my confidantes? Who are the people I can count on when I am in a jam? Who picks me up when I am down? Who do I trust with my life story? Who do I trust with my life? Who do I trust with you? I was at a friend's house—a woman who is definitely in my front row. I was resting on her bed and something made me get up to read quotes and affirmations on her board in her home office. I came across this beautiful quote:

"Observe the relationships around you. Pay attention to which ones lift and which ones lean? Which ones encourage and which ones discourage? Which ones are on a path of growth uphill and which ones are going downhill? When you leave certain people, do you feel better or feel worse?"
By Melanie Kissel

Who is in your inner circle? What are the circles you run with? How do you decide who sits in your inner circle? I have several circles, there's my NYC girls who have been here for me through it all, the "purging party" at my house where we threw out 35 bags of trash and donated fifteen bags of clothes. These are the friend's who bring me nourishment and love while I work, wipe my tears when I am in pain and are my constant sources of strength. My cousins, who are like my sisters their faith in me is beyond words. Then there is the constant presence of my your *abuela, abuelo, tia* Josie, *tia* Fabiana, and *tio* Fabio who are my biggest supporters, those who know me best and would die for me. There are people who love me sight unseen. They love me flaws and all. There are countless aunts and uncles who I love dearly. The NYCLWG are my sacred writing sisters. Then there is the circle of you and my relationship with Luz. You two are the closest to female soul mates I have ever had.

The people in my *true circle* want nothing from me but what I am willing to share. They take me as I am. How do we pick who's allowed in our inner circle? I think for me there is one constant. The deciding factor is *do you come in LOVE?* I am less concerned with having an exclusive inner circle with only the select few who make the cut automatically because we share a bloodline. I have met people recently that I love deeply. While I do have a small circle of people I go to FIRST. I am more inclined these days to have a circle of LOVE. Luz taught me how to have a true friendship with a woman. In NYC I was searching for sisterhood and solidarity. Solidarity is a union or fellowship built from common responsibilities and interests shared between groups of people. Sisterhood is an association of women for a common cause. I was looking for unity within my community of women. I wanted a sense of oneness in my connections.

"A friend is a person who dislikes the same people you do." ~ Anonymous
When I met my spiritual soul mate I was in college in the early 90's and I was extremely insecure. Luz was vibrant, confident and incredibly interesting. She was exactly the person sent to walk with me on this journey of self-discovery. We spent hours talking about life, love,

men, sex, spirituality, art and music. It was the first time I really heard Ella Fitzgerald.

We talked about what my issue was when I called the school that day and why I was so rude to her. So many years later I wondered about that and tried to answer that question. What was it about where I was in my life that had me so angry? What was I afraid she was going to take from me? Why didn't I trust her intention? Why didn't I trust her truth immediately? What scared me about her strength? Was I envious or jealous of her and this *thing* she possessed and walked with that words can't describe?

As I was taking self inventory the immediate answer was that I wanted some of what she possessed. She taught me that there is always a reason people come into your life and these reason may not be revealed immediately, but that there was *always* a reason and a lesson to be learned from everyone. There were even lessons from people we may not like. During the time when we met I was in a place in my life where I was searching for an outlet. I needed something different. I wasn't happy. I needed a place to retreat to and my relationship with this woman was very sacred and special to me. I would always protect our friendship with everything I am.

We used to say that if we were lesbians we would be married. We joked like that all the time. But the reality is that we do have a union. We have a bond that is unbreakable. We have an unshakable connection that no man or woman could ever sever and people have tried. People will show up who do not have the best intentions. Some will show up with ulterior motives. There are people who never show us who they are. Then there are those who enter our lives to share love, life and wisdom expecting nothing in return. These people who have so much love, that it just overflows. And if you have never experienced this kind of love you don't know how to receive it. If you've never loved yourself this deeply it makes sense that you would definitely not trust it. There are people who exist who will NEVER judge you and love you no matter what you do. These people are gifts to the world. These are the people who come into our lives JUST for the sole purpose of leaving gifts expecting nothing in return. My spiritual soul mate is one of these people.

The things that I have learned from Luz about life, love, spirituality, faith, living, sharing, teaching, counseling, healing and unconditional love are gifts that she has passed down to me that I will love her for ALWAYS. She was the first relationship I have had with a person who accepted me as I am, with all my flaws no questions asked. She had no desire to change me. Luz has never put me down.

There is a mutual respect and love between us. Every experience and every moment with her is uplifting for the both of us. All of our conversations are a spiritual experience. Our time together has been filled with laughter, reminiscing and passing down of wisdom. And she asks for nothing from me and I want nothing from her... but we give to one another in abundance. She is the definition of friendship, of solidarity, of sisterhood and of what unity looks like. *To one of the GREATEST loves of my life, my spiritual soul mate, my sister who I will love, cherish and honor always... a love letter~*

Letter: Amiga, What up? Shparkee... Shpark me up???

You are one of the most important people in my life. You are my bestest friend in the whole world.
"I have words that do not come from children's books~ everything I've got belongs to you~ you for me and me for you~ I'll give you plenty of nothing~ I have a terrible tongue a temper for two" ~ by Ella Fitzgerald.
I wish I had a cigarette right now while typing. Aaaaahhhhh the good ol' days when we bonded in the attic... when we would go on long drives and the

many spots we had that were OUR spots across two states. Baby, there playing our song... Ella and Frank: "That's why the lady is a tramp!" Another fav... "Bewitched, Bothered and Bewildered."

My dear friend, I wanted to write you a letter of gratitude for all you've been, given, shared, done and symbolized in my life. Thank you. You have been there for me through so much. You would not allow me to fall deeper into a hole with Terrance. You pushed me to see the truth about that relationship and for that and for everything you are I am eternally grateful. These days I am asking that you see now. These days I just want to return the favor. I am asking you to see all the beauty and strength that you possess. You are a healer. You have healing gifts. You were born to share those gifts with the world.

Thank you for the constant reminders that the power I seek is inside of me. That power is inside of you too. Thank you for reminding me that ALL that I need will arrive when I get silent and ask to be heard... you can do the same. Thank you for pointing me in the direction of my source... my force. I always go that place - - you taught me this. You are light. You did show me the way. You showed me the way back to me. You are love. We have such a beautiful connection and I am thrilled nothing has severed it. Not even our husbands and I know yours is dying to get rid of me once and for all.

Remember when I shared the story with you about Marc Anthony. I cried and cried that night... because it was exactly the message I needed to hear in that moment.

EVERYTHING HAPPENS FOR A REASON... That's your voice in my head. That moment was the first time that I accepted that I could be proud of who I am and where I come from. It was a moment that transformed me and you told me that I would meet Marc Anthony one day and tell him that story... and a few months later I did. I am so glad you are in my life. Please know that you are full of light, love and laughter. You are patient and incredibly kind. Your faith is unparalleled. You have many gifts to share with the world. When you gonna fly girl? Let's fly... I'll meet you in Spain. I miss you very much. I love you my dear friend and I know you will be back. I love you and I am praying for you. Thank you for the memories we have shared and the many more that have yet to come. Tu Amiga Alicia

CHAPTER TWENTY-ONE

2007 was the *"Year of Transformation"* for me. I was no longer this *"Organized Mess."* The Alicia now lived by the mantras *"Get it together,"* *"Everything happens for a reason,"* *"Everything will be revealed in due time,"* and *"You can't move forward unless you look backwards."* Luz knew me when every conversation started with, "Today was the day from hell!"

Luz knew me when my life was FULL of drama. She knew me when I never kept a promise. She knew me when I wanted to do a little bit of everything but never completed anything. She knew me when my life was upside down. She knew me when I was a disaster. She knew me when I lied to myself and loved me anyway. She knew me when I was hard on myself. She knew me when I was always angry and full of rage. She knew me when I was self-destructive. She knew me when I didn't trust myself to make the right decisions and relied on my friends to help me process and make the right choices for MY life because I didn't know how to.

It's so important to keep those people in our lives - - those who KNEW us when...

When I first told Luz about my writing dreams and how we were moving to NYC. I thought she would be like everyone else who told me that chasing after my dreams was unrealistic. I told her about all we had accomplished in New York so far and what she said surprised me. I could hear her excitement for us. She yelled, "Are you fucking kidding me~ I am so happy for you!" I just smiled and laughed listening to how full of joy she was and then she said, "YOU DID IT! You did what you said you were going to do. You stuck it out. You didn't let anyone get in your way. You didn't listen to words like, "get a real job" or "why don't you find something steady with benefits." She kept screaming, "Alicia you did it!"

Luz knew me when my conversations all started the same way. She knew me when I would go on and on about how unfair life was. I would bitch about how miserable my life was regularly and complained often about how unfulfilling my job was. Yet I was never doing anything to change my situation. I would just ramble and complain everyday. Everyday was "a day from hell!" She would always tell me the same thing "There is a reason for everything. There is a lesson in this." I was listening to the words but missing the message.

During that time my life was exactly the way I was painting it. I was the artist who at any moment could have chosen a different brush and color for a more precise stroke. I could have trashed that old painting and started with a new canvas. I could have added more yellows, oranges, light blues and pinks. For a long time I kept painting the same picture over and over again. It was full of reds, oranges and yellows. The portrait resembled FIRE my moments from hell. I was in pain when I was having days from hell. I kept painting myself there. I needed a new canvas. It was time to paint my way out of hell.

There is an order to things. I was developing in order. Everything happens right on time. I was unfolding right on time. I *needed* to be in hell to decide for myself if hell was the way I wanted to continue living. My days started changing. I am not sure when it happened. I was having fewer days from hell and more days filled with happiness. I guess it must have started when I realized I was born to write. I read today that *my force assures me that the divine plan for my life will unfold in an orderly manner according to my level of development.* How many times have I thought I was ready only to find out later that I was NOT ready? I was repeating a lot of the same mistakes. But what I know is that when I do fall that too was in ORDER. I needed to have those days from hell so that I could continue getting ready.

The word I am meditating on today is ORDER I read today that, "the condition or order of the environment demonstrates what I have learned, what I am thinking and what I am ready to receive." I am getting there. I am learning to release what doesn't serve me. I understand that the place where I am physically, mentally, and emotionally IS a reflection of the order or disorder in my thoughts, beliefs and emotions. In some cases the cleanliness of spaces is a cover for the real mess that resides in the crevices. Just like my mess shows the world that I don't have it all together being overly OCD can be a way of hiding things also.

Order for me means that I am exactly where I need to be in this moment in time. I can admit that my life in some ways is still in disorder that there is still work to do. For me to have order means that I will continue to do the work to get THERE. My life is being ordered when I see and recognize that I am exactly where I need to be doing what I am supposed to do. I know that everything I require will be provided. For this knowing I am so grateful. Today all of my paintings are still filled with reds, oranges and yellows but these colors symbolize the sunset, the end of an amazing day also filled with purples, pinks and sky blues.

There was a friendship I made in NYC that was special. We were kindred spirits. There was a connection that was undeniable. But something changed during our relationship. I had to make a decision as to whether the change was something that was good for me. I needed to decide whether the friendship was good for me. *Do we know how to ask for what we want? Do we know our worth?* When we make a decision we must be able to stand by that decision and not feel guilty about how the other person is going to take it.

The relationship between my kindred spirit and I was filled with friction. There were things I noticed that I wasn't really feeling. I started to see competitiveness and jealousy on her part towards women in our lives. It was a side of her that I didn't like. I needed to be honest about what I was seeing. We spoke about it but she wasn't ready to hear me. Perhaps she saw it as an attack. What I realized was that her actions were not aligning with who I am and were directly affecting me. I needed to let her know that I was uncomfortable with it.

The partnership called for us to be able to meet each other on the same level. I was hearing my voice for the first time and she wasn't ready for that. I no longer had the need to withhold my feelings nor was I afraid to speak my mind. And because I am no longer afraid of endings it was not difficult for me to know what I needed to do. It's freeing when you speak your truth.

"Don't hang with people who are where you don't want to be. Your friends and the environment reflect what you really feel about yourself. Winners hang out with winners. Losers hang out with losers. When you are on the move, you need people and an environment that supports and encourages your dream. You won't find that among people who are helpless and hopeless. You won't find support for your goals among people who whine and complain. You must know and believe that there are people waiting for you in the places you want to be. They will nurture, support and encourage you to keep moving. People you know may not always support your growth. For you to move on means you leave them behind. It also means that you prove what they claim to be impossible is definitely possible." ~Acts of Faith, Iyanla Vanzant

During a conversation with Rock I cried so much over the loss of several relationships that were important to me. We talked about the circles that I was in. When my friendship ended with this woman I felt like other women from that circle abandoned me.

Rock taught me that some circles are like churning butter. We get so wrapped up in being in these circles that we end up just churning and churning, going round and round, consumed and worried solely about the circle and the people within that circle. We get caught up in what everyone in the circle is doing. We keep churning and churning until we've dug a hole all the way to China. The most important thing I learned from that conversation was that sometimes we have to stop churning and leave the circle if we are serious about having anything. Otherwise the years will pass us by and we are still churning butter.

People come into your life for a season, a reason or a lifetime. Which people lift and which ones lean? Which people encourage and which ones discourage? Which people are on a path of growth uphill and which ones are going downhill? When you leave certain people, do you feel better or feel worse? Which people always have drama? Which people know and appreciate you and your gifts?

Sometimes you just have to let people go.

I met a woman who would change my life forever. This person came into my life at the exact moment that I needed an angel to guard me. She was someone who was sent to guard my soul and hug my spirit. While I was writing this I could see the scars from where they removed her tumor. The incisions were in several places on her scalp. Mostly what I saw was the light shining through her eyes and her smiling back at me. I saw the strength in the image she sent me after her surgery. I saw her happy in what must have been a frightening situation.

That morning I was in bed and didn't want to get up. I didn't want to get up because I was sad. *Why am I so depressed when everything in my life is going extremely well? Why am I sad when my writing is strong? Why am I crying when I'm blessed with incredible opportunity and have people in my life who love me? Why am I sad?*

I realized that I was mourning a loss. Loss can show up in so many forms. We lose people that we love dearly and I have had tremendous losses of people. I have had losses of relationships, losses of jobs, losses of opportunity, loss of faith, loss of hope, losses of friendships. It is the loss of a friendship that made me sad that day.

While I was sad an amazing thing happened the universe sent me someone to pull me out of my depression. This woman was sent to remind me to SMILE passed my scars, to smile passed my pains, to just *smile* but I will get to that. That morning I was reading a blog about PURPOSE—finding your purpose and knowing your purpose. Why am I here? What is my purpose? I wrote those words at the top of a blank page – **WHY AM I HERE?**

I lay back down and while I was lying down I started to think about the women in my life. The writers that I know, friendships that I have formed, my relationship with you, my sisters, cousins, aunts, Lulu and just the everyday people I have had conversations with about FINDING OUR PURPOSE or FINDING YOUR FORCE and the many different ways that people describe what purpose means to them. Purpose = vision, mission, goal, passion, dream and personal legend. There are so many ways to define purpose.

I continued thinking about my own purpose. *WHY is Alicia here?* And what is it that I should be doing while I am here? I lay back down and that's when the phone rang. I answered and it was a person I had never met, a person that I do not KNOW, but nevertheless it's a phone call from a person that is incredibly important for my life story and who arrived to my life in the precise moment that I needed her.

The woman called me by my first name like she'd known me for years and we just started talking. I didn't even ask her how she got my number. We spent I don't know how long on the phone. She told me about herself and how she would like to attend one of our writers groups one day.

During that conversation I started crying but I didn't allow her to hear me. Even though I didn't know her I felt connected to her. She was telling me wonderful things about how inspired she was by me. As I listened to her share *her* testimonial about her life that's when I realized that SHE was an inspiration to ME. In that moment I understood that—THAT IS my purpose. My purpose is to connect to people and provide them with a space to share their stories. I am here to support them on their journey and help them with healing through words. My purpose is to connect, to listen and to love. And while *they* may believe that *I inspire them* - it's the other way around. They are brought into my life to inspire me. So to that woman I say thank you.

181

Thank you for being exactly what I needed to get me out of bed that day. Your phone call was exactly what I needed to give me perspective. You were exactly what I needed to write about that day. This piece that I dedicate to you woman I haven't met yet! Thank you. Today you showed up as an angel on my front doorstep disguised as an anonymous phone call. Thank you for reaching out to me and reminding me that my purpose is and always has been to reach out to others. To that *angel* I am so grateful she reminded me of WHO I AM! ACHE~

One evening, I ran into that friend, my kindred spirit that I was mourning and she stood in front of me and said, "I feel as if you are always trying to one up me. I feel like you're competing against me."

What I wanted to say to her was, *you're no competition. You are not my competition. I have no competition! When you understand that there is NO competition for what you are doing you are free of jealousy, envy and competitiveness – they just don't exist. I don't have a competitive bone in my body.*

I wanted to say that to her but I knew she would not be open to that conversation. She might have taken that completely wrong and heard it as arrogant and combative. What I know is that there is no competition for where I am going and who I am meant to become. She was not ready to hear what I had to say.

She was not going to hear me and I honestly wasn't ready to hear her.

Becoming aware of how we impact the world is not an easy task, not for the weak minded. It's a process of self-awareness and self-actualization that requires determination. It's a constant willingness to listen. When we're aware of how we show up in the world we reach a place of complete acceptance, understanding, compassion, openness, humility and self-love.

"If you are on the path to self awareness and personal growth, criticism can provide you with very profound insights into yourself."
~ Author Unknown

CHAPTER TWENTY-TWO ~ *January 2007*

It was the night before New Years Eve. I had been writing all day at my writing spot at Grand Central Station and it was time for a break. I was participating in a competition *write your novel in 3 days*. I decided to take a break and headed home. While I was writing on the train, I felt this person looking at me but I continued writing.

That day I wasn't really in the mood for making connections on the train. I arrived at my stop and I heard this voice say something to me, "Hi there!"

It was the guy that was watching me the entire ride. We walked off the train together and he engaged me in conversation. He asked me what I was writing about and I just started yapping about my writer's life, my novel and my upcoming project.

Once I started talking he couldn't shut me up. I didn't even know what direction he was headed in or if at any point we were going to part ways. I told him I was going to grab something to eat and he offered to walk with me. He seemed harmless. Michael told me that he too was a writer. We shared small bits of information while I waited for my food. When the waitress came over I told him that I needed to get home and back to my writing competition.

I asked him were he lived. He told me he lived in Queens that he only got on the train to meet me.

I went with it. I allowed myself yet again to be open to what the universe was sending me. I allowed myself to be open to the possibilities of this new man in my life. In the beginning, I was saying things to him like, *slow down.... we're still learning each other. This is new. I am just enjoying each moment. All I can offer you is truth, sincerity, genuineness and time to know me. I was like the song, "Closer to my dreams~"* He told me he was like the Lionel Richie song, "*Easy.*"

He was jumping, leaping too soon. We were becoming an US and I was trying to hold onto me. He kept saying he would wait that he could be patient. But I felt pressure. He was overwhelming me with love. It was too much. It was too soon. I was suffocating. And while he was learning that he can love again. I was learning that I don't believe I've ever known what it feels like to actually find the person that I'm supposed to be with. At that point I had never met the person who was made for me.

He got real comfortable real quick. I have that affect on men. He said things like: "I am so swept up in you right now. There's a familiarity and comfort in you. I'm flying with you."

After two weeks of dating I told Michael that I loved him. He wanted to give me ALL of *his* **LOVE!** I was scared to death. We rushed. We leaped. I told him that I needed to breathe. I needed him to let go of me a little and allow it all unfold. I started to fear that I would spend the rest of my life showing him he is worthy of my love.

I gave him the test that I was accustomed to giving people I would meet on the journey. There were two books, *The Alchemist* and *Mastery of Love*. I didn't want to continue making the same mistakes in relationships. I knew right away when something didn't align. There were chapters in both books that were very significant for me in knowing if the person I was dealing with was on my level spiritually.

One was the story about Fatima meeting Santiago. There is a point in the *Alchemist* where Fatima encourages him to leave the desert and continue in pursuit of his treasure. Fatima told him that she would wait for him. Santiago didn't want to leave her. He was madly in love with Fatima but she didn't want him to look back at his life and have regrets.

The second story was from, *Mastery of Love*, about a man who didn't believe in love. The man who didn't believe in love spent his entire life studying and speaking on his theory that love doesn't exist. One day he was walking down the street and saw a woman crying on a bench. He stopped to ask her what was wrong? She said crying, "I don't believe in love."

He thought he met the woman of his dreams. They became best friends. They believed in the same things. They made a pact that they would be together as long as it was clear that neither of them believed in love.

One night the man was walking and the most beautiful thing happened. A star came down from the sky and landed in his hands. He started feeling something amazing. He believed that it was love. He was so excited that he rushed home to tell her about his discovery. When he arrived he said to her, "Look! Look at what I brought back for you."

He went to place the star in her hands and it dropped and shattered into a million pieces.

I asked Michael to share with me his interpretation of both stories. He called Fatima a bitch for pushing Santiago away, *"Didn't she see how much he loved her. How could she do that? What if she was his treasure?"*

I just listened. Then I asked him what he thought of the couple that didn't believe in love. The question at the end of the story asked, "Is the man or the woman to blame for the relationship not working?"

He blamed the woman, *"Didn't she see that he was willing to give her ALL of his love. She's selfish and fucked up."*

187

That night I asked him where he saw himself in five years. He told me, "I don't see myself."

So I asked another question, "What is your life purpose? Where do you see yourself headed? What do you want?"

"What if my life's purpose is to love you?"

That might have flattered a younger me. Right then and there I knew that it was time to let him go.

Letter: To the man who could love again,

I give off a powerful magnetic energy that says, come on in! "I'll love you... let me take care of you!"

I love to give myself distractions that will keep me from what's important to me like my healing or working on my writing projects. I almost made you my project. I wanted to show you how to love yourself. You wanted a little bit of what I have. But the thing is I'm still not whole. I'm good but I'm getting better.

Forgive me for having to release you. I must honor myself. I had to honor my heart and you were not the one. Being with you reminded me that I am closer to my dreams and I can not allow anything that doesn't contribute to forward movement and personal growth to get in my way. When you make someone your everything telling the person you're with that their life is in your hands that's a lot of pressure to put on someone else. I'm afraid I cannot and will not live up to all that.

While I'm willing to share my happiness with someone – I am happy with me! And it has taken me a long time to get here. I can't be responsible for healing your heart – that's your job. I can't give you your love. I can't give you your happiness. I can't give you a sense of worth or a sense of place. I can't give you your creativity.

I want to share my life with someone not give my life to anyone. SHARE is the operative word here. When you GIVE someone ALL your love you give him or her a lot of power. At least I think so.

I thank you for the music. In such a short time you have given me many gifts, encouragement, motivation, inspiration, support, and love. I was lying to myself. I was not ready to receive ALL THE LOVE you wanted to give me especially at a time when I made men my projects.

You would have become just another distraction to keep me from what's most important to me.

I forgive you for lying to yourself that you were ready to receive me and I forgive myself for lying about being ready for love. I wish you every blessing. I'm moving closer to my dreams. Love, Alicia

There were just a few more lessons I needed to learn. Just a few more men needed to appear before I got this shit right. I was sitting at a club and there was a Latin group performing. There was this person that walked by me. Something made me reach out and grab him. I felt him so strongly. I didn't know him. I didn't know his name but I was compelled to touch him. I got up and asked him, *can I hug you?* He accepted.

After I watched *Roots* perform I understood that I was supposed to meet him.

I didn't realize at the time but he had recently lost someone very close to him. The person he lost was his muse, his inspiration, his love, she was his beloved sister. His loss is what I felt that night and it was powerful. He was filled with an incredible amount of pain. After his performance I left. I took a cab home and cried all the way to our house. I was feeling so much of his pain. That evening I received an email from him.

Roots and I dated briefly. There was an attraction. But we were just friends. We only hung out. One night he was lying on my bed and I was sitting in the corner chair when we had one of those, *let's talk about where this relationship is headed conversations.*

189

"Alicia, what is that you want? What is that you want from me?" he asked.

"I want what we have. I love our connection. I enjoy our conversations. I want this."

"Well, I just need you to know that I'm experiencing *this* kind of connection with several different women."

I don't know what he thought I was going to say to that. I just started laughing. Was he serious? Did he think that I'd be ok with that? While I respected his honesty I needed him to know that I am not one of those women who has connections *like that* with all kinds of men. And I certainly wasn't about having sex with him.

I was at a place where I was beginning to master loving me. When I met Roots he knew I was abstinent and at that point in my life it was laughable the thought that I would even consider moving backwards and repeating the mistakes from my past. That's when I decided I would continue marrying myself until I got it right.

July 26, 2007 ~ Wedding vows~

Alicia, our courtship has not been an easy one. It *has* been a bumpy road, filled with twists and turns and climaxes that haven't always been so pleasurable. There have been failures and huge successes. We've had some incredibly great highs and some bad lows. I've been through some dark places but have always come up to find light. So this time around it feels like *this* is the perfect time, it's certainly the perfect date for my rebirth. July 26th my birthday. This is the perfect spot for my wedding our beautiful apartment in Harlem. There's no better place to marry me than in my home surrounded by everyone and everything that I love.

Today I give birth to a new way of loving me, to a new way of living. What I want most out of this marriage to *me* is GENTLENESS. I can take things slow. I understand that there is no need to rush. I am one day at a time.

I can live my life with compassion, understanding, patience and all the love that I have for me. This remarriage is one of truth, to honor, to love and to respect me. The good thing about marrying me today is that I no longer feel this need to mold myself into this perfect image of a person. I can just be me and I take me as I am.

Without a doubt I know that this is going to be a challenging marriage because Alicia my dear you can be a little intense, complex and some might argue a tad bit difficult. But I love me anyway!

To the old Alicia, I love you & thank you!

There was a moment where you were on such a desperate search to find the love of your life. I'm so glad you stopped searching for him so that you could find me in YOU! I'm glad you were finally able to be still and listen and know that I have always loved you Alicia, flaws and all. I take you as you are!

I give thanks for everything you've brought to my life. I'm grateful for all the painful and loving lessons that you've encountered. I'm grateful for every bad event you've had to endured... they truly were blessings in disguise. Your moments of brokenness have truly made you whole! I love you when you're vulnerable it truly displays your strength. Together we will continue to prepare ourselves for the love that is worthy of us. I vow that even when our person does arrive we will continue to do the work internally to keep our spirit and soul fed. Together we will only attract gentle life lessons, gentle people and gentle experiences that add to our life not drain us. Together we will continue to work at setting boundaries for the person you are today. We are truly one in body, mind and spirit.

We have a mission to spread love and light. There is no need to worry about how we'll get there, just trust and know that we will. Keep your faith bright. Know that I got you! I accept you, I love you, and I wouldn't change you for anything. Keep taking us forward. You are a force. I vow to keep my focus inwards and upwards and I will try not to get lost somewhere in the middle. I vow to give you all of me. I love who you are and I love who you are becoming!!! I vow to be patient with you and with others... to love, respect, accept, and honor the truth of others, while honoring what's true for me. I am no longer afraid of endings because I know that the end of anything is the beginning of something new, something beautiful and something magnificent. May the words I speak, and put onto the page be received with all the love intended. My vow as a mother is that I will raise Courtney to be the most magnificent, divine image of perfection this lifetime has ever seen. The gift that is my beloved daughter is the greatest blessing and best love I've ever known. She is the purest, truest and most perfect image of me. As I love her I will love all of the children who are sent to me for guidance.

Creator, I thank you for all of the blessings in my life, for all the gifts bestowed upon me especially for the gift of my family and friends. Creator, thank you for all of the spiritual teachers and guides you've sent on my journey. I am grateful for all of the experiences you've provided me with and gotten me through. I know that every moment you walk at my side. I'm no longer waiting for love to show up because I already found her in me.

CHAPTER TWENTY-THREE

Courtney's Quinceanera - 2007

She's only 15 but was born a LEADER~

Today is a pride filled day. For the past week I've been teasing you about being inducted into the Rock n' Roll Hall of Fame (which was really you being inducted into the Student Body Association at your High School). The ceremony was serious. It was like a real life swearing in ceremony after an election (presidential, governor, senator, any of those positions). You and over 90 girls (mostly Latina and Black - - that's whassup) were honored and sworn in this morning and inducted into the Student Body Association and the National Honor Society.

The event was called: "Installation of Student Leaders"

I sat watching you in awe. I wondered if you knew how big this was. I wondered if you were proud of yourself and your accomplishments. I wondered if you were bored sitting there just listening to all of the speeches. You were probably only thinking about getting it over with so you could get on with your day and get ready for Halloween. As I watched you I just sat there hoping that you would hold onto that moment for just a little while longer.

To me that moment was such a big deal. The themes of the speeches spoke about leaders, leadership, scholars and a person's character.

"A leader is one who goes forward when others hesitate." "Character is the force that distinguishes one from another - - it's a person's individuality." "A good leader leads by example and action."

They talked about serving and calls to action…about answering your call…
*The thought that flooded me the most was WOW – **MY** daughter is a*
LEADER! I have always told you you're a leader ever since you were in the
crib. How incredible to feel that you are somehow a reflection of me. When the
FUCK did that happen?

The ME at 15 was not an honors student. When I was 15 I definitely wasn't
student body president. At 15 I didn't care about being anybody's role model.
I certainly didn't care about leading anything or anyone. Alicia at 15 only
cared about one thing – FREEDOM. I wanted freedom from my parent's
regime, freedom from school, freedom from child-adult like responsibilities.
The me at 15 didn't care about what was happening to the world around me
because it felt like I was living in my own hell, dealing with my own shit,
fighting my own war and fighting my parents all at the same time. At 15 I
certainly didn't want to be anyone's momma.

During your ceremony, while I was celebrating you. I was thinking about my
own upbringing. I was pondering the things that bring me UP… to bring up
as in to elevate or be lifted up. How was I brought up? How was I lifted up?
These were the questions that filled me that morning in the midst of such an
incredible moment – a moment honoring the most important person in my
life. What I realized as I sat there was that I was never lifted up at 15. I was
never told how much power I truly possessed at 15. I was only told all the
wrong things I would never get right at 15. So I watched you… my beautiful
daughter sitting in the aisle about to be called up to receive your pin as I lis-
tened intently when they said:

President of the Sophomore Class COURTNIANA~

I didn't know whether to take a picture of the moment or applaud you. I was
so very proud of you. I cried the entire time I sat there. I cried for you and I
cried for the 15-year-old girl in me who never knew her greatness. I cried for
the 15-year-old girl I am BRINGING UP who is a powerhouse. You are
amazing. I can't say enough good things about you. It scares me sometimes
how connected we are – it's powerful. I had NO words for you (a first) when
it came time to our embrace at the end of the ceremony. I know that there is
nothing I could have said that day that I haven't told you everyday of your
life. I'll never know what it feels like to be you. I hope you know how great
you are. I hope you see the force that I see. It's so important to tell a 15-year-
old the truth about who they are.

I wanted to throw you the most beautiful *Quinceanera*. You deserved one of those Sweet Fifteen's that you see on TV where the big gift at the end is a brand new car. Your *quince* was such a special moment in our lives. I wanted it to be the most special day for you. We invited over 100 people. All our family and friends came from several states. It took months to plan. There were sixteen candles that you would light and dedicate to several people in the family. You wrote out such a beautiful speech filled with words of gratitude and love to each of us.

My relationship with you was changing right before my eyes. I never thought it would happen. I guess I always thought you would remain my little girl. We went away for the weekend to our private spot in Newport and everything was wonderful. We had so much fun going to dinners, museums, walking and laughing.

Something was changing. I felt you pulling away from me. I knew that I shouldn't take it personal but I did. A part of me wanted to remain so close to you but you were resistant because you were searching for your own place.

I think you are the coolest daughter. During that trip I felt like you wanted me to find my own way. You wanted me to find my own identity outside of you. I was torn because for your entire life I have always been, "Courtney's mom." For a long time my *own* way has been about you. I started to feel like I was going through an identity crisis of my own. I'm pretty grounded but it's started to hit me that I am more than just your mother.

That's why I was so sad that day because I no longer have my little girl who relied on me for everything. You were pulling away from me not because you don't love me but because you are in the process of trying to find yourself. You wanted your own identity separate from me. And I should want the same for me my own identity separate from you. So yes I was really sad that day because I knew that I had to let you go. But I didn't want to. Because once I let you go I'd have no choice but to figure out who ALICIA is. I could no longer hide behind just being your mother. This can be a scary place to be.

The days that led up to your *quince* were stressful. You were studying for finals and would come to *Businessweek* every day after school to do your homework. You got into this heated debate with a coworker about *quinces* and debutant balls.

You were joking with her but she didn't like how outspoken you were and stormed off at the comment you made. I was busy on the phone so I don't remember what you said to her but whatever it was it angered her so much that she wrote me an email. She told me that I was raising a disrespectful daughter who didn't know how to respect her elders.

She continued to say that her interaction with you was a direct reflection of my parenting abilities or lack there of. What infuriated her was that I didn't intervene during the conversation or check you for having an opinion. You stood your ground so I didn't feel I needed to jump in. What she didn't know was that in *our* house everyone is equal and even the kids have important things to say. I have always respected your mind, your ideas and your opinions.

Your opinion is the one I value most in my life. You are my go to person—FIRST. I trust and value you. Well needless to say she was not feeling that. In her email she insulted the both of us. I remember coming home and sharing her email with you and we both cried. We were so angry at the hateful words she spewed. We wanted to retaliate. You wanted to speak to her. Honestly, I didn't want to come into work and have to fight this woman. I was way passed all that shit.

This was a woman I considered a friend. We were both single mothers. We were both struggling. We both had dreams that we shared with one another.

My intention for that day was to surrender. I kept saying my intention to myself over and over again until I believed it. *Through the tears - - I surrender. Through the anger - - I surrender. Through the rage - - I surrender. Through the hateful thoughts - - I surrender. My intention was to surrender and continue walking in love.*

She wrote in her email: "I can't see when the words I used bring tears to your eyes or cause your fists to come together."

She wanted to know how her words affected me. As soon as I received the email in my inbox I felt it internally before even opening it. I didn't want to read it because I could feel that it didn't come from a loving place. It was filled with so much hatred and anger. I read the first two lines and stopped immediately.

You want to know what your words did to me. I was down for the count. The words felt like daggers aimed at my heart, mind and spirit. Fortunately, my heart will heal and my spirit remained untouched. But you're sphere hit its target... it went right through my chest... entered my heart and exited through my back. I looked like an abused child curled up in a ball in my bed. I asked Courtney to finish reading the words that were sent to me because I did not want to read them for myself. I was afraid - - afraid of what was to come. It took me right back to the days I was beat as a child. I felt like wounded animal. I felt every word. Your words hurt me, I cried, I got angry, and was full of rage. A few times I caught myself getting stuck on a statement wanting to retaliate. I had direct quotes imprinted in my brain that I wanted to come back to later to address. I wanted to defend myself. I wanted to destroy you an eye for an eye. So I affirmed… I surrender. I lifted the white flag… and surrendered… I kept repeating I SURRENDER as I read your words. I felt directly attacked and intentionally assaulted! I surrender! I call forth my strength and move forward. I surrender! Wherever I am, that's where my force is. I surrender! I breathe slowly, I release you and I surrender!

Words stay with us. The words that take the longest to heal are the ones that don't come from love. When you grow up in a house that's filled with anger, yelling, tension, anxiety and stress it can be hard to heal in that environment. You're left with an overwhelming feeling of frustration, unhappiness, sadness and limiting thoughts. Surrounded by people fighting for respect but never giving it. In this kind of environment it can be hard to expand and grow. When you're surrounded by darkness and pain these kinds of relationships can be emotionally draining and abusive. The effects of this kind of upbringing can be difficult to release.

Certain moments in my life when I've been surrounded by yelling, lack of individual acceptance and respect for one another views, thoughts and beliefs, remind me often how I allowed darkness to be my most dominant emotion. I always believed I was right. I never cared what other people thought. I never listened. So when I'm around people who are not using loving words this feels familiar to me… it feels like home. These moments are like returning to a past so painful… so hurtful… so dark.

I have spent many years trying to find new words to help me heal which makes it difficult for me to be around people like that. I am a lot more sensitive to it. During meditation I was thinking about the words I use to affirm myself daily. You and I use beautiful words towards each other. We feed each other. Our relationship is truly amazing. We affirm one another constantly. We lift each other. We love each other. We point out each other's flaws but we acknowledge our strengths. We make each other feel good. Sometimes we can be a little conceited but it's all in fun like when we were in Providence on Thayer Street at Au bon pain. I was writing my blog and you were sitting across from me reading a book called, *A Separate Peace*. Out of nowhere I said, *man I love myself.* You just looked at me and smiled and went right back to reading. You got it. You understood what I was doing.

In the book, *One Day My Soul Just Opened Up*, by Iyanla Vanzant, there is a Maya Angelou quote about the power of words; WORDS are like little energy pellets that shoot forth into the invisible realm of life. Although we cannot *see* the words, she said, words become the energy that fills the room, home, environment and our minds. Maya described how words stick to the walls, the furniture, the curtains and our clothing. She believes that the words in our environment seep into our being and become a part of who we are. I agree. I know how the words of my past have formed the woman I am today.

I affirm: I speak words of truth, love and every good thing I desire to experience. I am a divine reflection of universal love! I am whole and complete! I am unlimited and abundant - - my life is so good! I am joy in motion and my words are gifts. I am all that I am, and life is graced by my presence. The truth of who I am cannot be altered or changed. The way I treat myself determines how others will treat me.

My co-worker was a broken human being. Broken is defined as being reduced to fragments, infringed or violated, ruptured, torn, incomplete, weakened in strength or spirit, reduced to submission. So much about my past was broken. I was a broken child! I was a broken teen! I was a broken adolescent! I've had my heart broken! Teachers, adults, lovers, supervisors, superiors and family members have all played a part in breaking me! Men have broken me! I've had my innocence broken into and torn down! I've been violated and left broken! There are many moments to draw examples from to confirm that I was broken. It's really easy for me to recognize the broken girl since I too have been HER!

Letter: Dear Broken Girl,

We met at work and I believed you and I were friends. Until insanity hit us! You lost your mother-fucking mind! You were so out of line! You disrespected me. You betrayed my trust and said hurtful things about my daughter and me. I didn't know how to help you. I didn't how to be your friend. You made it so hard. You pushed me away. You verbally assaulted my daughter and I.

Girl, I LOVE YOU but I wanted to beat your ass. When you insulted my daughter that was a low point. I'm a lion girl... my claws were out and I wanted to attack! You went for the one thing you hoped would get a rise out of me. Your words had a choke hold at my throat and after so many weeks of pondering what this was all about and why it was that you were intentionally trying to hurt me I realized how weak you truly are.

What must YOU have been going through that I became your punching bag! I understood how much pain you must be in. You felt powerless and you wanted to break me down. And I know you saw that after all you did to try to get a rise out of me it didn't work. I never responded to you. You will never have my power! No one will ever take my power again! Trust and believe that! And even with all the rage I wanted to release on you – I surrendered – I prayed for you. I prayed for strength. I forgive you for the things you put in that letter intentionally hurt my daughter and I.

I forgive myself for not recognizing that you were a broken girl who just wanted to be loved... a broken girl just like me who was looking for healing. A broken girl who just wanted her power back! I surrender and I let you go. I release you. I forgive you for trying to hurt me and I forgive myself for wanting an apology. With love, Alicia Anabel

200

Believing the words and experiences that we have endured are the very things that keep us completely broken. We allow the past to paralyze us to block us. We are the ones holding ourselves back. We keep ourselves broken. It takes tremendous courage to face ourselves, deal with whatever demons we have, look deeply at our pains and all the darkness. If we look closely enough *that demon we're looking to blame* may be as close as looking in the mirror. If we can endure whatever comes our way we grow stronger and get closer to finding our force.

I realized something at the end of writing this (my aha moment) is that the thing that has kept me broken is the loss of trust, the loss of innocence and how I would spend the majority of my adult life searching for that thing to piece together all that was broken and robbed from me. It would take me many years to find that force within me - - that strength in me that never fails. I had finally found my force!

We decided not to respond to my coworkers email. In the house we performed a ritual. We were going to handle it spiritually. I allowed you to respond to her and say everything you needed to say her including using profanity if need be. We were going to burn the letter inch by inch releasing it into the universe.

As we read each line and burned all the pieces of paper, while the paper went up in flames I noticed something. I started blowing on a sheet of paper when these words jumped out at me, "How dare you want to write for *Essence,* you ain't black! Why don't you write for *Latina* magazine? It's not your place!"

She knew my dreams. She knew that I wanted to write for *Essence* magazine. She knew exactly how to hurt me. When she told me it wasn't "MY PLACE," I saw that as a direct message. It was a sign. She would never know that her email would be the inspiration for my greatest gift.

CHAPTER TWENTY-FOUR ~ *It's not your place~ August 2007*

I have been preparing for this moment for what must have been my entire life. Never really knowing what it was I was preparing for, when or if my dreams were ever really going to come true. I was so inspired after we burned that email. I believed that I was onto something really special I had an amazing story idea.

I sat with the words *Its NOT your Place!* It's not my place! It reminded me of the times when I was a little girl and would go to Santo Domingo where the kids would make fun of me. *Mira esa gringita.* Because I was born in the United States they called me *gringa.* To me the word *gringa* felt very unwelcoming. They weren't trying to compliment me. I felt excluded. They thought that this *gringa* couldn't speak Spanish and that I couldn't dance. I kicked all their asses dancing to every kind of music every time I went.

When you're a little girl you want so much to belong. I think I grew up my entire life trying to find that place where *I* belonged. Coming up in the 70's in New York, there was one of two groups

I could belong to. You were either black or white. I wasn't light enough to be white and I wasn't dark enough to be black. There was no Latino. Those who were a hint of beige darker than the average white person were automatically black. So hearing as an adult *it's not your place* threw me. It jumpstarted my heart and pushed me towards finding my place. It was a moment of revelation and self-acceptance. For me it became, wait a minute, not only am I Latina, but I am black too. Not only is it *my* right, it's *my* place to write *our* story.

So in June 2007, I pitched my very first story idea titled, "Will the Real Black Girl Please Stand Up," to *Essence* Magazine. The story for me was about unifying this divide that seemed to exist between African Americans and Latinos. I wanted to tell the story of the shared history that existed within both our cultures. The story was about Afrolatinos the 150 million Afro descendants that currently exist in Latin America. I never got back so much as an acknowledgement for that email. I was little disappointed. REJECTION SUCKS.

I had a great idea and nowhere to publish it. I decided to write the story anyway. I spent the summer working on it. I still didn't have the article sold. But I continued learning about the subject. In August 2007, when I still hadn't heard back from them I decided to pitch the story to another magazine. I sent it to the Editor-in-Chief of *Urban Latino* Magazine. She responded the very next day, telling me she loved my story idea and wanted to run it. Dream come true right? Wrong! When I received the email that she was interested in the story I knew that I needed to begin writing it. There was so much work to do. First, I needed to transcribe hours of interviews from my five experts and then fact check research.

After the initial email of interest I hadn't heard back from the editor at *Urban Latino*. I was a little disappointed but I said fuck it. I'm still going to write this story if not for anyone but me. I interviewed the last expert in mid-September and continued working on some other writing for my blog as well as working my fulltime job at *BusinessWeek*. Every chance I got I was working on the story. It seemed like it was never going to be published. I decided that I wasn't going to work on another story idea until I finished what I started. A writer friend kept saying to me, "Move on woman. Let that idea go. Start working on another story idea."

I was hearing her, but I didn't want to let it go. The story seemed too important to just abandon.

In the midst of working with over a 100 pages of transcribed notes from my experts for this story, I was also preparing for the first year anniversary of the NYC Latina Writers Group, which was going to be held on October 16th and that's when it happened... two months later, exactly like we've read about it... exactly like we've heard so many people say that "IT" happens when you least expect it! Exactly as it says in the *Alchemist*, when one walks towards their dreams the universe conspires to make it happen. It happened to me...the very next day on October 17th around noon. There it was an email on my blackberry from the editor, "Sorry it took so long to get back to you. I definitely want to print your story as a social feature in our November issue. Can you get me a 2000 word draft by Monday, October 22nd?"

I sat with that question for a minute. *Can I get her a 2000 word story?* A minute is all I gave that thought I was way too excited to be still. This was the opportunity of a lifetime. This was my moment. The door was open and I needed to walk through it. This was my time to shine. This was an incredible gift and blessing being sent my way. This was a gift that only arrived because I would not let go of it and kept getting ready. Here it was and now I only had five days to write a 2000 word story. Now I needed to step up my game and show what I'm made of.

HEY, LOOK AT ME WORLD, HERE I AM...

When I hit the send button at 7:44pm, Monday October 22, 2007, I just sat there in front of my computer for about 15 minutes in complete silence, prayer and gratitude. For me it had nothing to do with being published. It didn't have anything to do with the editor liking the story or the fact that the title of my story would appear in the cover of the magazine. It wasn't about the photo and bio of me that would appear in the contributors page. *The moment for me was when* I HIT SAVE AND SEND. That was the moment of pure *achievement* and *exhilaration*. In that moment I FINISHED it! That moment was the greatest accomplishment and best feeling in the world. I did it! I had no idea when it would be out on stands but I was ecstatic.

A week later I left my office and needed to run an errand. It was really dreary out. I was wearing my yellow raincoat... bright ass yellow... you could see me coming from miles away. I was walking up 7th Avenue with the biggest smile, I had on my iPod and I was listening to Barbra Streisand. The song I was listening to was from her album, *"The Concert."* Our favorite song... *"I'm Still Here/Everybody Say's Don't'/Don't Rain On My Parade."* This song is so very special to us. When you were about four years old and we were living near Brown University, I would do this performance for you while you were taking a bath. As Barbra was playing I would do a Rockettes number, their famous kick line dance routine. As I would be kicking my leg up in the air you would just smile and laugh and ask me to do it again and again and again.

> *I've heard them say song writing, acting, producing,*
> *What makes her think that she can?*
> *Or better yet song writing, acting, producing*
> *What does she think, she's a man?*
> *One day a Tony, Tuesday you're top of the Bill*
> *So I'm here!*

> *Everybody says don't, everybody says don't*
> *Everybody says don't, it isn't right!*
> *Don't, it isn't nice!*
> *Everybody says don't, everybody says...*
> *Don't bring around a cloud don't rain on my parade.*

> *Get ready for me love, 'cause I'm a-comin'*
> *I simply gotta march, my heart's a-drummin'*

207

FINDING YOUR FORCE

Don't bring around a cloud don't rain on my parade,

HEY, LOOK AT ME WORLD, HERE I AM... (Rockettes kick)
- Barbra Streisand

As I was walking to the bank I was thinking about ALL that we've been through together and all that it has taken us to finally MAKE IT in New York. I am so thrilled to finally know what it feels like to say that I have MADE IT. WE'VE MADE IT!!! While I was listening to Barbra's incredible voice telling me, "HEY, LOOK AT ME WORLD, HERE I AM..." that's when it happened, that's when I realized all I've been through, what the payoff has been for all the pain I've endured. It was about the lessons learned. It was about me appreciating all that's beautiful that surrounds me. In that moment while I walked up 7th Avenue all I could see in front of me were the 1000's of people walking in my direction and this feeling of complete and total happiness entering me. It was this feeling of joy and love that I was emitting. It was electricity that everyone who walked by me took notice to and smiled at because my smile touched them.

HEY, LOOK AT ME WORLD, HERE I AM... I felt like Barbra singing and Mary Tyler Moore flipping her hat up in the air ALL at the same time. I finally arrived. I am so very proud, blessed and grateful for every gift and every person I have ever met. My writing career is born!

CHAPTER TWENTY-FIVE ~ *November 2007*

We were visiting Rhode Island for thanksgiving. I went out with Emma and Colleen to the Roxy in Providence. We looked so *fly*. We were there for a while looking around checking out the prospects. That night I wasn't interested in any of the men in the club. Not one guy stood out to me.

Later in the evening there *was* someone who caught my eyes. I couldn't keep my eyes off this person. I was watching a dancer at the club. She was beautiful. I was enjoying her. I had never looked at women in that way before. But I was locked in. As I watched her movement I felt something happening to me. I was picking up an unfamiliar frequency. I enjoyed the view. That night I kept thinking about her. I felt an attraction to her. I had never felt this so strongly for women. There was this pull towards her.

Of course there were occasions where I had fantasized about being with women but I ignored all those thoughts. I used to have this reoccurring fantasy of going to a club, meeting a woman and bringing her back home with me. But I never gave into

into those feelings. That night after we left the Roxy I called a friend and had him pick me up. We went back to his house. I was feeling sexy. I wanted to be wanted. I was incredibly turned on. It had been nine months since I'd been intimate with anyone.

That night while I was with him... while we were making love... I thought of her. As he was on top of me I found myself wondering what the hell I was doing there. It didn't feel good. I wanted *her* to be touching me. When he entered me I wasn't enjoying it. That night all I wanted was for it to be over with. While I was with him that moment felt horrible to me — it felt wrong. *That night would be the last time I would ever give my body to a man.*

December 25, 2007

I had a conversation with God today and SHE told me SHE loved me! This evening I meditated on the words *Unconditional Love*. There was a moment in my life when I was truly afraid to be loved unconditionally. I was afraid of what it would do to me if I had it or it left me. I was afraid that love was painful. I believed that love hurts, love betrays, love beats, love disappoints, love demeans, love belittles, love breaks, that *true* love doesn't exist, that I would never be loved and that I would never find love. I was convinced that love destroys, that love leaves, that love lies, that love dies and worse that love ends.

I was being forced to look at where I've been and where I'm headed. I needed to ask myself, *Alicia, am I open to ALL the experiences of my life? Am I open to different expressions of LOVE? Will I allow opportunities to pass me by? Will I allow my soul mate to just walk by me on the street without even so much as a hello?*

I cannot control what is happening to me. What I do know is that I will not run away from love. I won't fear love. I know that I am worthy of love WE ALL ARE. I accept that love is my state of mind.

With these letters that I've been writing I have been expressing the deepest form of self-love. I understand that I was born to love. I act and speak in love. When I admit to myself what I really want in my life — its love. Love is always present. I love others and myself unconditionally.

Prayer: Creator, please send me a love unlike anything I've ever experienced... a love unlike anything I've ever known.

Everyday during meditation I prayed for the same things. I gave thanks for everything. You hated that I prayed before every meal, saying, "c'mon mom! I'm starving! You don't have to say thank you for your jeans, your sneakers and your t-shirt... c'mon lets eat." It was important for me to give thanks for everything we had and all that we were receiving because I know what life has been like for me without having faith and expressing gratitude.

I didn't care what you said—I prayed everyday. I was thankful to the creator for another opportunity to begin again. Thankful that you were always protected and guided. God brought you home to me safe everyday and I was grateful. I prayed for the protection of my family and for everyone I know. I prayed for all those I don't know. I prayed for the homeless that they would have food to eat and some place warm to sleep. I prayed for all the little children who have been abused or broken that they would hold onto their innocence and know that they are loved. And during my daily prayers I would ask my creator to send me a love unlike anything I've ever experienced... a love unlike anything I've ever known.

"Most of us remain strangers to ourselves, hiding who we are, and ask other strangers, hiding who they are, to love us." ~ *Leo Buscaglia*

"I think this person's the one!" How many times have you heard me say this? I don't have to tell you. You know that I never get tired of talking about love. This moment in my life I am learning a new way of loving... a new way of loving me.

I love being one with LOVE. Love to me is that ageless love. It's that REAL LOVE. It's that lasting love. It's the older couple I see dancing in Central Park smiling at one another and me just sitting there in awe of them wondering just how long they have been living their love story and wishing that same kind of love for me.

"We must take into consideration the pretenses and defenses that threaten LOVE. For our part, we should welcome the mystery, enthusiasm and challenge which will make us lovers for a lifetime." from Born for love, Reflections on LOVING, by Leo Buscaglia

I WELCOME THE MYSTERY! Isn't it amazing that when we are in that, "IN LOVE" feeling what we FEEL and how we see the world and everyone around us seems to be through clear eyes and a completely open heart FREE OF FEARS, free of prejudice, free of judgment, free of hate, free of cares. When we are in that state of *love* all is beautiful and no one else matters. Nothing else exists. I've been told, *Alicia you need to be in love.*

I sit with those words *Alicia needs to be in love.* I don't know many people who have shared or allowed themselves, to experience the kind of love I've had in my lifetime. I have LOVED... LOVED... LOVED... every moment of being LOVE, being IN LOVE, having love, sharing love and am looking forward to giving my love again and again and again.

I am looking forward to being with the ONE being prepared for me. I want to feel the levels of love that extend further than the initial feeling of falling for the first time. I want it to last longer than even the highest sense of being in love. It will extend further and further than anything I can possibly imagine. The object of *my* affection in my eyes will be PURE PERFECTION.

213

The kind of IN LOVE I am talking about has no definition. Love HAS NO WORDS~ but it IS DEEP and it is COMING.

Careful what you wish for. You just might get it. I can't tell you how many yoga sessions I've had where my closing prayer ended the same. I would ask the universe to send me the most magnificent expression of love. So when she arrived... she was definitely A LOVE UNLIKE ANYTHING I HAVE EVER EXPERIENCED. Those first conversations seemed fluid. We connected on a spiritual level. We were both writers, both single mothers raising teenagers. We talked every day for weeks. At first it was just about writing. We shared poetry. Then something started happening. I started to feel things. This was brand new.

Was I attracted to her? Was I feeling her in the same way that I had always felt men? Did I like her – like her... in that way? Was I having romantic feelings for her?

I had never felt this way before. Things were happening to me and I was confused. What I felt was beautiful. It scared me. It felt wrong. My upbringing was blocking the love I was receiving and feeling.

Then it happened one day. I was at war with myself. I was so confused. There was so much against me. I was feeling things for this person but I was torn. I was in the middle of yoga and I could not hold my poses. I kept falling. I was crying throughout

214

my entire meditation. My chest was tight. I didn't understand what was happening to me. This was foreign to me. So I did what I always do I prayed on it.

I prayed for understanding and healing. I began reading excerpts from the bible and every passage that I read was about how women would be stoned for this or that. *Honor thy man!!! God made Eve for Adam... men and women were made to procreate...* and anything outside of that was a sin.

I wanted to push what I was feeling out of my body. I wanted to resist and deny what I was feeling for this woman. I really believed that I was going to hell for loving her. *That day* while I was an hour into yoga and my eyes were closed, I continued crying and praying. I knew that my creator would want me to feel love. I could no longer deny myself who I am. Finally, I gave in... I allowed myself to feel everything. I released my religious and spiritual battle and gave into what was happening to me. I accepted that I was gay.

We were in bed when I told you. We held each other. I looked over at you and said, "Baby, I need to tell you something."

"What's up mom?"

"I'm in love with a woman... I'm gay!"

You looked at me and said, "Are you sure momma?"

"Yes! I am sure."

"Are you happy?"

"Yes... I'm very happy!"

"If you're happy... then I'm happy for you. That's cool!!! My momma's gay." You smiled and hugged me.

Your opinion and approval was the only one that mattered to me. Once I came out to you I felt free. I was liberated. I was so excited about this new chapter of my life. It was like I was born again. Everything was new to me. It always felt like there was just one piece missing to my puzzle and now I *finally* figured it out.

The moment I came out to you was one of the most special days of my life. The moment that I accepted that I was a lesbian was a moment of COMPLETION. It felt like I was finally a complete being. I wanted to share it the world. I wanted to shout it from the highest building. Once I knew that I had *your love* and support, I figured everyone else would just follow. I believed that the entire family would love me anyway.

We were in Washington, DC for the weekend. I was on the phone with abuela and I just came right out with it, "Mami can I ask you a question? *Que tu piensas de relaciones entre mujer y mujer?* What do you think about women relationships?"

"Are you asking about lesbian relationships?" she responded in total shock.

"Yes mami. What do you think about gay relationships?"

"Bueno mi hija? I have nothing against gay people. You know that my hairdresser in NY was gay, but I could never accept someone gay in my family. It's against the bible. Women are made for men."

Then she started quoting excerpts from the bible to me. As she spoke all I kept thinking was that for my entire life I'd never seen her open a bible once and now she was telling me *exactly where* it says in the bible that being gay is a sin. I decided that coming out to her during that conversation was a bad idea. I needed to wait for the right time.

Super Bowl XLII it was New York Giants 17 – New England Patriots 14. Sunday, February 3, 2008. I was standing in the hallway of our apartment talking on phone with your uncle about the game. There was a lot of back and forth… a lot of talking smack about who we thought would win. Our house wanted the Patriots and he was rooting for the Giants.

"What up sis?"

"Hey what's up bro? Yo! I gotta tell you something." I said.

"Spit it…"

"I met someone. I'm in a relationship."

"Oh word! What's his name?"

"Her name is Max."

His response was classic, "Max as in Maxwell or Max as in Maxine?"

"Max as in Max and yes she's a woman."

"Yo! I figured as much. I get it. I understand how you could be with a woman. You've had some pretty fucked up relationships with men."

"Hold on bro! It's not even like that. It's not about me hating men. I don't hate men."

He stopped me as I spoke, "Look Lee! I got your back. If you're happy then I'm happy for you."

That was the last he and I ever spoke about my relationship with Max. Your uncle never brought it up again. He didn't want to know anything else about her. Sure he said he had my back, but he wasn't really interested in hearing about Max. He certainly didn't ask me about my coming out. It was business as usual in the Santos family. If we don't talk about it then it doesn't exist. They didn't take it seriously because to them it was just a fad anyway. *She's not really gay. She'll come to her senses. She just needs a good man. It will pass.* They pretended to not really hear that I just told them that **I AM a lesbian**.

At that point I came out to everyone. I told your aunts, your cousins and Tia. For me it was like all the beautiful revelations of my life. It was a moment of transformation for me. I was finally complete. I was whole. *Send me a love unlike anything I've ever experienced... unlike anything I've ever known.* And finally *she* arrived.

CHAPTER TWENTY-SIX

I no longer had the need to be in a relationship. I wasn't looking for anyone.

We were doing fantastic. I was more inspired than I'd ever been. I was writing everyday. I was attracting abundance in everything. Our lives were about to change. I could feel it. We were at dinner at our favorite African restaurant when you said to me, "Mom, you did it! It's amazing. Everything you said you were going to do you did! We've done it. The move to New York, apartment in the city, published writer, and you're working on the *Daughters of the Revolution*. I'm so proud of you!"

I've tried so hard to be a good role model for you. I have spent my life thinking about how every choice, every decision and every move would affect you. Our entire family especially Tia always had something to say about how I treated you and how much I respected you. They couldn't understand our relationship. It was so fucking foreign to them how close we are. Tia could not accept why I was treating you like my equal, almost as if I should be treating you like a useless piece of shit. They believed that you should be invisible and have no thoughts of your own. I didn't care – no one could tell me shit about how to raise you. We have built a pretty great life together. It's been you and me for such a long time. We were better than good. We were happy.

We think we know when things will happen or why they happen but we have no idea. This is what I have told myself time and time again and most recently, that I would know when the love I've been waiting for has arrived. I just knew that I would recognize the love that was being sent and prepared for me the moment it got here. I believed that I would know when I met *him*. We think we know what love will look like when it arrives. We create this idea of how they will be packaged creating check-lists of the things we're looking for. We write down ALL the things, qualities, characteristics, similar beliefs and careers that we expect and want our potential life partner to have. We even keep a separate list of the things that we might consider letting slide. That second list contains the things that we might overlook in order to have love. These things that we settle for just to say we've found THE ONE.

Whenever I meet someone that I'm considering having a romantic relationship with, the issue of having children always comes up. I'm not perfect and certainly have many flaws but starting my life over with an infant was something that I've resisted for a long time. I think as far back as when you were a baby.

One night you and I were talking about love and relationships and you said, "Maybe we need to find someone who has everything we want even if they don't blow our minds or we're not madly in love with them."

You were telling me that maybe we shouldn't be so picky and be open to the potential of what people bring and not what we believe they can offer us. That really has settled inside of me.

I was having a problem accepting how I was feeling. I was conflicted about accepting a partner in my life. I am absolutely crazy about this new person. I see so many things in her that I'm looking for in a life companion and so many things I never knew I wanted.

We connected on a mental, spiritual, emotional and intellectual level; we had a similar history, a mutual respect and understanding. It was an instant bond. It was amazing... I had never felt this before.

There was a part of me that felt like I was dying in order to make room for this new love. What am I afraid of? All that I've been looking for has arrived, a partner who is strong, kind, generous, emotionally available, confident, honest, incredibly loving, passionate and sexually compatible. Will she be here for me always and *in* ALL WAYS? Will she give me my space when I ask for it? Will she be present in ALL my/our moments? Will she walk at my side even when she can't be at my side? Is she the mirror image of me?

FINDING YOUR FORCE

The Seduction~
YOU took me~
YOU had your way with me~
Whispering succulence into my ear...
YOU did things...
You made me want to...
WALK

By the water and
WAIT
For the sun to set~
I'm left with
thoughts...
Your greatest conquest
obsession ~
I the accused intruder~
the girl in the dream~

I'm no dream come true~
part of me still fears you...
You're seducing me~
With words~
Luring me~
Taking me~
Pleasing me~
And I succumb~
If I allowed you
to have me
in that way...
Then what?
Am I yours?
SEE...

me...
I don't give it up to JUST anyone
like that~
YES~
do tell me what I wanna hear~
The words...

how I LOVE WORDS~

My feet are firmly planted~
your words~
Entrance...
arouse...
Rise in me...
This sense of uncertainty~
Suspicion
Questioning la verdad~
Quien eres tu?
Passion
that's what I'll call you~
What do you want from me?
Whisper sweet nothings
Taking from me those things
that make me...
ME!

The words make me want to
open myself up
OPEN my...
Yeah~
That's it
right there...
My soul~
Like I said I don't know you~
But I know words~
LOVE will know...
How to win my heart~
The right words~
But words alone~
Can't sustain me~
They'll never obtain me~
The pleasure I seek is deeper than a hands touch...
There's a spot~
That spot...
where ONLY few know how to receive me~
Reserved for ONE~

FINDING YOUR FORCE

February 2008

I was completely in my head with a million thoughts, ideas, plans, dreams and my fears about our future! I was a writer, a newly out lesbian, a spiritual being and I was trying to balance it all. There have been so many things that held me back. I did not want this new relationship to be one of those things. I wanted to continue my momentum. There has always been this voice dominating my thoughts—FEAR. It has taken so much to get here. I have had to combat my fears every moment I begin a project. While I was on the phone with Max at exactly midnight I received an email on my blackberry that made me stop and pay very close attention.

"Congratulations to one of the writers of the NYC Latina Writer's Group!!! Our very own Alicia Anabel Santos was just published in Urban Latino Magazine."

I was without words. As I read it I couldn't believe it. I immediately went to the *Urban Latino* website to see the story. I was crazy excited. I could barely sleep at all. I kept my laptop on all night. I just looked at the computer screen. I thought I had dreamt that I received a note that the story I wrote several months ago was published. I sent messages to everyone in my circle I tried calling my family but NO ONE was awake to jump up and down with. At around 1:30am I went to sleep with a smile on my face and tears in my eyes.

224

NO ONE will ever really know what that moment felt like for me. It was a combination of shock, surprise, excitement, timing, recognition, validation, LOVE, achievement, accomplishment, gratitude and pure joy. I woke up at 5:00am and went to look at the computer again just to see if it was in fact true that I was finally a PUBLISHED WRITER! I read the words to my first published story, *Two Cultures Marching to One Drum*, by Alicia Anabel Santos.

MAN it felt amazing! I was just trying to take it all in and breathe slowly. I was inhaling this moment and allowing it to live inside of me. I wanted to enjoy this. I didn't want to rush myself out of this state. I have been known to just move quickly to the next thing always the stealth fighter. *Not TODAY! Just for today I will live in this moment... I will BE this moment.* I was filled with so much gratitude.

This writing thing means so much to me. It has never been about money or fame. For me it's about sharing the gifts that I've been blessed with. Everything that I write is an offering. This writing thing is the only thing I've ever wanted to do. WRITING and YOU are the *only* things that I have wanted to be GREAT at. That moment in my life was one of those moments I will always remember.

The first phone call I received was at 5:54am from your Tia Josie. She wanted to shout it from the rooftops. She just expressed how proud she was of me and when we hung up this was what she wrote me, "I've never been so proud of you! YOU freaking worked your ass off and finally we get to see it. You go Afro Latina girl...save the day!"

I love my sister she is my rock. SOLID. Hearing those words from her meant so much to me. Everything that I am and all that I have is because of my family, my parents, sisters, brother, cousins, tia's, tio's and all my ancestors. All that I do, write and give to the world is for *them* and comes from *them*.

The history, culture, life experiences, music and traditions exist in me because they never let me forget how deep being me really is. I am constantly reminded of what I am supposed to do with my gifts and what being here in this place is *really* about. My parents leaving their beautiful island of Santo Domingo to come to *this* country was not without cost. I would savor this moment. I was incredibly overwhelmed.

When I received that call from Josie I got so emotional. Our family has never really read anything that I've written. They've never understood my writer's life and why it has been so important for me to do this. All they know about my writing and me is that when I am working I never answer the phone and I never call back. They didn't understand my NEED and CALL to *create*.

When I realized I was a writer we lived in Florida and I would spend a lot of time away from my family and that hasn't changed. I am doing what it takes to achieve my dreams. I hope that they will see that all that I did was preparing me.

I was being prepared to give and share these gifts about our culture and history with them and the world. This is what I am doing and what I will continue to do until my last breathe.

226

When I look back at that part of my journey the moment my FIRST story was published. I will remember the hours I spent transcribing notes. How I had just over 100 pages. I will remember that the process towards the final draft was long it went from 100 pages, to 60, to 30, to 16, to 9 pages and finally to 3 pages — three pages and 13 drafts later. Yes I will enjoy this moment. I worked my ass off. I am grateful that I have so many people around me who love me, who GET IT and who have my back.

CHAPTER TWENTY-SEVEN

I wasn't always someone who completes things. People in my life *love* to remind me of who I was in the past. I was starting my relationship with Max and while it was beautiful there were moments she accused me of being selfish. It was only at this point in my life that I was just beginning to learn to put the time in necessary to have what I want.

What Max and my family didn't understand was ALL that it takes to achieve the type of greatness I was working towards. I was being asked to step up my game in a completely unfamiliar way. I was pushing myself and working the hardest I've ever worked. The moment I said, "I AM A WRITER," was the moment I answered my call to serve. I was being asked to show what I am made of! I was summoned to bring it! It was time for me to use everything I've learned on this journey.

There is something that I do when I know that I have an important deadline and it is to allow fear to paralyze me. I do everything but what I'm supposed to be doing. I am the queen procrastinator! There have been moments when I've missed deadlines. There was always something keeping me from stepping my game up. Something in my head was always keeping me from achieving what was so important to me. *Put up or shut up!* I'm a firm believer and hold this shit against people. *It's important to keep your word! Do what you say you're going to do! When you commit follow it through to the end!*

Before I met that deadline for the magazine article I started stressing myself out. I was spending more hours than I needed doing research on Afrolatinos than actually writing the story. I began obsessing over all the ways I needed to make this story better.

I was giving myself an anxiety attack and in that moment I stopped. I stopped doing all that I was doing! "Step away from the laptop ALICIA!" I took a break and sat with you to watch TV. We talked about how I was feeling. I said, "I'm so mad at myself. I'm supposed to get this done and sent. I don't want the editor to think I'm not serious or that I'm not working hard on this story."

Lovingly you said, "You are serious mommy! You are working hard! You're not giving yourself credit! You're not even paying attention to me because you're thinking about this project! You're doing stuff!"

We sat and watched TV a little longer. After I said good night to you I got on the phone and started complaining about all that I needed to get done. All my insecurities and vulnerabilities were just pouring out of me. While I was on the phone I no longer heard what the person on the other line was saying to me. I

I heard myself say, *you don't understand how badly I want this.* As I said that I was looking around our house at all of the projects that I am working on. I see my novel, Eva Peron, Mirabal Sisters, the history of PR, DR, Chile, Venezuela, Argentina, Mexico, Cuba, Isabel Allende's note to me, the photos of you and me in DC when we met Barack Obama. When I look around our house I saw just how much I've accomplished. I was surrounded by everything that we have accomplished together.

During the end of that phone conversation I said, *I have never wanted anything this badly. I have never worked this hard on anything. You just don't understand. I don't want to be good at this – I WANT TO BE GREAT AT IT!*

As soon as those words left my mouth I paused. I got quiet. I had never said that shit to myself before that moment. I've never said that out loud to anyone. Of course I have wished for greatness in affirmations and silent prayers always wishing that it would be realized. But this time it felt different.

This time, the internal feelings and emotions were overwhelmingly powerful. It was almost too much for my body to take without wanting to breakdown. And I did break down. I cried a little and finally said *is this what greatness feels like? Is this what greatness tastes like?*

As I was saying those words in that exact moment I actually believed them! In that very moment it no longer was about *achieving greatness* for anyone else. It was about pushing past that feeling, releasing all the words that don't serve me, kicking fear right in the crack of its ass and pushing myself beyond my own

230

limitations or the limits that others have placed on me. It became about ME pushing me and doing it FOR ME. It was about completion. As I've completed project after project I am no longer AFRAID OF MY GREATNESS!

Max started to ask me often *when I would start telling the family about our relationship.* I told her that I wanted to tell each person individually. I told her that I wanted to handle it with care.

I remember calling your *abuelo* in Florida. We were on the phone for a long time catching up. Your *abuela* was in the Dominican Republic. During the conversation I told *abuelo* that I needed to tell him something. He asked me what it was. I told him that I was in a relationship with a woman. The phone got quiet. He didn't say a word. I asked him if he was ok. The only thing he said was that several weeks prior to our conversation he was watching an episode of *la Doctora* and that there was a family on the show... a son or daughter was telling the family that they were gay.

He said that as he watched the show he remembered saying *if one of my children ever came out I would love them no matter what.* And now his eldest daughter was the one telling him that she is a lesbian. He never expected that. He was extremely upset and told me he had to go. He couldn't speak to me anymore and hung up. My mother was flying back from DR that very day and he was the one who told her. When she called me she was ex-

231

tremely upset. She could not believe what I had done to my father. She blamed me for him being depressed over my news. She made it perfectly clear to me that they would never accept me as a lesbian.

Abuela told me that she would never accept my partner in her home for any holiday. I was devastated. I honestly thought that I was going to get the, *Mi hija, we love you just the way you are. We accept you! If you're happy that's all we've ever wanted for you.*

In my fantasy we would hug and I would think I had the coolest parents on the planet. NOPE! They were devastated and that's when I started to pull away from them. I was sad that I didn't have their support. Only one of my sisters was supportive. Everyone else in the family was incredibly devastated. Whatever illusions they had about my finding the perfect man was now long gone.

My emotions were up in down. So many wonderful things were happening to me. I had to go back and look at my life. I needed to make sense of all the relationships I'd been in with men that were based on these ideals passed down to me. I was in the process of processing what my life would now be like.

There was no marching in demonstrations or fighting on the front lines for gay rights. I was allowing the revelation to live in me while learning what being a lesbian means to me. I had no intention on being anyone's definition of what being gay is. I was defining being a lesbian on my own terms and in my time.

Max had been an out lesbian for over 17 years. She spent a lot of time telling me how worried she was about being my *first* female relationship. She never liked being anyone's first. And she never liked being with bisexual women. To her these women were iffy. Her constant fear and most of our conversations were around this idea that I would one day wake up and say that I was really straight. She was always concerned that I would want to be with men again. I always found myself reassuring her that I was positive that I am gay and that I wanted to be with her.

I still wanted to "do the right thing" for my family and for you. It had less to do with any confusion about my sexuality than it did about acceptance from those that meant most to me. My doing the right thing for them means that I wouldn't be gay. If I thought that my coming out was going to harm you or affect you in any way I was going to live my life in the closet to protect you. It was never going to be about leaving *her* for a man. I was living my life for everyone but me.

During our first visit together I brought you with me to meet her. Max brought her son. As soon as she sat down at the restaurant she put two boxes in front of me. They were rings. She mentioned that she bought me a gift but the way she presented them felt heavy. We had only been together a month.

The newness of our love was amazing. It was beautiful. She was tender, soft, strong and smart. I enjoyed the limited time we had together because she lived in Georgia. The distance seemed to work well for me. I wanted slow, steady progress and was not in a rush. I was still going through so much and needed her to be patient with me. I was balancing a lot at this point of my life. I was trying to hold onto my spirit and feed myself positive things. I was feeling pulled. I felt myself starting to put up walls and protect myself. At the same time there were so many blessings entering my life. Things were happening and something huge was about to happen. I spent an entire day one weekend roaming the streets of New York City trying to find the perfect place to write. It felt like I was looking for the perfect place to HIDE!

I recently finished reading, *The Alchemist*, by Paulo Coelho for like the 4th time. Each time I've picked it up I've been in a new place in my life and something in my life always draws me back to this book. So when I picked up the book this time it was a way for me to check in with myself. To remind myself of what I needed at this point to go forward on this journey. It helps me confirm that I AM on *my* journey or pushes me in the right direction if I seem to fall off. On two different occasions I have been in romantic relationships while reading *The Alchemist*. It seems like when things are going great in my life, when I'm making pro-

234

gress, while I'm moving forward, I tend to attract things that *seem* wonderful. While these things seem amazing on the outside they also have served to move me away from my journey — away from my *Personal Legend*.

I had to ask myself, *how do I continue on my journey towards my personal legend while building a relationship? How do I NOT allow for distractions to take me off track? How do I NOT allow for things to enter my life and move me away from my journey? How does my journey get altered? And is it always for the better? What is my role in it? What do I need to understand here? What is my lesson?* What I know for certain is that every person that I meet on this journey I am meant to meet. Everything that I experience on this journey I am meant to experience (good and bad -- especially the bad). Sometimes while on this journey there are people you have to let go of in order to move forward.

The journey teaches us how to turn our dreams into reality. Reminding us that there are many tools we must pick up along the way. Tools that we learn from others, learn in school, pick up from elders, read in books, hear in songs and get from TV. The most important tool I think any of us can pick up on the journey is PATIENCE. Patience is very necessary on the journey. Somehow we forget this or fail to practice patience. We walk with this sense of urgency and frustration that what we want hasn't arrived. This lack of patience, lack of faith because we want things in the immediate, we want it *now* looking for fast results in the present.

While I was walking aimlessly lost in the city I started to think about the people I have met on my journey. Those who are in my inner circle and just associations I have made along the way. People can get *real* comfortable with the US they're used to. People aren't always ready for that change in us. They will not always be welcoming and supportive. They will want the old Alicia - straight Alicia. They accepted that Alicia. The new Alicia makes them uncomfortable. When you're doing that inner work and start to change the people around you sometimes will no longer fit who you're becoming. They will want the old you because it's safe for them. It's safe because they don't have to look at themselves.

When you're on that journey of finding your own personal legend it might feel lonely. People who are not living their dreams won't know how to support you in reaching yours.

There are people who will try to convince you that it is impossible to realize your personal legend. HOW DARE WE GO IN SEARCH OF OUR PERSONAL LEGEND? There have been countless people who have told me that my writing is silly and not a real job. They will want to fill us with self-doubt projecting their own fears of achieving or reaching their own potential. And in the face of all those who doubt you – you MUST continue to prepare your *spirit* and your *will* to carry on. It takes a lot to continue on the journey. You must honor what you've been called to do... but first you must figure out what that is.

"And when you want something, all the universe conspires in helping you to achieve it." The Alchemist

This was longest walk ever. I had been all over the place and I don't just mean emotionally and mentally, but physically. I still didn't have a spot to write. I took the bus cross-town to the 6 train. I headed downtown and took the L to Union Square. I walked into the Barnes and Noble. I get there, settle in, unpack all my shit, I'm in flow, I'm ready to go and my laptop battery is about to die. I leave all my stuff and go looking for a new place to sit where I could plug in. No such luck. Apparently this location has sealed their outlets for the past two years.

I packed up my lunch, laptop and journals and decided that what I needed was a new location. I considered for a moment heading home but you were there and I needed to release some things on the page. There were things I needed to get out of my body. I knew that if I came home you would want some quality time and attention. I decided to go to the spot that never fails me 113. I headed to Grand Central Station to MY SPOT. Track 113, is where much of my novel has been written. It's where most of the book was born, the letters, my blogs so many wonderful hours spent writing there. I just knew that my spot wouldn't let me down.

I get there and there's a man sitting in my seat. I stand there patiently waiting for him to finish eating because I didn't want to sit anywhere else. Plus it's the only spot that has an outlet.

After thirty minutes the table near him frees up. I jump in that seat and wait I don't even un-pack. I am sitting there patiently waiting with my coat on, bags on my lap and I'm just watching him. I'm trying not to stare him down because as soon as he got up I was in there. He collects his trash, I stand up, he leaves and I jump to that table quickly. I start unpacking slowly. I was spreading out all my stuff like I do at home. I take out my laptop and I start smiling because *finally* I am about to get started with my writing. I pull out the chord to my computer, untangle it, plug into the back of the laptop and assume my position.

I look under the table and start to push the cord through the holes. The chord wouldn't go in all the way. I was like, *what the fuck!* So I get real close to the wall. I'm now under the table and what do I see? The outlet was stuffed with this white substance. What I discovered was that Grand Central Station is no longer allowing patrons to plug in their electronics. If they see anyone with cords connected the NYPD will give you a summons.

I sat there for a moment and thought to myself this can NOT be happening. What was the universe trying to tell me? So I stood up pissed off. Put on my hat, scarf, and jacket. Packed up all my SHIT AGAIN and stormed off. I was walking out of Grand Central Station and went underground to the trains. I was talking to myself, thinking *MAN today is NOT my day…maybe I should just take my black ass home?* I kept feeling like something was keeping me from writing today. I believed that everything that was happening to me was trying to get in my way. There was something pushing me away from what was important to

me like my WRITING. There was something interfering or inter-
vening in my process. I believed that I somehow was the one in
control. I felt like I was being tested. I definitely felt like my patience and peacefulness was being tried. I was being called to
look at something. I was underground walking towards the
shuttle train when I see this group singing. I kept walking.

> *People will come in*
> *At times*
> *Unwelcome*
> *With words*
> *To test you*
> DON'T STOP BELIEVIN'

> *THEY*
> *WILL*
> *Say things*
> *Infer*
> *Imply*
> DON'T STOP BELIEVIN'

> *Things will happen*
> *make you question*
> *second guess*
> *Doubt*
> *self*
> *And then there's*
> *TIMING~*
> *ALL happens*
> *right on time~*
> DON'T STOP BELIEVIN'

I was reminded of this that day. The voices coming from those
girls made me do a double take. They had just finished a song
and were about to start another. There was one girl whose voice

239

made me stop. I was frozen. They pulled me back. I turned around and stood in front of them. I figured why rush now things weren't going my way anyway. As far as I was concerned my day wasn't going according to MY plan. The sounds that came from this group, took my breath away. They had no music backing them. They were beat boxing... hitting notes that I swear I thought some of these girls were black. They were amazing. Then one of the singers started with these words...

> Just a small town girl, livin in a lonely world
> She took the midnight train goin anywhere
> Their shadows searching in the night
> Working hard to get my fill,
> Everybody wants a thrill
> Some will win, some will lose
> Some were born to sing the blues
> Oh, the movie never ends
> It goes on and on and on and on
> Don't stop believin
> Hold on to the feelin
> By Journey

I felt like I was that small town girl living in this lonely world. I felt like I was going nowhere. I swore that they were singing that song directly to me. I cried the entire time they sang. I knew that there was a message sent directly for me. *Alicia! Don't ever stop believing.* When I stopped there were only four of us listening. By the end of the song there were thirty people. They were absolutely amazing. I had to thank the universe for these angels who were sent to remind me, DON'T STOP BELIEVIN'!

When they finished I immediately bought their CD and walked to the shuttle train and as I sat there I cried and cried. At that moment I released all those thoughts that I believed were stopping me. I released my belief that I was being intentionally delayed. I removed all sabotaging thoughts. Something else was slowing me down. There was something greater happening. All of it was part of a bigger plan if I only I stopped to BELIEVE! All was happening to me that day so that I could arrive *right on time*!

That's what was missing for me the ME that believes. I needed to hold onto my faith. I needed to be reminded that I should never stop believing. I needed to remember who I am and not allow what others say to influence or affect me. We walk around spending our days missing the many blessings sent our way. We listen to the words of others when we should really be listening to *our* force. That day I was tested in so many ways or at least that was my perception. The universe sent me a message in the form of that amazing chorus, *The Middlebury Mischords.*

I affirm: I believe in the good in others. I believe in love. I believe that everything that happens in my life happens for a reason even if the reasons aren't revealed to me immediately. I believe in me. I believe in you. I believe that if you hurt me… I must let you go and I will. I believe in quiet, tranquility, and space. I believe in peace.

CHAPTER TWENTY-EIGHT

"Don't you check your voicemail?" That's what Kelly said to me as we were driving to Rhode Island for a visit.

I was so excited because we were going to go the cemetery to visit Diamondz. I was going to share the news of being published in *Urban Latino* magazine. I wanted to read him some of the article. As we headed North on 95 there was a voicemail from the editor in chief. She received a phone call from a television producer who wanted to interview me on the story I wrote.

He was the executive producer for television shows American Latino TV and LatinNation. She asked me if it was ok for her to give my contact information to him. Of course I said yes. We were screaming in the car so excited. We didn't know what this interview was, but Kelly had my outfit picked out. She had me with my entourage on the red carpet. We laughed that entire time. We felt that what was starting to happen to my career was a testament of my hard work paying off. When we arrived to RI we went directly to the cemetery. We sat by his grave. I shared my news and read some excerpts from the story. When we got up to leave Kelly's son said, *Alicia, he gave you the thumbs up!* We all just stood there in shock. But we understood that there was something he saw that we knew to take as truth. Diamondz was proud and was protecting me.

I had a meeting scheduled with the TV producer the following week. This was when I met Renzo Devia. He was incredibly welcoming and excited to speak to me about the inspiration for my story. As I looked around his office I noticed all of his awards for TV producing, videos with segments, pictures and books.

There was one book that jumped out at me. It was sitting on his windowsill... it was *the Alchemist*. I took that as a sign, it was an omen that I was in good company and I knew we were going to get along. As we spoke we talked about the importance of knowing ones history. Renzo had done a segment for American Latino TV on Afrolatinos and was very interested in the subject.

We shared our background and talked about our careers. He mentioned to me that he was about to make a huge move. He was getting ready to sell his company and relocate to Bogota, Colombia. Renzo shared with me his plans to work on a documentary about Afrolatinos. He informed me that he wasn't sure how I fit into his plan but perhaps we could work together in the future. I wished him luck and told him that I was available for whatever he needed, if he needed me to write anything to reach out.

He walked me to the elevator and said, "Alicia, I really wanted to meet you for two reasons, I wanted to congratulate you for you for telling this story, but I also wanted to commend you for being Latina and a single mother doing great things." We hugged and that was that.

One week later he called me and asked me if I would be interested in working with him. At the time, I didn't fully grasp that he was asking me to be the head writer on the project and travel with him throughout Latin America. This was a huge honor and the biggest writing opportunity of my life. We had much to discuss and I had a lot to think about.

What makes a relationship work? When is togetherness too much? How do we become a WE and hold on to the ME? How do we hold onto our individualism while honoring the UNION?

"But the most exciting, challenging and significant relationship of all is the one you have with yourself. And if you can find someone to love the YOU that you love, well, that's just fabulous." ~ Carrie, Sex in the City

Our lives were changing fast. So much was happening at the same time. In just a matter of few days I had just come out as a lesbian and my first article was published. I was in my first relationship with a woman and my writing career was going to the next level. I had big decisions to make as to whether or not I should leave you.

When Renzo offered me the position everything in our life stopped. This was a BIG moment! Now more than ever I needed to be with someone who was strong enough to stand at my side. This was the time I needed someone who could stand beside me. I needed someone who would understand all of the work it had taken for me to get to this point. I needed a partner who could be there for me through all of it.

Love creates an "us" without destroying the "me" - Leo Buscaglia

You and I had countless conversations about whether or not it was the right time for me to accept Renzo's offer to work on this documentary. I wasn't sure if I could do it. I would have to quit my job. I would no longer have benefits or a steady income. You were starting your junior year of high school. You were only 16 years old. We were going to begin a new chapter in our lives. There was so much to do over the next few weeks. I had never left the country or you for months at a time like this. *Who would take care of you? Would you be ok without me? Was this really responsible of me?*

This was such a critical time in your life! This new chapter was very intimidating. I was part nervous and part excited. I was filled with so much fear. I wanted to release all of it and kept reminding myself that I was about to embark on an amazing adventure.

May 22, 2008 was my last day at *BusinessWeek*. This was such a big move for me financially. The decision was emotionally draining. To leave a stable job in pursuit of my dreams when

245

everyone thought it was crazy and irresponsible? It was a HUGE leap – a big risk. It was a decision that I didn't regret not even for one moment because I understood that where I was headed was far better than anything I could have ever dreamt of for us. Plus I had your blessing. You were the only person that could have asked me to stay and I would have.

Every ending is a new beginning... I began writing the treatment for the documentary *Afrolatinos: The Untaught Story.* It was Wednesday; May 28, 2008 we were celebrating your 16th birthday. We were on the West Coast. What a wonderful time we had together. We stayed at *la Chicana's* house in LA. This was our last get away weekend together for a while. We went to the Bay Area so you could tour Berkeley. We hung out on Venice Beach and went to Santa Monica. We even went to the club were Green Day played for the first time. You fell madly in love with San Francisco. You were crazy excited about going back and living there. Once we got back from California the documentary was beginning to feel very real. There was a part of me that was so scared about this new phase in my life. It didn't seem real. But I was leaving. I was about to live my dreams. It felt like I was dreaming. I was scared of the unknown? *What is it about the unknown that is so FRIGHTENING? What if I decided to SEE the unknown in a completely different way... what if I chose to look at the unknown as WONDERFUL? What if I decided to see this as an adventure?* I am about to embark on an incredible adventure~ I am going to be living my NOVEL. This moment was AMAZING!

June 2008

I felt like shit. I had muscle spasms that kept me in bed for a week. We had only been back from California two weeks ago. I had horrible back pain where I couldn't even dress myself. My stomach was upset everyday. I didn't feel strong. I was weak. I definitely needed a cleansing/detox/personal trainer to get me in shape. I felt like I needed to prepare physically and spiritually for this trip. My body was starting to react to my decision to leave. All my fears about leaving you were affecting my health.

There was so much I needed to do and I wasn't sure where to start. I needed to figure out your living arrangements while I was gone — which alone had me stressed out. I needed to leave the finances in order and our rent paid. I only had two weeks before I left the country. I was feeling blocked and paralyzed. I kept hearing myself saying, *just keep moving... just keep moving... keep getting ready Alicia.* This was an incredible gift and opportunity. *Why was I afraid? What is it that I'm most afraid of?* FAILING!!! I am afraid of failing you, failing my family, failing myself, failing my friends and failing at life. *What is it that I'm worried about?* Am I doing the right thing?

When Renzo invited me to work on the documentary I was *petrified.* I would be out of the country for six months. This was truly a dream come true. I was going to be a part of something amazing. This was a project that would tell the story of who we really are. I would be learning about different Latin American cultures, our history, our people, our politics and our love for our individual countries.

I was discussing with a friend the areas where we feel stuck in life. It was as if we both hit a wall. Nobody said it would be easy! No one said this journey would be easy. It requires perseverance, determination, patience, willingness, faith, endurance and a tremendous amount of courage to go in search of our personal legends. I needed to get ready. It's not an easy task to follow our hearts desire when we allow fear to set in. Believing that it's not meant to be or that we're not worthy of having it. There will be moments where it hurts. In the end it's NOT seeking, NOT searching, NOT going for it and NOT realizing our FULL potential that is the greatest pain of ALL. Out of everything I was doing to myself physically, allowing fear to stop me, it's NOT accepting this opportunity that would have affected me the most.

I was thinking about the many times I've hit the same wall over and over again. I've discovered that one of the reasons that happens to me is that I've been distracted by life. I've allowed many little things to take my attention away from where I'm headed. And what I've learned is that I needed to get back to me. We must constantly and continuously keep getting ready.

CHAPTER TWENTY-NINE

Our relationship was exhausting me. That day I woke up a little before 7:00am with my body telling me a very familiar story. My body was sending me all kinds of messages. I always know exactly what it is I am going through by what my body is saying to me. It felt like a truck hit me. Where to I begin? I will begin with the end… with last night. I was completely drained from the day. I felt pushed around and beat down.

I took you to dinner and a movie for our special date and sat quietly I didn't say much. You looked at me and said, "Mommy why do you look so depressed?"

I just smiled at you and said, "I'm not depressed. Everything is fine. I'm just tired." I guess you weren't the only person I was lying to. I was lying to myself. I was fooling myself that the events of the day didn't affect me. I was being bullied and pushed around. The body gives us all kinds of messages if we really listen to it. Not only does it tell you to feed it, make love to it, rest, exercise, sleep, and play. *That day* my body was screaming messages to me saying LISTEN HERE LADY... pay close attention! What's going on here does not feel good!!!

I got out of bed and just sat there feeling really sore for a minute. I was feeling like, *DAMN... why do I feel like I was just hit by a car?* I got on my computer like I always do first thing in the morning. I handled some business then looked at my floor at the spot where I do my yoga. Our house was quiet and I felt at peace. I decided to do some yoga and work out the soreness from my body. I got down on the floor laid on my back with my mask on my eyes and got quiet. I was meditating on the words *"God is always in complete and perfect control...I will not judge."*

My word during meditation was NONJUDGEMENT. I was coming to the end of my session and was in prayer position when the words that came into my mind stopped me mid-thought. I stopped to write them down: YOU PUSH ME~

You push me to show you. You push me to say. You push me to speak. You push me to prove. You push me to share. You push me to love. You push me to tell you. You push me around. You push too hard. You push me to push you back. You push me to pull away. STOP PUSHING!!!

And the word that followed those thoughts was: PATIENCE~

Be patient Alicia. But PATIENCE does not mean push over. Patience does not mean I allow you to walk all over me. So here I am again in a familiar place. Am I going to walk away or step up and say DON'T PUSH ME! I will stand here and not walk away this time but I will let you know Max, please STOP pushing me I do PUSH BACK!

I accepted things from Max that I would never have tolerated from a man. I would have left from jump. I stayed because I was trying to love her past her pain. I wanted to show her how much I loved her. I wanted her to see that I was different. I was unlike any of the lovers she had ever been with. I wanted her to believe that she was worthy of me. I wanted her to know that she is worthy of love.

"Love is not concepts; love is action. Love in action can only produce happiness. Fear in action can only produce suffering." from the Mastery of Love by Don Miguel Ruiz

Are relationships really as complicated and as complex as we make them out to be? I feel like that old quote holds such truth, "treat others the way you would like to be treated." I think for me I look at a few things when I consider people to walk with on this journey. RESPECT is incredibly important. Then it would be ACCEPTANCE – take me as I am. Step to me in FAITH. Come to me in PEACE. Speak to me in LOVE. I don't think that I am *that* complicated or difficult to deal with. I am pretty much *what you see is what you get*! I believe my requests are simple treat me the way I treat you. Love me or leave me! The fights that we were having had nothing to do with me. It was about *her* personal history — yet it did affect me.

Leave your baggage at the door! That's what I wanted to say to her. We all have our shit! None of us are perfect. We're all works in progress. Relationships are filled with high and low points. That night was one of those low points during my conversation with Max. It's an interesting thing that men and women do in

251

relationships. Sometimes we take out our past on the new folks who come along. I decided a long time ago that I was NO LONGER going to do this to my potential suitors.

I decided that I wanted to give every new relationship the benefit of doubt allowing *them* to come as they are; credit reports and references not necessary. I decided that I would accept them for who they are flaws and all and see where it leads.

So with Max I was doing that. I was staying open. I came as I am. I came in love. I was sharing all of me. I was sharing all that I could with the time that we had left together. But there was something missing. TRUST seemed to be one sided. I began to feel like I was being put into a category created by her. I was put in this little box with all the people from her past that hurt her.

I'm NO punching bag~
I don't do rollercoaster's
They make me wanna throw up
I refuse
To pay
For your past
I'm not your ex
I'm ME
I'm new
NO comparison please
FEAR
Makes you walk
Quick
Away
From love
LOVE fears
nothing
To test love
Simply

Stand
Still
And wait
Face fear
Look in her eyes
You are loved
We'll know
During our
20th, 30th, 50th anniversary
"Life is too short"
Does not mean
Full steam ahead
Live fully
Walk slowly
Love deeply
Watch the flowers grow
Feed off the moments
Just because you've arrived
Doesn't mean my dream changes
Be here to add
Not take away
Love doesn't walk
It takes fear by the hand
You're worthy
Love has arrived
Be happy
When the ME is threatened
For the goal of an US
It never works
Love and fear
At war
Love always wins
I have no doubt
Accept who I am
Believe and know
I'm nobody's punching bag~

FINDING YOUR FORCE

Cielo was waking up. She started to discover gifts hidden in her box. It frightened her... but she was hearing something. As she put her ear to the corner of the box she could hear voices. She opened it slowly. The voice was whispering I want to scream... open the box Cielo... open me. The screaming was deafening.

I wanna SCREAM~
Why do your words hit so hard?
I'll love you
I'll whisper until you make me SCREAM!
Scream it girl
I wanna scream
FUCK girl
I'm screaming on the inside
The voice is deafening
It's like bombs exploding on the inside
A dragon
blazing fire with each breath
I wanna scream
I'm tired of speaking so softly
I'm through with you thinking I'm somehow soft
Yeah I'm nice
But don't be confused
I'm nothin nice
I wanna scream
Who's holding you back?
Who do you blame?
What do YOU want to do?
Where are you headed?
I wanna scream
Growth
Evolution
Forward movement
Expansion
I wanna scream
Are you with me?
Are you with me?
Are you with me?
Are you WITH me?
I wanna scream

My light
My life
My laughter
My love
My happiness
Don't fuck with that
I wanna scream
Are you in my life to add?
Are you in my life for the moment?
Are you in my life for now?
Are you in my life for LIFE?
I'm screaming on the inside
BACK THE FUCK OFF

Prayer: Is she the love reserved for ME? I'm thinking about my life partner and what that looks like for me. What does our partnership look like? Will you be threatened or jealous of other connections I make? Will you question my partnerships? Will you worry about my friendships? Will you ask me to change my writer's style? Will you dictate to me what I should write about and when? Will you try to control me, own me and keep me for your own pleasure? Will you love me unconditionally? Will we last a lifetime this time? Will you let me roam free when need be? Do you love me? Do you love YOU is a better question? Will you let me be ME? Or will you try to take it from me. Will you keep me under lock and key for the world NOT to see? Do you know that I was born to love you – if you let me? Do you know that I was born to share my love with many?

Why do women tolerate abuse? Why do women stay? I was finding myself in an abusive relationship. She was hurting me yet I believed that I could love her passed her pain. A dear friend asked me, *Alicia, how much will you take before you leave her?*

255

I cried as I responded, *I will stay until I can't take it any more.* It was so early in our relationship when I started feeling responsible for her past. I felt like I was paying for all of it.

ABUSE comes in all shapes, and colors. I was thinking about the different levels of abuse... from an argument with a loved one that can go from a heated debate and turn into words that cut. Then there is the condescending insults and sarcastic jabs disguised by saying, "I was just joking" or "I really didn't mean that." Then there are the extremes: sexual abuse, physical abuse, domestic violence, cruelty and rape. There is abuse of power in the work place, bullying in schools. An assault is exactly that AN ASSAULT on your PERSON.

I wrote in my journal in big letters, I WILL NEVER STAY IN AN ABUSIVE RELATIONSHIP with a man or a woman. I will never stay in an abusive situation...PERIOD! I was in an abusive relationship and I stayed because it was my first relationship with a woman and I believed that this relationship required more work than my past relationships with men. What I failed to recognize was that abuse has no gender.

CHAPTER THIRTY

I wrote Cielo a love letter... as of today you will no longer be silenced. Today I write for you my little girl who has put up with so much shit. Today you will speak up loud and not give a fuck what the adults think. Today I offer my writing to you.... the little girl in me~ the little girl in me with the loud voice... the little girl who has always wanted to be seen and heard... the little girl in me AFRAID to demand respect and recognition... the little girl in me who is so beautiful. You have so much to say. There is so much I want to show you and teach you. Come to me I will guide you. I will tell you all you need to know. You were born for greatness. Many will come to you... many will come to hear you speak.

Max made me want to run and hide. I wanted to protect my inner child. She didn't feel safe. What I needed at that point in my life was gentleness and understanding. During that time I was writing a lot about wanting to be a little girl. The little girl in me was afraid of the woman she was.

You've heard the joke: "What does a lesbian bring on a second date?"

"What?"

"A U-Haul!"

While I was making arrangements for my trip out of the country Max had rushed her move date to be in NYC. Originally, she was scheduled to move in the fall of 2008 but decided she wanted to come sooner. I made it perfectly clear to her that I hoped she wasn't coming to NYC for me because I wasn't ready for that kind of commitment. I told her that I had not lived with anyone since divorcing your father and that I would not live with anyone until you were off to college. That's just the way I was. I have always put you first.

I would be leaving for six months so I decided that I would allow her to move into our apartment. We would both do each other a favor. She would pay half the rent and the utilities. After thinking about it I decided that six months might be too long so I offered her three months because I knew I would be home in October and wanted our apartment back. I wanted you and I to be alone. She was upset about the change in plans. I was very serious about NOT LIVING TOGETHER.

July 2008

There is nothing better than arriving to your home after being away for so long. I had just come home from Mexico, Puerto Rico and the Dominican Republic. Max was so excited to have me home. I walked into the house at 5:00am after a long flight.

She greeted me at the door, "I've missed you baby... don't go to sleep. Lets' have breakfast together before I go to work. How was your flight? Was it long?"

"I just want to rest Max."

"No don't sleep I want to spend time with you."

I told her that I needed to sleep. I was so happy to be home in our sanctuary. I noticed that she had put some things up on my wall in the apartment. I felt such an invasion of our space. It didn't feel like home to me. I didn't feel welcomed. I no longer felt warm. It was not comfortable for me. The arrangement was supposed to be temporary. I remember not even taking off clothes that day.

That night when she got home from work she wanted to have this twelve-hour conversation about the status of our relationship, commitment and fidelity. "I know you're fucking your business partner Renzo."

"Where did that even come from? What are you talking about Max?"

"I know you're cheating on me. You've probably slept with men and women during your travels."

"Max, I am too tired for this shit. I need to rest. Home is where I come to rejuvenate, to refill. This is my sacred space. I don't need this. I wanted to come home and be filled with love. I am out there giving all of me in Latin America. I am working my ass off. I told you that the moment I decide to cheat I'd end things with you first. You won't ever have to worry. I will call you and break up with you before I ever do that."

I had been traveling for weeks and did not have one indiscretion. I was very faithful to her. In fact one of the jokes between Renzo and I was, "Yeah let's see how long you will be faithful with all the fine women in Latin America?" I didn't cheat once.

That night she accused me of being selfish. She went on and on about how I didn't know how to be in relationship. She complained that I didn't know how to be in a committed partnership. She called me narcissistic.

"I weep for Narcissus, but I never noticed that Narcissus was beautiful. I weep because, each time he knelt beside my banks, I could see, in the depths of his eyes, my own beauty reflected." ~ Author Unknown

The story of Narcissus… Narcissus was a boy who visited a lake to acknowledge his own beauty. As he sat by the lake talking to his own reflection he fell madly in love with himself.

I won't bore you with the psychological description of someone with Narcissistic Personality Disorder. What I will share with you is that Narcissism gets a bad wrap. There are healthy forms of narcissism that have more to do with a person achieving greatness. So for me in order to get to that a place of greatness I have had to be selfish. I have put myself first. I have put US first. It wasn't the first time someone had accused me of being narcissistic. I think the first time I heard that word was when I was married. When your dad bought me the Pretenders CD and played a song for me *you're so vain you probably think this song is about you.* Max thought I was selfish. And I thought that 2:00am was not the time to talk about my selfishness as I had just returned from traveling thousands of miles serving Latino communities. I was spiritually exhausted and had given all of me. I JUST WANTED TO SLEEP!

She stormed out of the house that night. I think she thought I was going to run after her. I just pulled the covers over my head and went to sleep.

"What a man thinks of himself, that is which determines, or rather indicates, his fate" ~ Henry David Thoreau

August 2, 2008

THE END! That morning I left the apartment at about 7:00am to meet with my personal trainer. I didn't come back home until around 7:00pm that evening. I wandered all over NYC. I wanted to be anywhere but home. I had never felt that way before. I met with two of my spiritual sisters and we talked about how I was feeling. I cried the entire time I was with them. I was only going to be in New York for two days. I was going to be meeting Renzo in Bogota and then we would be traveling to Barranquilla, Cartagena, San Basilio de Palenque, Panama, Honduras, and back to the Dominican Republic. From there we would be heading back to Colombia, flying to Peru and back to Colombia. I wouldn't be back in NYC until October. I was going to miss your first day of school. Your entire life I had never missed your first day.

After what happened the night before I was left feeling like shit. I was drained. I was spiritually spent. There was this pain in my heart. I was beyond exhausted. I needed to refill my cup. That's what those two days should have been for me. The past few weeks of travel were amazing. There was so much learning happening at such a rapid pace. It was information overload. We met with historians, religious experts, musicians and people in the community. Not to mention the hours of bus rides traveling from one side of the country to the other. You feel like your drowning. You're meeting amazing people who are passing on wisdom and sharing their experiences and it's just absolutely beautiful. I was depleted and came home on empty.

How do you balance it out? How do I hold onto my spirituality? How do I fill myself when I am giving all of me? How do you do great work and take time to rest? How you maintain a relationship that no longer feels good?

Two days... that's all I had to rest. I had so much running around to do. There were commitments I needed to keep. I was trying to make everyone happy. Everyone in my life wanted to see me. I needed to be selective. I didn't even get to see you because you were with your father. I was learning how to pull back and say no to people's demands for my time. I needed to keep some of what was left for me. It might have seemed like I was out there and it was fun all the time... this fact is that this project was a lot of work.

Max was right I was selfish... I needed to be. I needed to take care of *me*. During that conversation with my spirit sisters one of them said, "sometimes it feels like I'm holding onto someone else issues and baggage. Their shit is not my shit!"

Those were the words that freed me. I no longer needed to hold onto other peoples shit. I was feeling this weight on me that I needed to lift off of me completely. *Your shit – is not MY SHIT!*

That evening when Max returned to the apartment. I ended our relationship. We spent the night together... we made love for the last time. The gentleness was gone... it was filled with aggression, anger and hate. She wanted to hurt me, to punish me and she was successful. The way she entered me brought me back to the Terrance days. I felt violated. And I allowed it. I let her. I just wanted it to be over. I wanted us to be over and it was done. When she finished I went into the bathroom and cried.

PART III ~ REBIRTH

*"There can be no healing in our external world until we give
intensive care and healing to our internal wounds."*

Quote by Iyanla Vanzant

CHAPTER THIRTY-ONE ~ *August 10, 2008*

Cielo, you are like a butterfly just emerged from its cocoon. You are a baby just learned to walk. Everything is new for you. You see everything with new eyes! You are open, open to change, open to new things, open to new experiences and in time that may indeed leave you open for love.

Today I am feeling some pretty incredible vibes. I am receiving an incredible flow of love, strength and good wishes. My body feels strong. My heart is full. I feel ready. I feel blessed, happy… crazy happy. I am READY to continue getting ready. I am free. I feel this tremendous weight off my shoulders. I am on an amazing journey right now and want to experience every good thing that comes my way. I am more patient today than I have been lately. On this journey I have met so many wonderful people. I have heard stories, shared food and have been surrounded by magnificent views. This experience is so surreal. I've dreamt of all these places I have visited. It was real. I have been here before.

> *The end of us~*
> *It wasn't easy*
> *Calling it quits*
> *It never is*
> *But in honoring me*
> *I honor you~*
> *If you think I'm gonna write about us~*
> *I WON'T*
> *If you think I blame YOU~*
> *I DON'T*
> *What we had was OURS*
> *What I gave is YOURS*
> *What I received~*
> *I WILL CHERISH*
> *I'm grateful*
> *Thankful*
> *You arrived~*

TODAY IS A NEW DAY! I am grateful I can still be light after the break up. What tends to happen during a break up or what has happened to me in the past is that I allowed my self to fall apart. I would become paralyzed and lose focus. My footing tends to slip. I lose track of all that is important to me. I would allow the sadness to consume me. But not this time~ TODAY I AM A BUTTERFLY.

This time yes there were tears. Yes there was sadness. Yes there is something missing. I will miss her voice. I will miss her eyes. I will miss that someone you wake up every morning thinking about. That person who is the first thought of the day. The first call you want to make. The last voice you want to hear. It was wonderful to love her in that way. While something is missing... the love I have, the love I shared and gave is STILL INTACT! That love is still at HOME!

Prayer: Do I feel empty? Do I feel broken? Do I feel lost? Not today... that's not at all how I feel. I feel incredibly full. I can find beauty in the sadness. I can find hope in the aloneness. And my faith... my faith is strong. Our last day together was painful. I was completely drained but all is good. The universe is good to me always and in all ways. In licking my wounds my wings are healing. This butterfly is soaring. I still have much work to do and I realize I am not ready for a relationship. I am not done with me yet. So to that person thank you for coming into my life~ to that person thank you for being apart of my unfolding~

The word I'm meditating on today is, "Expansion" which basically means being open to natural growth. I'm going with the flow. Books are wonderful but how are we living our lives with the words we're fed? The difference between me then and me now is that now I am truly PATIENT. I know where to turn to for the answers. I can ask a question and WAIT patiently for the answer. I don't need to force it. I am expanding!

I affirm: I allow myself to expand beyond where I am. I allow myself to expand beyond who I am. I am expanding into my full potential. I am unfolding into what I want to be. I am willing to risk losing everything if I'm serious about getting anything.

Prayer: There is still some residue inside of me. Yesterday I was supposed to feel peaceful and open yet the day was met with anger and frustration. Today I release all of it. Today I make a conscious choice to choose another thought. Today I choose a different way of being. Today I release all that made me angry. I release all that brings me pain. I replace all feelings that have kept me incarcerated. I release all limiting thoughts. I replace all those negative thoughts with the knowledge that I am an unlimited and limitless being. I know with certainty that I am beautiful. I am love. I am kind. I am truth. I am made in your likeness. I am compassionate. I am generous and gracious. I am wise. I am creative. I am peace. I am light. I am strength. I am faith. I am abundant. I am walking with every GOOD thing the Creator has given me. I am not afraid because my FORCE is at my side. I am not alone. I have an opportunity to begin again. Today is a fresh start. Yesterday is gone. Today I choose to see my day unfold the way I want it to be. Thank you for allowing me to wake up and greet another day. I know that I was born to answer this call and that through my writing I am healed and will heal others. And perhaps that thought scares me a little... the thought that I am responsible to write in a way that affects others... but I can release all fear. I know that I control nothing. Allow me to be a vessel. Send the words through me that you would have me write. Reveal to me my path. Thy will be done... and so it is~ Ache~ Let it be filled with love.

En un solo dia~

I was staying at a hotel near *el parque* colonial near *el conde* in the capital. It was my only night off while we were filming in DR. I would be meeting up with Renzo to continue working on Afro-latinos. We were there to film *Santeria/21 Divisiones*. It was the perfect time to be in Santo Domingo since September is when we celebrate el *dia de San Miguel*. We wanted to shoot *Palo Dominicano*.

I took a shower and was relaxing when I decided that maybe I should go out and see the nightlife in DR. Actually what I wanted was to hit a lesbian spot. So I researched gay clubs in DR and three names came up in my search. I wrote them all down. I got in the cab and asked the driver to take me to the first club.

We arrived to this dark street and the spot was next to a *colmado*. It looked like it was in a house and it was kind of hidden. The building was black and there were no signs hanging outside of the club. There were some men standing in front. I wasn't sure if I was even in the right spot. I asked the cab driver to wait for me so that I could check it out. I walked up to the men standing outside and asked them if this was the *club de mujeres* / the women's club. I wasn't sure how to even go about looking for a gay club in DR with all the homophobia that exists in Latin America. The last thing I wanted was to get assaulted. The men told me that it was in fact a gay club. I walked back to the cab and told him that I was going to stay but that he should come back for me in like an hour in case I wasn't having a good time.

When I walked into *Amazonia* I just looked around it was filled with beautiful Dominican women. There were women dancing on the stage, women dancing together and women dancing alone. They were FINE, STUNNING and simply BEAUTIFUL! I was in heaven. I scanned the place and walked around to the other side of the bar. I sat on a stool and ordered a *Presidente*. As soon as the bartender placed the beer in front of me someone tapped my left shoulder. I turned around and this beautiful woman with an afro asked, "estas perdida?" she was wondering if I was lost. I just looked at her and said NO! I'm not lost. I know exactly where I am. She asked me if I was there alone. I responded yes. She invited me to join her and her friends. She asked me where I was from. She could smell the blue passport. We laughed... I played along with her games. She *thought* she was teaching me about Dominican culture. She thought I was just an American girl. There was a point when she asked me if I knew how to dance. I told her I didn't. I asked her if she would teach me. When we got on the dance floor and started moving she looked at me and said for someone who doesn't know how to dance you sure dance well. I just laughed. I told her I had been dancing way before she was even born.

We spent the entire evening talking. She invited me to grab something to eat after the club. We sat at a restaurant near my hotel. I invited her back to my room so we could continue speaking. "Just speaking!" I showed her pictures of you and our family. It was a night that I didn't want to end. It was 6:00am and I told her that I had a long day. I gave her my email and she left.

The next morning, I received a call from the front desk that there were flowers waiting for me in lobby. The arrangement was filled with red roses. When I received them there was a beautiful note thanking me for a lovely evening and she left her number. I immediately called her to thank her.

We spent that afternoon together. She was personal tour guide. She went with me to the *Archivo Nacional* to retrieve some archive footage for the documentary. We walked around the city and talked that entire afternoon. We shared our life story. We had coffee near *el Museo de Bellas Artes*. There was something about Mariposa. I felt so good around her. I felt so light. It felt like my spirit was safe. Instantly I felt like I could trust her. We had so much fun together. Mariposa is incredibly funny and easy to be around *totalmente uno de eso tigere de alla...* street-smart and intelligent.

Mi Leyenda Personal

With Mari everything was new. It was as if I had never been with anyone before *her*. On my last day she arranged for a car to drive me to the airport and went with me. I didn't want to leave the country. I wanted to stay with her forever.

I was playing around with the wedding ring that was on my finger. It was the special ring I bought for myself. It was the ring that I said I would *only* take off once I found the person who would love me just as much as I loved me. I kept twirling the ring around my finger in the cab... I felt like I wanted to give her something of mine to keep.

We drove to *Boca Chica* and had lunch at the beach before my flight took off. We stood in the ocean talking about life. Our time together felt so important. It was as if there was something I needed to understand about why *she was sent to me* at that exact moment in my life. Our love was exchanged that day. When we looked into each other's eyes there was no denying what was happening but I was leaving and what future could we possibly have? We stood face to face on the sand by the water and it felt like it was just to of us. Nothing in the world existed in that moment. The words that were shared felt like promises.

We were quiet the entire ride to the airport. As we sat next to each other I rested my head on her shoulder. She reached into her bag saying that she had a gift for me. Mari said that it was something small but that it came from her personal collection of books and that it was very special to her — it was her favorite book.

She gave me her copy of *the Alchemist*. My mouth dropped. I knew that that moment was a day I would never forget. In that moment I understood that she was a very important part of my personal legend and I gave her my ring. I married her that day.

During one of our phone conversations we talked about losing our virginity. I started to think about the ways I have given, shared and received love. Giving someone your virginity is something so sacred so special. It's that moment when you give yourself completely to someone. It's that moment when you can no longer wait. You are absolutely sure that *this* is right! There are no questions. There's hunger... desire... heat... passion.

That first time should be like no other experience. When we give our bodies over to someone for the first time that's when we show how much we trust them. We've chosen *them*. They've chosen *us*. We surrender to them completely. I could not wait to give Mari my virginity.

Our first time... was an innocent moment... that moment was SACRED. We were trembling. We were nervous. I felt her electricity with every touch. We released all fears and I gave myself over to her because I knew that she was treating this moment like the most precious jewel. I withheld nothing back. There were no inhibitions. My body responded to her in a way it had never responded to another human being and her body responded to me in the same way. Every single time we made love I cried. I felt like I was making love to one of the God's. It was as if my body was made for her. I felt so blessed to receive Mari in that way. I felt so connected to her. When we made love for the first time it lasted fifteen hours. They were hours filled with exploration, love, tenderness, honor and trust. The spiritual world was present. Our first time was *A Virgin Love.*

When love begins~ its beautiful
When love begins~ its light
When love begins~ it's a fairytale
When love begins~ past loves no longer exists
But virgin love
Aahhhh virgin love
this love is ~ Pure love
Innocent love
Unquestioning love
Trusting love
True love
Real love
Full of passion kind of love
Not caught up in the bullshit love
Lasting love
It's you and me love
Untainted love
Loving you freely love
Without conditions love
I feel you inside me in a way I have never felt anyone LOVE
You the mirror image of me LOVE
Ese momento when one gives themselves over and becomes ONE
now that's LOVE~

273

CHAPTER THIRTY-TWO ~ *December 2008*

When I got home from all my travels I was stuck in darkness. I felt like my *peace* was stolen from me. I didn't know how to get back to my core. I felt like I had lost my spirit somewhere on the journey. I have met many people and have felt all kinds of emotions. The issues that I have been exposed to like: *poverty, brutality, corruption, oppression, exploitation, hopelessness, sexual abuse, racism, segregation, marginalization, sexism, hombre machista and just outright ignorance.*

There were moments on the journey where I've had to assert myself and felt tremendous discomfort about speaking up to men. There was a morning while we were in Peru where I sat alone to record a private blog. I cried about how disrespected I felt by men and how I never wanted them to see me as emotional. I wanted them to see me as their equal. I never wanted them to see me as weak. This project has been instrumental in empowering and helping me to find my voice. In the first six months of filming we visited Mexico, Dominican Republic, Panama, Peru, Honduras, Guatemala, Puerto Rico, Haiti and

Colombia. I should have been so happy, yet depression set in when I returned home. Once I was back I had to deal with all kinds of drama. There was the residue from my relationship with Max still lingering. I was madly in love with Mari and I had so much work to do for Afrolatinos. At the same time I was readjusting to my life here in the United States. Courtney's mom was back.

I definitely went through culture shock. I was so used to a different way of life. I didn't know how to deal with being back. Everything seemed so different to me. You were different. You were so much more independent and mature. I was so proud of you. Your grades were amazing. You took care of yourself. You were all grown up. While I was out there traveling being exposed to a whole new world. You were left here fending for yourself.

Once home I started to realize that the things that I believed were so important about life *here* were so insignificant in the third world. In Latin America I found that there was more value placed on family than there was on money. There was this sense of community that seemed to be lacking *here,* which I longed for.

In Latin America, children were up at 5:00am so grateful to be attending school. They loved their books. Here at home I see all these ungrateful kids walking the streets with their latest gadgets and hating school. I started to see how much we really take for granted in this country. I came back with a new pair of eyes and was seeing the United States as if for the first time.

275

I found myself being very unhappy home. Other than having you to come back to there was nothing else that seemed to make me happy about being here. I was starting to see the world as so much bigger than this life we were living. We are so consumed by media and gossip. Most people *here* live in *their* little fish bowls. Not concerned about what is happening to the world around them. People are only concerned about the shit that directly affects them and *if it isn't happening in our backyard then why should we care?*

I started to get angry about what I was seeing in Latin America. It angered me how women were treated. It pissed me off at how men treated *me* working side by side with a man. "Is he your husband? Are you his secretary?" I can't tell you how many fucking times a man has asked me that question about my relationship with Renzo. It's interesting to see the male/female dynamic in a patriarchal society. Women are invisible and insignificant. It didn't matter that I was the writer and co producer on the film. I had breasts and that automatically put me in the category of being insignificant. I really appreciated the government officials and doctors we interviewed who I'd be interviewing and asking them questions but they would direct their responses and make eye contact with Renzo.

I was asked about my work relationship with men. There were questions that a young woman asked that made *me* question everything about who I am today, "Do you feel you are respected by your colleagues? How do you deal with men who do not allow you to speak? Have you ever felt undermined?"

276

I think for the most part I do have the respect of some men. The men in my life are all about empowering women or at least they say that they believe in the power of women. Some of the men in my life *are* sexist. As much as they love women, that machista bullshit is deep in the programming. I recognize that some men walk around with that tendency and need to save women.

There *have* been several occasions were I have felt disrespected on my journey, where my opinions have been questioned and where I have felt devalued. The challenge for me has been about speaking up when I've felt offended. In the beginning of this journey it was uncomfortable to speak up. That has changed.

I learned that there were important things to care about and fight for in the world. I started to understand that my real calling was to do important work that affects change in Latin America. I understood that there would be a point in my life where I would have to put my pen to good use and work on issues like Dominican-Haitian relations, sexism in the workplace and prostitution in Latin America. I was hearing from people daily about the things that were important to them like education, wanting more schools built, land and human rights violations, inequality and gender discrimination. It was going to take me time to readjust to my life back home. The world is so much bigger than what we keep in our peripheral. Things are just so trivial. We live in a country where we have everything and we're still miserable. Most of the places I visited compared to U.S. standards are poor, it seems like they have nothing. What I found was that they have everything... *they're* richer than us... *they're* happy.

I feel an intrusion. I feel as though my life is polluted. I need space. I want time alone. I need to be left alone. No one in my circle seemed to recognize this. No one seems to realize that I need time for me. How do I tell them what I need without hurting their feelings?

I was a walking fungus. It spread into all areas of my life and began to pollute me. The problem was that I wasn't speaking up for myself. I wasn't voicing what I needed and this fungus turned into an infection, which turned into rage and anger. I was angry because I didn't check people who needed to be checked. *What are the things that form me? What is it that I believe to be true about me? Why do I get nervous when I need to speak up on something? Why am I afraid to stand up for myself?* I was replaying in mind all the ways I have stayed quiet. *What have been the moments that have impacted me the most in my life?* Sometimes you have to sit in the darkness and feel everything. I needed to sit in the darkness. Darkness moves all around me and through me.

Everything from my past had seeped into my body. Everyone I met impacted me in some way. I was hearing stories about how women were treated and mistreated by men who say they love them. I was so angry. I had to sit back and watch as a school superintendent used a cowbell to summon his two secretaries so that they could bring him his water and turn on his computer. The rage completely filled me when I heard that a woman is asked if she has children at a job interview. If she does then that would disqualify her from getting the job. In most countries you'll find in the classifieds an employer asking in an ad for someone with *buena presencia* and they also have to attach a photo to their resume. If you're black you're probably not going to get the job and if you're a woman with coarse hair in the Dominican Republic you're definitely not getting the job.

Racism... discrimination... It felt like my hands were tied. How was I going to stand up to all of these men, institutions and governments? I didn't know what issue to work on first. I could hear *Cielo's whispers... You are not worthy of being heard. Your opinion doesn't matter. You will lose the job if you say anything. Just go along to get along.*

When I got back from traveling I felt so pulled by my circle to do things and go places. What I needed was to BE STILL and be home with you. I needed time to reflect and rest. I didn't want to talk to my EX. I didn't want to visit everyone. I didn't want people in our house all day everyday. I didn't want to respond to emails. I wanted time alone with you and I should have said that. When something bothers me I should say something. When I see injustice I must say something. We must say something. We must tell people what we feel and what we need. We must call people on their shit when their words are out of line.

This fungus was about me not honoring what I was feeling and all that I was afraid to say. I was not speaking up in the moments that something occurs. I was allowing things to build. I was always worried about how others would feel. Enough is enough. What has taken me so many years to learn is that I can

279

say everything I need to say exactly when I need to say it. If you are worried about how to deliver it say what you *need* to say in the way *you* would like to hear it. This journey has been a lesson in what freedom and justice means for me.

She told me that several months before we met she got married. She was married to a man and planning to move to Germany. She was waiting for her visa to finally be able to leave the Dominican Republic. Mari was married!!! I was heart broken. I was in love with her. I saw my future with her. I continued to pursue her. I still wanted to get to know her. I knew that she would have to leave me one day. But I didn't care.

You've got potential~

"There is an enormous potential in the human being, that it isn't out-landish to say if we really wanted to fly, we could fly." ~ Leo Buscaglia

I saw myself in her. That's what I loved the most about Mari. I saw the Alicia in her that existed before the beatings, before the abuse, before the constant violations and moments of betrayal. She *was* the Picasso painting mounted on our wall. She *is* the *Girl Before a Mirror*, 1932 oil on canvas. *We* are the images in that painting. Standing in front of each other sharing dreams, wishes and hopes for our future. And there is no one telling us that we can't achieve them. That's what I see when I look at that painting. I see her smile... her softness... I see who she is.

I was madly in love with Mari and with the potential for our beautiful future. I saw a life full of happiness. There was a part of her that didn't want to grow up and that's precisely what I found appealing. I felt like she hadn't been tainted, soiled or beat up by the world. She hadn't had too much bad shit happen yet that would change her perception of people. The world hadn't yet screwed her over to the point where she could not put her trust in people.

Mari still had so much living to do. She had so much growing to do. I found comfort in that she was just as trusting in me as I was in her. I trusted her with my life. *I met a little girl that I could play with and she wouldn't hurt me. I wanted her to be my girlfriend. I wanted her to be my first. Can you keep a secret? I gave her my virginity.*

When she and I made love it was like I had never been with a single partner male or female, before that moment. She was the definition of love that had been reserved for me. There was a combination of spiritual and physical connectivity when we were together. We became ONE! Each moment we were together I could feel myself enter her and she was entering me.

I have been accused that I fall in love with the *potential* of people and not the *actual* person. So in thinking about "this potential"

that I fall in love with; I accept that I am guilty as charged. I accept this about me and I make NO APOLOGIES. I can admit that there is absolute truth in that statement. When I meet someone I see past things. I don't measure them by their mistakes. I see past them. I see their greatness. I see their strength. I see their weakness. I see their potential even when they don't. I see the greatness that they possess. People might put me in that box of falling in love with something that I want to see... I disagree. However, what I will say is that an ALICIA in love... does fall in love with potential... I FUCKING LOVE LOVING~ and I give it freely. I love that I see in someone what they were born to be.

I fell madly in love with Mari. I believed in her potential for growth and expansion. I fell in love with her potential for greatness. I fell in love with her gifts, her heart, her kindness, her gentleness, her weaknesses and her ability to cry in front of me. I fell in love with her ability to fall down, clean her scrapes and get back up. I fell in love with the way she could make me laugh. I loved how I could trust that when I fall she could pick me up and never consider kicking me while I was down. I fell in love with her spirit. I fell in love with her innocence. Yes I fell in love with her potential. I fell in love with her potential to hold this love and stand with me. *That* potential is less about me and was all about her. I was already in love with the person she is I just wanted her to see that she had the potential to be even greater.

What happens if she NEVER sees her potential? We can want so many good things for the people we love but in the end they are the ones who have to want those things for themselves. When you're with someone who's afraid of reaching their potential the best thing you can do for them is give them room to figure it out for themselves. When you're with someone who has no idea of how to reach their potential it's important to tell them what you see in them in hopes that they will believe it for themselves. When people don't believe that they have any potential and YOU are on a continual journey of development and evolution sometimes the hardest thing you must do is walk away and allow them to find that potential on their own.

So I decided that I would be patient. I would wait for her. One night we were having dinner in Santo Domingo and we talked about our age difference. We talked about our future. I shared with her my thoughts on growth and growing as a couple. I shared with her my concerns. We had a fifteen year age gap. I was constantly moving, growing into my writing, traveling and expanding spiritually. I was nonstop and I was afraid that she would be left behind. I told her that I was willing to be patient that there was no pressure for her to reach me or to be where I'm at.

Expecting her to reach me overnight is unrealistic. She had living to do. At that stage I'd already had a full life filled with experience. I did share with her my need to be in a relationship that felt like there was forward movement. I told Mari that I had no desire to move backwards... that I could never do that. As long as she was moving with me we would be fine. I shared with her my biggest fear... that I'd continue moving and get so much further ahead that she would be left behind. I knew that if that happened our relationship would suffer.

I was moving slowly in this relationship but you had many concerns. You worried about me giving my heart to this woman. You were afraid that Mari would hurt me. You believed that she was too young for me and you were afraid that she would get bored of me because she didn't know what she wanted in life yet. But I knew that I wanted to spend my life with her.

When I met her I knew that if I were a man I would have married her and brought to the United States probably in those first few months of meeting her. That's how crazy about her I was.

During that time we saw each other every three months. We were very honest with each other about our expectations and what we were willing to give each other. I was ready to start my life with her immediately.

I have been quiet since the moment she told me she loved me. I love you are words that come easy for ME. I love many. I love quickly. I love passionately. I love immediately. I love loving. I love being in love. When she told me she loved me I felt it... I felt her... that message was received soft and tender... like a kiss on my forehead... I felt her love for me... I looked at the words from that text message for a long time... I went somewhere else... I wanted to be close to her... I wanted to see her face when she said it... I wanted her to be in my arms when I heard it... I wanted to be able to tell her, Mariposa I LOVE YOU TOO... Mariposa TE AMO~

2009

She was scheduled to take the German language exam at the consulate for her visa. Mari was preparing to leave the country and the pain of it was unbearable. I did not want to get in her way. I told Mari that there was no way I could stand by while she did this. I believed that she was making a huge mistake. I could not imagine another person touching her, making love to her, kissing her. I could not imagine a man entering her. It was too much for me to bear. I had to step aside.

Letting go of someone you love is the hardest thing you will ever be called to do. But *that* is how we love someone unconditionally. It's doing what is best for *them*. It may not be what we want—but it's not about us. This decision to move to Europe was not an easy one for her to make. Not only would she be denying herself something that was such a part of her essence, being a lesbian. She was going to be giving up having the love of a woman. She would be losing me.

This was an opportunity for her to be able to provide for her *entire* family. She would be able to send money home. Sleeping with this man would save her entire family. She would be able to prepare documents for her brother so that he could leave DR. Then I showed up and made her question everything about that decision. We argued all the time. I wondered how she could face herself. I came at her with all my feminist talk about self worth and how this decision was like prostituting herself. I was worried about her. *"He could take your passport and keep you hostage.*

285

You don't even know what you're headed for? You don't even know this man." I came at her strong and very aggressive. I really had no idea what this decision was doing to her insides. She must have been terrified. I don't know what life was like during her day to day that would make her consider for a moment that *this was her only option.* There is so much value placed on having *things* in the Dominican Republic... having things and this desperation to leave. *As if life is so much better en el extranjero!*

Mari and I fought anytime she brought up leaving or said his name. I spent hundreds of dollars on calling cards letting her know that I did not support her decision to move to Europe. I did not understand her reasoning and rationalizations about how *this wasn't a big deal so many women do it.* I would be lying to myself I if said I was strong enough to be with her while she had to go through with that. So I ended our relationship. It killed me. I called Mari and explained to her that while I loved her deeply, perhaps this was not the right time for us. I told her that one-day we would be together again. But that right now I had to let her go. I told her that I wanted to be her friend. I knew that I would make a better friend to her during this time. As her friend I could get on a plane to Germany and be there for her. As her lover and partner I couldn't do it. NO!!! I'm strong... but I'm not *that strong!* I told her that I would rather deal with the heartache of us ending now so we could move into our friendship. We cried together for days.

The end of that relationship was unbearable for me. I was hyperventilating. Not many people will ever experience the kind of love that we shared. I did not want to let her go. The death of that relationship felt like it would never heal.

The breakup only lasted *two days... in true lesbian form we were back together in no time.* I did not want to live without her. We weren't sure how we were going to do this or how we could possibly make this work. All we knew was that we were going to figure things out—together. I told Mari that I was moving forward with my plans to relocate to Santo Domingo and that I would be there as soon as we finished the documentary. I promised Mari that we would be together forever.

It wasn't enough. I wasn't moving fast enough. She was growing impatient. Age does that... she wanted evidence that I was serious about us NOW! Mari began complaining. She was feeling hopeless. She stayed in DR for *me* and began second-guessing her decision. She was talking crazy about an exit strategy. She just wanted to leave the island. She believed that things would be better for her and her family if only she could leave. Mari believed that there were more opportunities in Europe or in any other country that wasn't Santo Domingo. I tried helping her get into a film school in Cuba. It was incredibly competitive.

When she wasn't accepted she became discouraged and felt rejected. All she wanted to do was leave. So I helped her leave. I made arrangements for her to move to Colombia, work with us on the documentary and go to school there.

July 2009

I couldn't wait to get to Florida and see my sisters. We were going shopping for the perfect ring. I was excited to share that moment with the women I love most in my life. We looked at diamonds, thick bands, thin bands, yellow gold, white gold and platinum. The ring I wanted to give Mari would be the starter ring. I wanted to buy her a new ring every year to show her how committed I was. I wanted to remarry her every year on our anniversary. That's how much I loved her. I was planning to propose to Mari on her birthday in Bogota. When we found the ring I was so excited. I was really going to do this. We arrived to Colombia. Both loves of my life were going to be in the same place at the same time — my daughter and the woman I love.

It was our first vacation together out of the country. I was just a few days away from the proposal. You and Renzo were going to be my best men. I was crazy nervous that day. I wanted to *give her my life* and that would be the song I'd propose to… *Para Darte Mi Vida* by Milly Quezada. *Para darte mi vida yo volvere… Volando en una estrella y en ti renacer… Para darte mi vidaaaaaa — yo volvere!*

The day I was going to propose I was a mess. I had never done this before. *How would I do it? Would I get down on one knee?* I decided that I wanted us to be dancing a merengue when I proposed. That's how we met and fell in love… we were dancing a merengue in DR. I imagined us spinning and spinning… and then at the perfect moment I would get down on one knee. Renzo made a CD for us to take to the gay club that night. She kept

288

kept asking me what was wrong with me that day. "Why are you biting your nails... que te pasa negra?"

"I'm fine. My head is filled with so many thoughts. I'm good."

I wanted that night to be special. I bought her a birthday cake and balloons. We invited her friends. You were present which made the night perfect for me. It was going to be a moment she would never forget. I approached the DJ booth and told him what I was going to do. I asked him to play the song for me. He told me that his system didn't play CD's. I was freaking out. He tried to find some other song for me to propose to. One song was about this guy seducing and sleeping with his girl. Everything he recommended was *so not* working for me. I was not going to propose to a *vallenato*. I wanted a merengue and I was proposing to a Dominican woman. HELLO!!!!!!! There was a theme he was obviously missing. I asked him if he had anything by Juan Luis Guerra. Thank God he did. It was the song... *Travesia*...

Now I had to adjust my plan. I'd practiced the entire proposal to *Para darte mi* vida.... I would have to just wing it... *when are you going to propose? During what part of the song are you going to do it?* Everyone kept asking me... I told them that once the DJ started playing *Travesia* we all needed to be on the dance floor.

Como tu vida mia yo no encuentro en la tierra otra mujer... La e buscado... Camine por manhatan... Y llegue el empire state... Como tu no ay nadie en esta vida... Como tu no ay quien me comprenda... Como tu no ay ninguna...Para mi travesia... para buscar un amor igual que tu...no lo ay... no no no no ay nadie como tu en esta vida.

Then it was time. I looked at Renzo, he handed me the box. This was it! As my hands were trembling, as I was sweating... *Nadie como tuuuuuuuuuuuu.... jamas sin tu pedirme nada que tu me gusta...* I turned her... got on one knee... and asked, *Mariposa... tu sabes que yo te amo... quiero pasar el resto de mi vida mostrandote cuanto... casate conmigo?*

You *never* cry but I felt your tears on my cheek as I hugged you. You held me the tightest you've ever held me. *I wonder what you thought at that exact moment. How you felt about me wanting to marry someone.* You're entire life it has been *only* about you and me together. You're hug was so genuine. You were so happy for me. You were happy that I was happy. I could see it on your face. *How did you feel in that moment when you saw how serious I was about spending the rest of my life with someone other than you?*

It was such a beautiful night. We had so much fun. Everyone wanted to see her ring. We celebrated until the late hours. Renzo was so happy for us.

After the proposal, you wanted to leave Bogota. You didn't want to share me with her. You weren't having a good time. You had hoped that we would be alone more. The thing is that we were in a country where Mari was by herself. I didn't feel good about not including her in our plans. I wanted to marry this woman.

You could not stand that she was always around. I think after I proposed to her you had seen enough. You were ready to go.

All of it was way over the top. It was like a big ol' gay musical. I remember us talking about it. You have always been so supportive of every decision I've ever made, but this time you had reservations. I asked you for your blessing on my proposal. It was so important for me to know that you were on my side. You made me promise not to marry her right away. You wanted me to have a long engagement. After I asked Mari to marry me something changed in you. *Did you think you were losing me? Did you think that I was making a huge mistake? Did you think that I was somehow replacing you? Did you think that I was raising another daughter?*

You started to resent her. You didn't like that I paid for everything. You despised the fact that I bought her things for her apartment in Colombia. You didn't accept her as my partner. You didn't see it as an equal partnership. At that point in our relationship I believed that I was doing what people in relationships do. Sometimes there's *one* person in the relationship who takes on more of the provider role. I wanted to be supportive. I wanted to provide for her as long as I had the means to. I believed that I was in a better position than she was. For me that's how I viewed our relationship. I didn't see it any different than my marriage to your father.

When we were married I was always more of the provider and was supportive while he went to school fulltime. I did it all. I have always been the one who does it all.

You worried about me though. You worried that because Mari was so much younger than me that she would hurt me.

You worried that she could be using me. I think most people in our lives felt that way about my relationship with her. I didn't feel that way. I believed in her. I believed in our love. I don't think you even lasted a week in Colombia you couldn't wait to leave. I changed your flight. I felt horrible that you were leaving early and I stayed behind with Mari.

CHAPTER THIRTY-THREE ~*February 2, 2010*

When I got home from my Cuba trip you and I were having a horrible time together. We didn't like each other at all. Things between us were changing drastically. I would always joke around that for the first 16 years of your life we had a good run. For your entire life my parents, aunts and uncles would always say, *con esa tu la va pagar toda!* They told me that I would pay for everything I had ever done—with you. You would be my karma. That somehow you would be the payback for my being a bad kid. At least they hoped you would. You were bound to start messing up at some point. Having me home was new for you. You had spent so much time alone without me that it was hard to have to answer to me again. You were used to coming and going as you pleased. You had your own routine. When I returned I jumped right into my role and picked up where we left off.

You were not following the rules at home about calling me when I asked you to. You were coming home past curfew. I felt incredibly disrespected. You were beyond testing me. I didn't even know what to do with you. You were answering me back. We were knocking heads at every turn and I wanted to knock you the fuck out. With everything that was going on between us I still allowed you to have your space and independence. You asked me if you could throw a party one weekend and I allowed it. I even slept at la Chicana's house so you would have a good time.

After the infamous party I sat in our house completely devastated. Your computer was stolen along with my backup drive and a bunch of other shit. Who ever you invited went shopping. You expected me to not make a big deal about it. I had to ask you to leave the apartment that morning when I couldn't find the computer. I wanted to put my hands on you. I was going to fuck you up. I ended up putting a hole in the bathroom door. I was incredibly upset about losing everything that I had written for over two years.

This WAS a big deal to me. It was ALL of my work for the documentary, as well as, over 100 pages written for the *Daughters of the Revolution*. They stole everything. At the time I was working on your computer and moved everything onto your laptop and I backed everything up. Not only did they steal your computer but they took all of the originals and the back up. I wanted to die. I wanted to kill the little mothafucker's. This was all my writings, my blogs, the notes and research for my novel, and the scripts for the documentary. All of my work was gone.

There are images on that laptop. They stole all my Cuba stuff... my work... my words. My chest was incredibly tight—I felt terrible. When I sent you out of the house... I sent you on the hunt. It was your job to get in touch with the 35 heads you had in our house for your party of the year. I just kept praying that you would walk into our house with the laptop and hard drive. I was hoping that nothing was deleted. I prayed that it hadn't been sold. *Please creator let it be returned to me. Please creator let it be returned to me untouched--undeleted. Please creator...*

We were already having a difficult time in our relationship and this moment sealed the deal for how I wasn't sure that I could trust you anymore. I blamed you for it. I blamed you for being such a poor judge of character. I blamed you for allowing these people in our house. I blamed you for not being responsible with *our* things. While I was busy blaming you I was hoping that the person who took your computer would have a heart. I wanted the thieves to understand that what they stole was more than just a material item. *What they stole were works that were supposed to HELP the world. My work is supposed to HELP societies. My work is supposed to HELP the poor. My work is supposed to HELP abused women, gay women and children. My work is supposed to HELP heal racism and discrimination. My work is supposed to help release HATE and build community.*

WHAT YOU STOLE — was my VOICE! A voice that I've hidden behind words — in that laptop — backed up on that hard drive. YOU

295

STOLE the VOICE of words that are TO BE the voice of MILLIONS of people. MILLIONS... You didn't just steal from Courtney and I.

Although I felt hatred in my body and was completely consumed with rage. My thoughts were filled with venomous words that I wanted to spew and bodily harm that I wanted to inflict. I will leave NEW words. I forgive them. I forgive the kids that came into our house and stole from us. I forgive you. Up until this incident I have always considered you to be the most perfect child. I am sorry for hurting you.

Please forgive me for judging you. What you needed from me was compassion. This is one of the things I love the most about *you* how you have forgiven me countless times for hurting you in one way or another. All the moments where you have forgiven *me* for disappointing you and not being present. What you needed from me was forgiveness. How many times had I made a mistake? You didn't deserve to be assaulted by me like that. I'm sorry... and I love you.

Thursday, February 4, 2010

It's a few days after the computer mess and I was about to rush out of the house to go handle apartment stuff when I decided to sit at my altar before leaving. I needed to slow down and FEED myself. I always leave without eating. I needed get quiet, give thanks and be still. I needed to trust that ALL will get done. As I got quiet I asked the Divine what I needed before starting this day. *Do ONE thing at a time – DISCIPLINE.* This was my word for the day – discipline. Do my discipline. Do my morning practice. This is where I need to be in my sacred space honoring the day.

I needed to check in with myself. Every week I would do a weekly VISION check with my girls to see where we were all at with our individual goals. We held each other accountable for staying on task and moving towards our dream. When I looked at my week I realized that I had become paralyzed with the loss of the laptop. Sometimes it's hard to keep that smile on your face when shitty things happen. It can be challenging to be positive when you feel violated. That week I felt defeated. I didn't accomplish much of anything. I spent THREE days allowing the LOSS to drain me. I felt so horribly sad.

I did do my meditative practice everyday that week which *was* something positive. I spread out the pages of the *Daughters of the Revolution* to see where to pick up from and start again. So much of my new stuff for the novel was gone. You told me the greatest story that changed the way I was feeling.

"Ma, you know.... Green Day lost ALL their tracks when they were working on the last album. It was their 7th album. They had recorded every song for it and when they returned to the studio the masters were all GONE. Someone had STOLEN every track recorded. And you know what they did??? They went back to the drawing board. They went back into the studio and re-recorded that ENTIRE album. That album was AMERICAN IDIOT and it went triple platinum. So who knows momma??? This might be your best work yet!!!"

I guess that's the *real* lesson in all of this. Often times when things enter our lives disguised as the WORST possible event, the WORST possible moment... it might just be our most BEAUTIFUL lesson in disguise. We never did get the laptop back but I have you and your love and the story of the *Daughters* and *Afrolatinos* lives inside of me. So we will keep moving. Thanks baby for the reminder that my greatest work has NOT been stolen. It is still waiting to be born. I got nothing but time... time and the BEST daughter. Ache~

The Unfolding

I feel like for the most part I have always known what I want and who I am. I may not always know how I'm going to get there but I always believe all I desire will be mine. I believe that my life unfolds right on time. Mari was having an extremely difficult time in Bogota. She was homesick. She was broke. She had never been away from her family. This transition was not easy for her. I tried to be very supportive emotionally, spiritually and financially. There were moments that I would try to feed her positive words and she just didn't want to hear them. There were days that she just wanted to complain and feel bad about her situation. I didn't want to have any part of that. I didn't want to feed it. I didn't want go down with her.

All my positive spiritual messages were met with resistance and resentment. She didn't want to hear my, "JUST BELIEVE" bullshit. She wanted to feel bad and was making me feel bad in the process. I would support her in a lot of shit but putting down my spirituality and throwing back in my face the words I was sharing with her in hopes that it might help her—I could not accept that. I wasn't signed on for that. Talking about my spirituality is like talking about my mother... I reserve the right to say whatever I want about her... but anyone else might get cut.

I wanted her to realize her WHOLENESS~ I was on a path of spiritual unfolding. I thought that she was also. I wanted to have compassion for her. I wanted to be there to nurture her, comfort her, support her and love her. I never wanted to be her crutch. I needed to set aside my needs and understand that we all unfold in time... in OUR own time. I needed to decide how much time I was willing to wait.

We sat in your bedroom one day hanging out, talking and just laying on your bed. We talked about Mari and how discontented I was. I shared with you how my providing her financial support was hurting us a little. You had so many questions. You were angry that I was giving her money when we barely had any for ourselves. We were having some difficulty paying the rent. We talked about partnerships. "Mom, how long are you willing to wait for her? You deserve so much more."

"Look Court, I just want to be patient. I understand that she's not where I'm at and I don't expect her to be. I have almost twenty years of life over her. I want to be understanding and I'm willing to wait for her to become the woman she is meant to be."

"OK mom! Well *you're* almost 40! What if it takes her twenty years to get there? What if it takes her 20 years to figure it out? What if it takes her 20 years to find her purpose and discover her personal legend? Are you willing to wait that long? You will be 60 years old. And *what if* at that point she discovers that she doesn't want to be with you? *What if* the direction of her life takes her somewhere else? What happens to you? That would be like a waste."

"SHIT!!!! You have a good point. I don't know that I am willing to wait *that* long. Waiting a few years for her to catch up to me is one thing. But me being 60 and finally being able to begin my life with someone who's supposed to be my partner... I don't know that that would be fair to me. The thing is that I was aware of the age difference but there were some things that I believed she was giving me that were instrumental to the success of our relationship. I would never see my time with her as a waste. If she decided one day that I am not the one—I would have no regrets."

"Mom, you deserve to be with someone who's your equal. You deserve to be with someone who can give you what you give. You're getting closer mom... closer to having what you deserve. Don't settle mommy."

You gave me so much to think about but rather than focus on the relationship I threw myself into my work. I started working on an idea that I wrote about on December 25, 2009. It was a play called I WAS BORN. I was consumed by this story. So I began writing a one-woman show about LIA a journalist from the United States who travels throughout all of Latin America and meets seven women whose stories change her life forever.

I enrolled in a playwriting class at the FELT Lab to help. I was so inspired by the stories I'd heard from women throughout Latin America and wanted to write something that would pay homage to them. I wanted to give a voice to these women who are invisible in their countries. So while my relationship with Mari wasn't completely satisfying me I continued getting ready. I continued unfolding and moving towards my personal legend.

"It's not about making ourselves into what we think we should be – but unfolding into what we already are." by Iyanla Vanzant

There were questions I had to ask myself... *what do I need to do to reach my wholeness? How do I reach the fullness of my potential? What does it take? Do I know what I want? What do I want for my life? What do I want from my life partner? What do I want from my parents, family and friends? What do I want from my career? What do I want to be when I grow up? What do I want for my future? What do I want 1, 5, 10 years from now? What do I want today? Am I growing beyond where I am? Am I living my full potential? How do you grow into your highest, fullest and greatest potential if you don't even know what that potential is?*

There's was a time where I kept changing my mind about the kind of person I wanted to date, the kind of house I wanted to live in, the city I wanted to raise you in, what I wanted to study in college. I could never stick to one thing. I never finished anything. I could never be relied on. When I said I was going to do something I never followed through and when I did come through it was always late and I was always in some kind of trouble for it. I didn't know what I wanted. I always did what was expected and demanded of me (and sometimes failing was exactly what some folks wanted for me). I stayed in relationships that were all wrong for me. All because I didn't know what I wanted and I certainly wasn't living my full potential. I wasn't honoring me!!! Dishonoring me was the "in-thing" for a LONG time.

Later in life, immediately after the Twin Towers came down, after I dusted myself off from under the debris I realized it was important for me to get *really* clear. I began to focus. I wanted to hone my skills. I began to take *my self* and *my life* seriously. *Do I know myself well enough to answer the above questions?* It became about expanding my view of who I am and what I deserve so that I never find myself in limiting, uncomfortable, miserable and unhappy situations again. I finally knew what I wanted and who I was.

While reading *One Day My Soul Just Opened Up*, Iyanla Vanzant wrote that rather than *telling* God what I want. I should *ask*

God to *show me* what's in store for me. So everyday rather than telling my FORCE what *I want*. I asked my FORCE to show me what's in store for me. I asked daily for help in developing my skills. I asked to be guided and protected. I asked my FORCE to *use me* as a vessel. I allowed myself to unfold and I embraced the qualities necessary to arrive at where I want to be. To arrive at here I am meant to be.

CHAPTER THIRTY-FOUR ~ *My illusions*

Summer 2010

I was reading a book titled: *The Country Under My Skin*, by Gio-conda Belli and there was a line that jumped out at me, "My illusions of changing him into a happy man quickly evaporated. I was furious at the trap I found myself in—all because I had been so innocent, so romantic. In my terrible hurry to get on with life, I had married a man who longed to hide from it."

I went on to read, "It had never crossed my mind that a man could think he had the right to stop me from being who I was."

Mari wasn't stopping me from being *who I am*. I understood though that my presence in her life could have altering affects on the person she was born to be. I started to wonder if we aligned. I started to question whether or not we served each other in the relationship. I began to question my place in our union.

What does it take for a relationship to work? What does it take for a relationship to last? I started to think about the *illusion* that we can somehow make our relationships into what we'd like them to be. We fall into this trap that we can somehow change people. I strongly believe that when we love people we want the best for them and see the best in them.

I could not get Mari to see the greatness that I saw in her. I had no interest in molding her into the woman I wanted her to be. I didn't want to become that partner that constantly points out flaws. I did not want to fight with her about the place she was at in *her* life. It was her life to live. She was simply doing what someone her age does. Mari was learning. She was finding *her* force. I couldn't give her that. I couldn't show her how to do that.

You and I had a great conversation with my old boss from BusinessWeek about me, dating and finding a partner. He joked that I needed a woman who could take care of me. You both believed that I needed a woman who could provide for me. When he asked when the last time was that I went on a date, you responded, "Ask her when was the last time someone paid to take her on a date."

You looked at me and said, "When was the last time someone bought you something?"

You were referring to the fact that I always paid for everything. My response was that I couldn't remember the last time I was taken out but that I was less interested in that. I wasn't looking for someone to pay my way or support me economically. I told you both that I rather focus my efforts on becoming the woman that I want to attract for me. I want to be the woman that I want first.

305

We come up with so many excuses for not becoming the people we are meant to be. Mari had so many complaints about how hard life was. She held onto all kinds of excuses for not being where she wanted to be. When I think about our life—the many "what if's". What if we didn't move to NYC? Would I still be a writer today? I could have spent so much time complaining about how fucked up my life had turned out or I could change all of that and create the world that we currently live in. I could have made all kinds of excuses for not taking the risk and following my path.

What I've learned was that I needed to be willing to lose everything if I was serious about having anything. This included being willing to lose friends, looking stupid, falling, failing and getting out of my own way. Mari was getting in her own way and it was affecting me and I certainly didn't want to be another obstacle. Her unwillingness to grow was starting to get in *my* way. In honoring her I needed to honor me. I needed to keep getting ready.

God was playing a joke on me. The Divine was messing with me. We think we're ready. We think we're in control. We believe that we know exactly how life is going to turn out. There is a moment when you're just minding your own business and the universe throws you this curve ball that knocks you on your ass.

The NYCLWG had a performance at Camaradas on May 22nd 2010, in NYC. It was a beautiful event with incredibly talented poets and performers. It was hard for me to hear everyone's poetry because I was working the door. I was called to come up and perform. After I performed my *Quien Eres Tu* piece the last of the performers went up. I was taping the performances with a little camera, when this person started speaking.

The voice moved me. Literally I almost fell off the chair I was standing on. These words that I was hearing spoke of strength, pain, love, truth and courage. This spirit entered me with every word spoken. The piece was about a woman who had been molested, raped by her grandfather at a young age. I looked at Bloo and just gestured with my lips, "Who the fuck is this?"

No one has ever affected me that way. It was more than just the stories being shared and the beautiful poetry performed. There was a connection that only spirit could fill me with. I understood that I needed to pay attention to this blessing and gift standing before me. I knew that I was looking at God. I was looking at the God in me. And I fell in love with him in that moment. HIM! Seriously God... you sent me a man?

I had been an out lesbian over two-years and not once during that time had I felt any confusion about being gay. There was not a moment that I saw men in a romantic way. There was no physical or sexual attraction to men. I was done with men. Not because I hated them — but because I knew who I was and I was very comfortable in my skin. I was beginning a new life. I was

307

starting my true life. I was authentically becoming me and proud to be a lesbian. I was madly in love with Mari and then the universe puts this human in my path that would change the direction of my world. That next morning after the performance I remember emailing him that I loved him.

When Rock reached out to me on facebook I knew nothing about him. We had never met before. I had a writer's session a few weeks before the Camaradas event and asked all the women in the session if they knew this Rock WILK person. Everyone in the circle yelled, "of course we know Rock!"

I felt like I was the last to hear the greatest secret. Apparently, this Rock character was making a lot of noise in the poetry world. A friend told me that Rock was also writing a play about *his* life. I was immediately interested in meeting him because I too was working on a play. The girls spoke so highly of him that I couldn't wait to meet. It was like being around a bunch of schoolgirls talking about the boy in class we have a crush on. Rock and I shared a few words on facebook but I still didn't know him. In fact, I had never watched a single video of him or seen his pictures or read his work. I had no idea what he was about. When he asked me if he could come and support the NYC Latina Writers Group I told him of course come on through.

So when I met him, I was super surprised. I was talking to Bloo when this man steps to me and says, "Hi! I'm Rock WILK!!!"

"You're ROCK??? It's so nice to meet you." I gave him a hug and jokingly said, "I gotta go and collect money from motha-fucka's at the door. Catch up with you later!"

I don't know what I expected. With a name like Rock I was sure he was black not this short white Jewish boy.

He was *inside of me* from the moment we locked eyes. After the show ended you and I went home. Our cousins slept over and we talked about this guy all night. I wanted to know every-thing about him. I NEVER DO THAT! When I woke up he was my first thought. I wanted to see him. I wanted him in my life. I wanted to be close to him. I didn't want to do the whole... let's keep in touch thing. Not with Rock. I wanted him in my life permanently.

I called Mari to tell her about this man that I'd met. I went on and on about how inspired I felt by him. I told her that I wanted to get to know him. I shared with her that I was starting to feel things for him. "Are you attracted to him?" she asked. I told her that I wasn't sure what I was feeling but that I understood that the universe was sending me a gift in him and I wanted to ex-plore it. She asked me if I wanted to sleep with him. It wasn't that at all. That's not what I wanted from him. It was so much deeper than that. It was a spiritual connection that I had never felt with another human being. It was a connection that seemed to match my own. It was the closest to mirroring *my soul* than I have come. "What are you saying to me Alicia? Do you want to explore these feelings?"

"I'm not sure what this is Mari. All I know is that what I'm feeling is incredibly powerful and we always said we'd be honest with one another."

"Alicia, is this something you want to pursue?"

"I think I need to. The universe sent him and I want to honor what I'm feeling."

"I never worried! Alicia, *yo salia y volvia donde ti. Tu saliste y no volviste.* You left and never came back."

She wanted to know why it was so easy for me to walk away from us. She was furious that I ended things with her. We were engaged. We were getting married. I was going through so much during that time. I met a man that was bringing me everything that I needed in that exact moment. I was being fed spiritually and intellectually. The support I was getting from Rock during that time I had never received from another person. EVER!

I was devastated when she gave me an ultimatum and forbade me from seeing Rock. After everything we had been through together. I will never understand how she thought that threats would keep me. Leaving her was the most painful loss I've ever gone through. As I was going through my mourning period of losing Mari, Rock just stood back and tried to be there for me. He never tried to put pressure on me. He gave me the room to go through whatever it was I was going through.

I was questioning everything. *What was this that I was feeling for this man? What was this attraction? Why was he the one sent to me? What about the fact that I was complete? What about the fact that I am gay? What was this? What was happening to me?*

Mari was putting me through hell. As much as I tried to have a loving ending to our union she was devastated and angry. I was being pulled. I never expected that she and I would end. That was not the plan I had for our future. Meeting Rock was never a part of the plan.

This time... tu saliste y no volviste. Mari wanted to know why I chose to not return? Why did I leave her?

We were both sitting in a waiting room. She was waiting for me and I was waiting for her to catch up with me and be the woman that I needed and wanted at my side. I've been waiting for my life partner my entire life. I've been waiting for my equal. I was waiting for her to see the greatness that I see in her. I was waiting for her to create the future for us that I was planning and walking towards alone. I was waiting for her to get there. I was waiting for her to get it. I was waiting for her to have a revelation so that we could start a revolution. She was waiting for me at the airport to make it all better. She was always waiting for me. She was waiting for me to arrive, rescue her and save the day.

It was all wrong. I wanted to take care of her. I was not allowing her to take care of herself. We have to allow people to be grown. I wanted to protect her. I wanted to be her shero. I wanted to provide for her. I wanted to give her a life. I wanted forever with her.

We have to allow people to be grown. When I step in and do it for her I take away the good that is coming to her. When I am doing everything for her... what messages am I sending her... that I really don't

311

respect her... that she's not capable of doing it on her own. This is where resentment is born. I didn't want to resent her. I wanted to get out while it was still beautiful and virgin like.

Mari wanted a superhero and I wanted my equal. She was waiting for me to save her because that's just what I do. I save people. But who's here to save me? I've never been saved. Well you came in and saved my life on more than one occasion. But who throws me a life vest when I am drowning? As I write this I'm feeling a little nauseous my stomach is doing flips. This feels uncomfortable... there's this tightness in my chest. I feel very present in this moment allowing myself to go back and feel what I felt that day. I am feeling numbness in my arms and I can barely feel my toes. The tightness in my chest is making it difficult to get air. There's heat rising from my rib cage. This hurts. She will never know how deeply I love her. How this is destroying me.

I wanted her to be a force standing at my side going for it. I wanted the projects that Mari and I worked on together to change the world. I didn't want to be her mother scolding her for not doing what I thought she needed to be doing. I didn't want to be in a relationship where I would be criticizing her for not meeting her goals. I wanted us to transform societies and move people to do more. I wanted our work to mean something and to achieve all that we've ever dreamed of together. I wanted to be like *"yeah we did that – two women did that... two lesbian women... you doubted us and look we don't give a fuck what you think... we're still moving."*

But this dream doesn't work if it's just one person dreaming it. Mari needed to want it too. I am sad because I saw all of that in her. I saw all of that *with* her. She was the person in the audience when I won my first award, sitting right next to you. I saw us walking the red carpet at the Oscars sharing my acceptance speech telling the whole world how much I love Mari and how grateful I was for her support and love. I wrote her in my life, in my future and now I must write a new chapter where I am walking towards that revolution alone.

I didn't know what to do with everything I was feeling. I was a lesbian in love with a man and I had no idea what that meant. It wasn't as simple as saying maybe I'm bi-sexual. I knew I wasn't bi. I had no desire nor did I want a penis inside of me. The ending of my relationship with Mari put me in a really dark place. I was feeling a tremendous amount of loss. My thoughts were all off. The feelings were very familiar. This time it was the worst death I had ever gone through. I was falling and falling... there seemed to be no end.

The day I fell into quick sand was scary. It was dark. It was cold. The dirt was squeezing around my skin. I had just come home from volunteering at el Museo del Barrio. I didn't want to talk to anyone. I was in the middle of the horrible break up with Mari but I still managed to get up and go to work that day. I wanted to surround myself with kids. It was a welcomed distraction. Bloo picked me up from work and we sat in Central Park for a while talking and then she drove me home.

When I got home I just wanted to sleep. I remember telling Rock that I didn't want to speak to him that I just wanted to sleep the pain away. He left me alone. He didn't bother me. I was scheduled to have a spirit date that evening with a woman I wanted to work with but I wasn't feeling strong at all. I took off my clothes and fell asleep on your bed.

I knocked out pretty quickly. I was in a deep sleep and dreaming. I heard the doorbell ring. I jumped up. I didn't realize I had slept that long. I thought my friend was the one ringing. I went to the buzzer asked who it was. I heard nothing. I ran to put on my pants I didn't want her to catch me in panties. I went back to the door and opened it. I waited for a while and nothing. It wasn't her. My heart was racing. I was out of breath. I grabbed my cell to call Rock. I wanted to tell him about this dream I just had. "Hey Rock! How long have I been asleep?"

"Like ten minutes."

"Ten minutes??? Wow... let me tell you about this dream I just had. I was running and running and running and running. I fell into quick sand. I was being sucked in. The sand was covering my body fast. It was around my neck. It was over my mouth. The sand passed my eyes and covered my head. I only had one arm raised..."

As I was speaking I was out of breath. It sounded like a matter of life and death. It felt so real to me. I didn't think I was going to make it. Rock was so scared when he heard me describing this dream. I was suffocating. I was putting everyone before me. I was taking care of everyone but me. I was giving all of my love away. There was nothing left. I was completely empty. I was sucked dry. I felt like I wanted to give up. I was done. I was tired. I was so very tired and that's when he interrupted me from my dream state.

"Alicia!!! NO you will not fall. I will not let you!" No rope needed. With one hand he yanked me the fuck out. *Alicia you are important. Alicia you have a responsibility to Courtney, to Afro-Latinos, to I WAS BORN and to these women. You are a leader. You will not have a nervous breakdown. I will never allow that.*

In a writing session one of the writing prompts the girls gave me was, why do I have to save people? My immediate response in silence as I wrote was; *I want them to love me. If I save you then you somehow are obligated to me. You somehow owe me something for my kindness. No! That's not right. That's not it – that's what I expect... but that's not me. The love thing is real... of course I want love and to be loved.*

As I wrote those words they never felt more honest and true in my stomach and in my heart. I save people always with the best of intentions. I want to fix it for them. I want to be important to them. I want them to need me. I want them to love me.

Why do I have to save people? I guess I'm not giving people enough credit that they are capable of saving themselves that they can't get themselves out of it. I save people because I want to help them. I want to show them the way out it. I want them to realize their potential. I want them to see themselves. I have made myself responsible for showing them what I see in them and for them. But is that all about me. Am I seeing what I want to see or the person that I want them to be?

Mari wasn't ready for me. She was on *her own* journey trying to discover who *she is* and why *she's here*. It was up to *her* to figure all of that out. I was becoming a crutch and she was becoming dependent.

There were things that I needed. I needed help. I needed to be saved. I needed support. I needed a partner who could match what I bring. I needed someone to fly with me.

It was my turn to allow for someone to come in and rescue me. I could not get out of the quick sand alone. I needed help before it ate me alive. I needed Mari to be strong enough to carry me when I couldn't walk. So I chose me. I chose to not wait for her to change for me. I gave up a *virgin love* to love her in the deepest way possible. I allowed her to live. I chose to allow her to continue getting ready on her terms and with out me.

And Rock... well he came in and saved me. He came in and loved me through all of that. I have never needed anyone and he quickly became *just* what I needed. So to him I am forever grateful - grateful to have shared that moment and grateful that he was strong enough to be MYROCK. He wasn't going anywhere.

316

CHAPTER THIRTY-FIVE

Today's hug~
When you hugged me today
The nervousness was GONE~
Replaced by
familiarity
Safe
HOME
Emotions running through me
Every part of me
OPEN
To receive
Welcome
I SEE YOU
NEWEST LOVE
OPEN To the truth of this
And the truth is
that you are HOME
Anywhere where love lives is my residence
Of course we've been here before
Children always return home
This is where we're intended to be
I
love
you
loving me~
Something changed me today

A simple HUG
While DENIAL fly's all around us
TEMPTING
It spoke of
TRUST
Respect
Honor
Loyalty
LOVE
That's what I felt
I felt my friend holding me
Head resting on shoulder
At the crease of his neck
And it was home
It calmed me
Heart rate slowed
Pieces fall into place
DISASTER no where to be found
I smile now
I do love you
I'm not running
I'm not pushing you away
I'm standing still
READY
For the love you bring
Not scared
Let's share
Let's love
We are soul mates~
Friends for life~
I LOVE YOU~

We had a date at sunset. He wasn't present but I took him anyway. I invited Rock my favorite spot in all of New York City, my pier on 72nd and Riverside Park. We hadn't been alone yet. Most of our dates were phones calls that started at 11:00pm and ended at 6:00am every morning. We sat together as the sun went down and I played for him my favorite songs. We talked about everything. This was different than the other relationships. This felt like forward movement. This was deeper than that fantastical falling in love state. This was on some real shit. THIS WAS HOME!

He knew who he was and I knew who I was and together we were unstoppable. His grandmother told him that he needed to find someone who could deal with him because he *was a lot*. She told him he needed "Such a such a girl." She warned him that the girl for him would be someone incredibly strong that could match what he brings. And so he met his match.

Now all we needed was to get to the task at hand of understanding how a lesbian could be in love with a man and how he could love her back. From the beginning our relationship was incredibly complicated. His past combined with my past and our present—extremely complicated. How the hell were we going to make this work? One day you said to us, "Good luck on your twisted journey."

There's no place like home. We were connected for life. He made me feel comfortable and safe. Nothing like him and I—has ever existed. I told him once, "Do you realize most people NEVER get to feel this?"

His response, "Most people will never be brave enough to ALLOW for this type of connection. You and I have been very brave; we are connected for life because of that."

Good morning pages, I cannot deny that I am feeling amazing things right now. My thoughts are with Rock. I am attracted to him… that's the truth… I will not try and stop what I am feeling. I have to believe. I believe in this love. I believe in LOVE. Why am I trying to deny or prevent myself from feeling this? I have always stayed to true to me. I have always remained open. Rock, when you hugged me today the nervousness was gone. All my fears were replaced with a familiarity — like I'd been here before. With you I felt a sense of security that I have never felt with anyone. I was home for the first time. I am feeling so much right now. My emotions are everywhere. I feel him all over me. I feel every cell vibrate. I am open to receiving and being present in this newest love. I am open to the truth of who he is and why he is here. Love… is that you? Are we home? Anywhere were love lives that is my residence. Of course we've been here before this is where we are intended to be. And we are brave… no one has this… No one gets to experience a love like this… Loving you is easy.

Something was changing in me. Although I was filled with confusion, worry and doubt the truth of us was that the foundation we were building on was based on trust, respect, honor, loyalty, friendship, partnership, understanding, equality and LOVE. I met my soul mate. I wished that he had been *my first love, my first experience with a man.*

I never admitted before now, but all the men that *had* my body *took* something from me. It was hard to really *give* myself to Rock. From the moment we met we were adding amazing things to each other's lives. With him my heart felt so full — so alive. We would spend countless hours talking about love and loving. There is not a day we don't feed each other with encouragement towards reaching our dreams. We were defining love for ourselves. There were moments I was concerned about how I would

320

show up in the world being in love with this man. I was worried about what lesbians would say about me. Concerned more with what the women who respected me would say about me?

Those initial conversations about my sexuality were very difficult for us. This person is perfect for me he is about shit. He is kind and gentle. He's good for me. *He loves you.* He cares about everything that's important to me. We spent the first few months of our relationship trying to strip away everything that people expected from us. Our conversations were painfully honest. Yet the love that was shared between us was the truth. My life started taking new shape because of him. I was turning into the most beautiful butterfly about to take flight. He loves my stories and I love his voice.

The connection between him and I was unmatched. We knew exactly when the other needed the other. There were letters and messages that came in at the exact moment we needed to receive them. Rock and I talked so much about how we do shit at the same time... FEELING me... feeling him... feeling us... that was how connected we were.

The day of your high school graduation; what was supposed to be a beautiful day turned into something stressful. We got into a fight with your father, which made it hard for us to enjoy the day. Rock will never know how sad that day was becoming for us until he felt my sadness. Something made Rock stop and document the day with us. Something made him stop to fill us with love. There was no way he could have known that during the car ride to your graduation you cried making me cry because we have never known how to love your father.

We have never figured out why your dad does things that hurt us. *How could Rock have known how we were feeling?* While we was in that cab I was telling you how beautiful you looked and how proud I was at the person you are. But deep down I knew that it didn't matter how much I have tried to lift you... for your entire life you've only wished that your father would be the one saying those things to you.

No one will ever know how desperate I was to find the right words. I wanted to erase, remove and cleanse you of the pain you were feeling on your graduation day. As I sat in that car and told you that your life begins today. I told you that it was not your job to parent your parents. This new chapter was all about YOU! You would be starting at Syracuse. This was *your* moment not your dad's... not mine.

And like clock work and right on time we received a message on my phone from MYROCK.

she is ready
like sweet Papaya
her curtain raised
the most beautiful sunrise
this is her day
and you built this Taj Mahal
this Grand Canyon
this Jerusalem
Harlem
she is your world wonder
your Picasso
and today you.....

322

you are ablaze
rich
glowing
a cloudless sky
you are endless
onward and upward
a rocket ship
you are frontier
This is your day
Be STILL in this
BREATHE in this
close your eyes
be journey
Magellan
conception
new born baby
you crawl again
talk again
fresh sand to walk again
be THIS
be THIS moment
unidentified
so YOU name it
call it YOU
call it whatever you want to call it
hear it calling back
and LISTEN
like Bed Stuy church bells
Far Rock seagulls
Hispaniola
Rio Damajagua
27 Charcos
Puerto Plata
Santo Domingo
Merengue makes you dance
like Harlem
like Harlem
you are home
you are home
and so stop.......

and listen to the taste of your Papaya
she's Ripe
she's Aurora
she's Spring
You are a bouquet
you are delivered
you are arrived
you are one
This day is yours
This day is hers
This day is beautiful
Graduation Day, by Rock WILK~

He reminded me that we had so much to proud of. Together you and I have gotten through the most difficult moments of our lives. This moment was so incredibly significant. It had been 18 years of your life getting to this day. My beautiful daughter is about to fly for the first time. This is your life. I hope that I have left you with great lessons and that I have prepared you for the world. Our life truly has been about raising each other. Rock wrote me this beautiful note:

"Courtney just taught you to remove yourself so that you could watch from the outside in, see all of the love that comes from inside of you growing into another person, being all that YOU are, and over the years, becoming all the SHE is, ready to live her life now, with you forever, firmly planted inside of her, and giving you a part of you back for yourself. Saying, "thanks mommie, you did well, I am prepared to rock this [no pun intended... well, maybe a little], ready to change the world JUST LIKE YOU mommie...... just in my own, Courtney kinda way"

I was thinking about a baby picture I have with you in my arms. You were so little. I was still in a lot of pain because I had a c-section. I'm just holding you. I was a little jealous because I felt like everyone wanted to visit you and not me. But today I realize that they also came because of me. They came because I brought you into this world and they wanted to share that moment with me. My tears on your graduation day are joy filled and filled with sadness. You are so amazing. I am so proud of you. I love hearing you call me mommy. You are an incredibly brilliant woman. Courtney you are truly the reason why I know how to love as deeply as I do. You showed me how to love, you are the reason I was born and because of you my life is *all that it is and it will never be the same.*

There was so much happening. It was too much change all at the same time. It was hard to be happy because things were so fucked up. We were celebrating all of your achievements gradu-ating, starting college and I was maneuvering through my beautiful, complicated relationship with Rock. But the com-ments... I couldn't ignore the comments. *All she needs is a good man~*

Rock felt horrible about how quickly they accepted him and disregarded the fact that I am a lesbian. I was so angry at their comments. While the family was here for your graduation it was so painful for me. They all showered him with so much love.

325

And I was happy about that. But they only did that because he was a man. It made me question everything that I am and what I believed to be true about me. *Que desperdisio de mujer. What a waste of a woman. What she needs is a good man.*

The family was so happy that Rock and I were together. They were happy that I was with a man—any man. *What I needed was someone to fuck me straight.* I was so angry with them. They believed I was questioning my sexuality. They hoped I'd returned to the correct side. They believed that all I needed was the right guy.

They say that they love me. They say that they're supportive. They say they want the best for me. They pretend to love me when they only accept parts of me. What they love are the parts that *they* are comfortable with. They love me now because there's a man in the picture. They were happy that Mari was no longer here.

What they didn't understand was that I was engaged to her. I wanted to spend the rest of my life with her. They were the ones who are confused. Just because I love a man doesn't mean I stopped loving women. It wasn't that simple!

CHAPTER THIRTY-SIX

I was at the end of the playwriting class. I had advanced so much on I WAS BORN. Every week when the class met I'd introduce a new character. I remember when I introduced Clara, an 8-year-old from Chile who had been molested and raped by her own father and Mara, a 32-year-old Puerto Rican woman who self mutilates.

As I progressed I was developing the story of these characters at an incredible rate. I wrote about Caya, an indigenous woman from Colombia who was dealing with land rights violations and wanted desperately to preserve her land and history.

Everyone fell in love with Priscilla, a hip-hop artist from la Habana, Cuba who inspired women and gave them hope. There was Bella la bailarina, Veronica the lesbian and Milagros the prostitute. The facilitator told the class that she would be selecting works at the end of the session that were completed or close to completion. The plays selected would be a part of that year's staged readings. I had two weeks to complete my play.

Rock was pushing me hard. I asked him to hold me accountable for making my deadline and completing I WAS BORN. I needed to have the script to him by 5:00pm on June 23, 2010. I was writing everyday all day. I wrote from 11:00am to 5:00am the next day.

The evening before the due date at 10:18pm I was on page 108 editing the script. It was the second to the last character and I was editing for twelve hours straight. I was pushing myself hard to get to finish line. I wanted to quit. I was uncomfortable. My eyes were burning. I had backache. All I kept thinking was that *this* was too difficult, I wanted to give up and then I remembered that he DARED ME.

I DARE you to use all you are
to attend to your work everyday
in a very specific manner
to set goals
to rise above the circle you are currently living inside of
because there are greater things for you

My body hurt, my neck was sore and my eyes were having trouble focusing. I don't think I've ever pushed myself this hard. I don't think I've ever wanted anything so badly. I needed to push myself *beyond* the limits. I was pushing myself until it hurts. I pushed myself while on the brink of tears. I couldn't stop. I needed to push past my perception of what I can take and release those self-defeating thoughts about whether I have what it

328

takes. I learned that I could take so much more. I will push harder; move faster I will surpass the exhaustion.

It took every ounce of energy from my body, mind, spirit and soul to get to the end. When you push yourself you *truly* see what you are made of. The things I believed were *unattainable* are in the past. Those thoughts no longer serve me.

I wanted to thank him for pushing me. In those final hours I could feel his spirit and energy all around me. I felt him next to me. He was lifting me. He was rubbing my back. He was telling me that I could do this. I wanted to remember that moment. I wanted to acknowledge the fact that I was in so much pain and wanted to turn off everything—but I did not. I kept moving. I pushed even harder. When I finished editing the last monologue and arrived to the last lines of my first play I immediately wrote him an email... MET MY DEADLINE, KEPT MY PROMISE... I WAS BORN~

"I can't do it!" is no longer in my vocabulary... it's replaced by: I CAN'T FAIL! I WILL NOT FAIL! I WILL DO IT! I WOULD DIE FOR IT! I WILL HAVE IT! I CAN DO THIS! I BELIEVE IN ME! I WAS BORN TO DO THIS! I BELIEVE IN MY ABILITY!

"I'm tired!" is replaced with FINISH IT! There is NO time to be tired! MEET your deadlines! DO what you set out to do! Do what you say you're going to do! "I am exhausted!" turns into I still have a little bit more... SO KEEP PUSHING! How about the housework, the errands, the dishes that have been in the sink for two days after working 12-hour days? All excuses I've made to stop my momentum and procrastinate. Just FINISH IT... Finish what I set out to do. Finish what I start. The dishes will still be there tomorrow. The only thing we need to practice is perseverance, tenacity, determination, never quitting, working harder, commitment, effort, motivation, drive, achievement, goal setting, have a team, constant movement, work, endure, attitude, inspire, courage, ambition and challenge.

It takes great courage to wake up everyday and go after what you want. It takes endurance to be able to take whatever comes your way and still have the strength to move forward even when you're kicked down. Know that anything worth having requires hard work and many moments of working hard for what you want! I have been non-stop and I am not stopping. I am pushing myself harder than I ever have and this pain feels good. An incredible amount of commitment is necessary. Without it we're just full of shit and fooling ourselves. We have to believe we can achieve a certain goal.

It took everything that I was made of and shit I didn't know I had. That moment was pure exhilaration. I finished it. I got to the end of it. *I needed to remember why I do this. Why it is I want this. I needed to call up everything from my arsenal of truth. What made me want to write? Why must I write?*

You made me write. You made me a great writer. The first time I even thought about writing something it was for you. This journey has always been about giving you a gift. It's about leaving you with something to repay you for everything you've given me. I wanted my words to be with you always. I write because I can't imagine myself *not writing*. Writing is my voice. I don't need to search for it because it's already here.

Rock and I take turns giving each other mouth-to-mouth. He takes my hands and I take his. I say to him, "Bring your mouth to mine." He replies, "My mouth is open." I take a deep breath and breathe into him every good wish that I want for his life and then he sends it back to me. We do this a few more times. And after a few breaths my head is clear. I am calm. I am ready. I am open. I am present. I am this moment. I OWN this. I am LOVE. I am grateful. I am guided and protected. *Thank you for the air underneath me and for restoring my wings. I love you Rock!*

After spending so much time writing about the seven women from my play I laid in bed completely exhausted. There were things I wanted to say to him about thoughts I was avoiding feeling. There were things I wanted. There were things I needed. There were things that were too confusing to even begin to understand. I meditated so much on all of it. I prayed everyday that my feelings would change. I wanted to understand how I could love someone so deeply, how he could be everything that I would want and need in a human being but I could not get past the fact that he wasn't a woman.

As I was writing about the women in my play their voices spoke through me. The characters made me question the person that I am and how I show up in the world. *What do I stand for?*

Who am I? What are the issues that matter to me? Where do I stand politically? What did I want to be for him? How did I want to show up for him? What would I give up to be in this relationship? What I am able to give him without losing me? And what the fuck does it matter what the world thinks?

I was getting ready for my move to Bogota and we decided that we would stay together for as long as it made sense for us. We were good for each other. Whenever I would question our relationship I would push those feelings aside because I loved him. Like clockwork when I'd begin to question us I would get an email from him. He asked me to stop and stand still with him:

I feel you flying
shifting
twisting in the wind
you are a juggler
a magician on point
you are the homeland
you are the ultimate
but you are a carrier
you do the heavy lifting all the time
and so you know how to breathe
in and out
slowly
quietly
so you can hear yourself
because therein lies your truth
and you need to remember that
that you are perfect
you are exactly where you need to be
that everything is falling into place

in precisely the way things need to float down
so take a minute to slow it all down
right now
just for a few minutes
and watch is all fall like feathers
slowly
gently
and now the feathers turn into butterflies
like beautiful
brilliant
just like you
flying around
cascading luminous colors
you are centered now
you are focused
you are clear
you are in the pit of my stomach
the center of my universe
you make my heart beat
you are home now
take a deep breath
let it out slowly
you are HOME
now spread your wings again.....
and FLY~
I love you
YOUR Rock WILK

CHAPTER THIRTY-SEVEN

In the *Alchemist*, Paulo Coelho writes that *there will be a point where we will want to give up on following our personal legend*. There will be a point where it will be incredibly grueling, difficult, painful, unbearable and just plain HARD. These are the moments where we must believe. It *is* hard work and at that the exact moment when it hurts you must press on. You've got two choices. Do what you've always done and get the same results or take a risk and say fuck it! I'm going try it anyway and actually DO something NEW, something different and go for it.

We get so used to doing what feels SAFE. We do what's familiar. We do what we know. We do what people are used to us doing. We do the same thing everyday. When we do this we miss an important lesson. We miss out on NEWNESS of EVERY—DAY.

I am allowing my life to UNFOLD into what IT will become and not what I force it to become. The greatest understanding and gain for me, is that I know exactly what I came here to do. I feel myself changing. Today I started to think about my life and all the ways I've changed in the past 40 years. I went back to the days where I constantly needed to *see* proof that change was happening. In my past I believed that I needed validation and recognition for the changes that were happening in me. I was always looking and desperately searching for *that someone* to come enter my life and tell me how proud *they* were of me.

But today I feel different. I am different person. I *could* spend my life resenting the people who fed me words that poisoned me trying to prove to them who I AM. Or I can simply just be me and not worry about them. I am no longer waiting for those people to tell me *they* SEE ME.

People are funny... they say they want the best for you. Some people get comfortable with the mediocrity of things. When we start to show them something different. When we start growing. When we get better. When those things that they believed about us is no longer the truth of who we are... nor is mediocrity a sentiment we will ever settle for. They tend to become a tad bit uncomfortable and resentful about *"this NEW change"* in us.

Some people won't like it. Our changes will make people uncomfortable because it's like holding a mirror up and people are resistant. Today I look at my life and I notice the change in me. It's a good change. I am in no way perfect. I still mess up. But everyday I am expanding.

Over the past few years I have been on quite the rollercoaster ride one that has forced me to purge things from my life that were harmful to my health. There have been moments when my life was out of control? There are things that happen on this journey that are out of our control. I was trying to find balance. I've spent so much time healing and cleaning my wounds. I have been growing through some changes that have brought me tremendous understanding and clarity. These changes have served to teach me what it means for me to be a woman in this world. Afrolatinos has provided me understanding in what it means for me to be an Afro Dominican woman in this world. I WAS BORN has provided understanding about how everyone's story is important and how that story is a *shared* story. It's *OUR* story. I have gained understanding in what it means for me to be YOUR mother, a Latina, a lesbian and writer in this world and that there is an order to all of it that I have nothing to do with.

I needed to get my stuff in order. Ordering my writers life was crucial to my success. This is why I was able to finish I WAS BORN. I needed to teach myself to plan and order my day. I needed to commit to one thing at a time. I needed to learn how to complete large projects without allowing distractions to consume me. I was so proud at how hard I worked to complete I WAS BORN. I was ecstatic when the play was selected by the playwriting teacher for a reading. Only three plays were chosen and I got my own night. Everyone that I loved was there. The theatre was completely full to capacity. It was the first time I had ever heard my words read. I sat back as my spirit sister delivered each line and told the story of these seven women brilliantly. She gave birth to them that night. Their stories were no longer kept quiet. The actor was amazing. I was so proud of

336

her for being brave enough to share their story with the world. I watched her in awe.

In that moment, *I WAS BORN*... something changed in me... something shifted. I could feel how uncomfortable the audience was. The response to the work was beautiful. I was so grateful to be able to share that experience with that first group of people. You were there. Our entire family was there. Rock was there. My friends, confidants and sisters were there. I will always carry that moment. After that performance I decided to workshop the play. I envisioned having seven women each performing the entire play. We had a casting call but it was very difficult to find seven actors, so I settled for five including me. We were each going to have our own night to perform I WAS BORN on book (meaning we would have the script in front of us). We spent two months rehearsing for our October play readings. The girls were excited about having there own one-woman show to perform.

October 13, 2010

During yoga my neck was in a lot of pain. It was hard to breathe. I was thinking a lot about my problems, financial matters and everything that I needed to get done. I was trying to figure out ways to make more money. I tried to stop my thoughts... they were racing... *where do I go? How do I start? Who should I call? What do I do?* I knew I needed to meditate for the answer. I was

337

saying things like be still, clarity, release. BREATHE on the INHALE I used positive words like *INHALE peace. Exhale chaos. INHALE love. Exhale hate. INHALE strength. Exhale weakness. INHALE abundance. Exhale limitation.* It wasn't working. My mind was filling up with all kinds of things like *what about the rent, bills, food shopping, chores, responsibilities, travel, work, money, making money, stress... inhale... exhale... release it!*

Have you ever taken the time to really feel what happens to your body as fear creeps in? More importantly do you know how to push it away? Do you know how to release it, how to get it out your body, how to get out of your own way? For me this morning my stomach was upset, as if something bad was going to happen. It was like a premonition of something terrible to come. I was felt like I wanted to throw up. I was distracted during my practice by so many thoughts of unworthiness. For every negative thing that would try to get inside of me I would remind myself that I have been here before. I have felt this before. This feeling wasn't new. This tightness in my chest was familiar. It was all a part of the, "prevent Alicia from achieving true greatness plan." I had to push past those negative thoughts just to get through yoga.

I got through yoga and still didn't feel like I reached that place where I could begin my day with clarity and perspective. I tried again. I went to a calm space... a safe place inside of me and asked; *what is it that I need? What is my body responding to?* The word that came up for me was WORRY. I am worried. I am worrying. I must release all worry. My words during meditation were, "*Uncover and unleash your best by worrying less.*" Here it was a direct message for me not to worry that *all* will be ok. Everything will work out. Trust that I am guided and protected. I needed to TRUST that we would be fine.

I focused on something else... WHY WORRY... Don't I always get myself out of a jam...DOESN'T MY FORCE ALWAYS GET ME OUT OF IT? Rather than worry, why not look for the solution. The other word I meditated on was *patience*. I am connected to a force greater than me. The people I have met, the lessons I have learned and everything in between has brought me to *this* moment. I need not WORRY. I can TRUST and believe that my blessings are manifesting and that all will be ok. I had allowed for our finances to get all fucked up. Things were not looking good. I was scared.

I finally found a job. I started temping and could finally catch up on my bills. Those first days of work I didn't have money for food. The girl I was going to be replacing invited me to the cafeteria to pick up lunch so we could eat at her desk while she was training me. I didn't want her to know that I didn't have any money so I joined her. Once up there I made an excuse for why I wasn't getting anything to eat telling her that I didn't see anything I liked. I was eating an oatmeal packet for lunch everyday. I saved my breakfast to eat at around noon so that it would sustain me. I was in and out of housing court making arrangements.

I believed that as long as I was making some form of payment everything would be fine.

Just when you think you're done growing, done learning, have got all the lessons down. BAM! You get knocked the fuck out. You weren't home this day. I was leaving to go to the court-house. This had become my regular routine as of late. As I was gathering all my stuff, looking for house keys, my bag, a book, my journal and a pen. I was just about to walk out when I no-ticed a white envelope sitting on our floor. There was nothing interesting about this envelope and it's not *unlike us* to leave shit on the floor unopened. *Something* told me to open up this white envelope. I bent down and picked it up. When I pulled out the letter I saw on this white form in big bold black lettering... **NOTICE OF EVICTION!!!**

I didn't tell anyone about the eviction notice. I didn't share it with you or anybody for a while. I only told Rock. I was thinking about all the writers in my writing group, all the young girls who inspire me and all the women who look up to me. I was thinking about all the people who don't really know me and how they think that my life is so glamorous and wonderful all the time. No one knew that there were days I didn't have money to buy food.

Over the past few year's people have said to me that they wish they had my adventure. But do they know all that we have been through to have it. Do people know the sacrifice that we've had to make for everything? I've had some women say to me,

340

"WOW I envy you. I wish I had your life. You're so lucky." *They want my life?* They have NO idea!

While I was walking to the courthouse I received a phone call from a friend who is an attorney. She was calling to talk to me about last night's performance of I WAS BORN. Even though I was dealing with so much heavy shit I still managed to wear a mask and be present for these girls who had worked so hard at studying and preparing for their individual performances. None of them had any idea that I was about to be evicted from my house. My attorney friend went on and on sharing her feedback and offered suggestions on how to make the show better. I thanked her for her thoughts. I shared with her that I was on my way to the courthouse to deal with a housing issue. She asked me if I wanted to talk about it. I ended up telling her the entire story. She made me stop. She told me not to go into the courthouse yet. She started screaming at me, "What do you mean you don't have an attorney. Don't you know that New York has laws that protect the tenant? What did you sign?"

She was telling me about all the things that I should have done and I just listened. First thing she said was that I needed to go see an attorney at the housing court. She told me to speak with someone and see what I could do and to call her as soon as I got out. I went to the office of court appointed attorneys and approached the counter. I had the eviction letter in my hand and the clerk just took it from me saying, "Let me see if you're on the list?" I was thinking, THE LIST what is she talking about? She dialed a number and I just stood there listening to her say, "Hi!

This is Jane from the housing court. Can you look up a name and tell me if she's on the list to be removed?" I just stood there in disbelief. "Her name is Alicia Santos." Right in that moment I just started crying.

"You're not on the list for today. When did you get your letter?"

"I just saw the letter today. It's dated October 6th."

"You had nine days from the date of your letter to pay what you owed or you would be removed from the premises. You are on the Marshall's schedule for removal on October 19, 2010."

At this point I was hyperventilating I couldn't catch my breath. She told me to go and sit down in the waiting area that an attorney would be with me shortly. When I sat down the attorney brought me a box of Kleenex and told me what I needed to do. Two attorneys later, I was told that my options were limited. They recommended that I file an order to show cause with the housing court but if the judge denied it that I would need to go to the Supreme Court and file an appeal to overturn the housing courts decision. This moment was hard enough without feeling completely demeaned and demoralized.

> *Dear Mr. Clerk,*
> *Did it excite you?*
> *When you spoke to me today*
> *In that way*
> *Looking down*
> *At me*
> *Making NO eye contact*
> *'cause according to you*
> *I'm*

of no value
My presence
A waste
Of your time
My reasons
Irrelevant
My issues
insignificant
Forms to fill
Done incorrectly
You called me
An idiot
Stupid
Careless
"people like me"
can't read
or follow
instructions
and I
well I stayed SILENT
quiet
because SEE
you sit
hide
behind your glass wall
and I.....................................
just wanted to reach in and TOUCH you
do you feel good?
Did it feel good to make me cry?
And its not that you have any power over me...
It's only that there is something that I need – FOR ME!
So I CHOSE
To stay silent
Because you see
It doesn't serve ME
To tell YOU
About YOU and YOUR LIFE
All the things I could say
And where you can go
I let YOU BE

343

I can see that YOU
are EMPTY
Yet I
the love
that resides in me
IS FREE
I AM free...
You are a clerk
Doing the same thing
everyday
Dreading
The people you meet
Never seeing
Not realizing
Disregarding
the presence of LOVE
that paid you a visit today
What's your career without it?
How's your life?
Who are you?
And me
Well I am HAPPY
As I am facing this legal situation
This moment too shall pass
My moments always do
Not at all affected by you
Yes I AM SAD
Perhaps a little broken
But MY LIFE IS FULL
I have love
And you
What do you have?
How do I see you?
Like this case
I face
closed~

DENIED!!! I went directly to the Supreme Court to their appeals office and was there for three hours filling out forms and writing out everything that I had done and agreed to pay on my case. They asked me if I wanted to wait for the decision and I did. As I sat in the juror's room I cried and cried. I spent an hour writing my statement.

I held my prayer beads and prayed that the creator would give me the strength to handle this situation. I prayed to every orisha and guardian angel. I was so scared. This felt so real and unreal at the same time. *How did I allow this to happen*? I had my head between legs trying to breathe. The clerk who was helping came by to check on me. He brought me a box of Kleenex. At 4:00pm, I went back to the clerk's office to find out the decision. I walked slowly to that office. When I arrived to the front door I took a deep breath and walked in. I stepped up to the counter and the clerk asked me to wait for a moment while he looked up the decision. When he came back he told me that my judgment was denied. I thanked him and left.

I walked out onto Court Street and didn't know what I was going to do. I needed to come up with $3,000 before the 19th or we would be kicked out. I don't think you understood the severity of the situation. This was not some easy fix for your mother. My prayers alone weren't going to get us out of this mess. We were on a list! This was not a good list. This was the list where the Marshall comes and puts a lock on our door. This list meant that we would never be allowed back in. Our personal belongings would be touched by complete strangers. It would not be handled with care. They would take our shit and put it ALL in storage. A storage where I was told most people can never afford to get their items out of because of how expensive it is. This was serious. This was devastating. I was completely destroyed.

I called a cousin and the only other person I knew who could help me out of this situation; my ex boss. He lent us the money and of course yelled at me for my poor management of money and supporting a girlfriend who lived in another country. He was furious that I wasn't worrying about you and our house. I just sat there and took it because he was right.

I went back to housing court the next day with a letter from him and the money I needed in the form of a personal check. The judge did not accept it. He denied me again. He needed a bank check or money order. My boss was leaving town. I would not be able to get a bank check from him. Now I was freaking out. There was no way that check would clear in enough time. I was on the phone with Kelly. I was a mess. This was it. This was my last chance to try and save our apartment. I had tried everything. I wanted to throw my hands up in defeat. I've LOST! I'm DONE! As I was crying she was walking to her bank to deposit the money in my account.

The very next day, October 15th, I went to court with the money orders. The judge then told me that I would be put on the calendar for October 22nd, at which time my management office would be the one to decide whether or not we could keep our apartment. All I kept thinking was that I was going to be packing our things. I imagined that we would be going back to

346

Florida. I figured that we would need to rent a truck and head back to *abuela's* house. As I was dealing with all this, it was the anniversary of the writers group the very next day. October 16th we celebrated our 4th year and it was also my going away party. I was scheduled to move to Bogota, Colombia on October 18th to finish the documentary. With all that was going on personally, the plans changed. I was too embarrassed to tell anyone what was really going on. I decided that the best thing for me was to stay in New York and get myself out of this mess. Actually, I had no other choice!

As my world was crumbling around me I kept moving. I attended a new playwriting session to further develop my script. This time I would be focusing on one character Lia. From the stage reading during the summer one of the questions posed was about Lia. *Who is Lia? We want to know more about Lia.* People wanted to know why these women in I WAS BORN, impacted Lia so much. How did meeting these women change Lia? Since Lia was based on my life and experiences I knew that it would require a lot more time and effort. It seemed like telling the stories of these other remarkable women came easier for me, yet when it came to exploring ME — not so much. There were things about Lia I wasn't ready to face. Lia's story was too heavy, too much, too close to home. I continued to rehearse for the last two performances of the play. I was scheduled to perform my own interpretation of I WAS BORN at the closing on October 21st. It was finally my turn to deliver this one-woman show. I would be standing in front of an audience and sharing the stories of these incredible women. I would be playing 20+ characters.

I don't know how I did it. I don't know where the strength came from to get me through that night. I had nothing left to give. As I stood there the evening of my show, everything went wrong, the multimedia and the music. I didn't care. I was incredibly weak and I was terrified. I was just barely hanging on. I gave every ounce of me. I gave all the love I have for these women. I just needed a little more strength to get to the end of the show. And finally, I did. I gave everything that I had in that moment. For the entire run I was the director, writer, producer, stage manager, sound and light person. It was so important to me that the girls have great shows. And they did. They had so much fun. Their performances were each so special. We all grew and learned so much.

The very next day I would find out if we were going to be evicted from our home.

October 22, 2010

As I sat in the courthouse I tried to have faith. I had my Iyanla book with me. I had my prayer cards with me. I called forth eve-

every positive message I had ever heard to get me through this moment. My angel Patricia was praying for me. All those in my life were praying for me. Abuelo and abuela were so sad to learn I was dealing with this and could lose our house. All they said to me was, "you've always been so responsible with your money what happened?"

Sitting there in the courtroom waiting for my name to be called felt like I was on trial. I looked around at everyone. I observed everything. There were people of all colors all walks of life. We were all dealing with housing issues. Housing Court has 75 cases per court session. They have four sessions per day. They meet five days a week, that's over 1,500 people in NYC, on a weekly basis dealing with what could be an eviction. In that moment I understood how someone could become homeless. Homelessness isn't about alcoholics and drug addicts. They are people just like me trying to do the best they can in life. Yet often its just poor choices that put us in these situations. It can happen to anyone. It was happening to me. I cried so much as I sat there. I had no idea how the judge would rule or whether the management office would accept my payment. As I sat there praying, I heard my name called, ALISHA SANTOS, "yes that's me." (Why bother correcting him — not the time or place).

"Do you have some money for me?" he said.

"Yes I do."

"I'm the attorney for the management office. Let's step outside and move down the hall."

I took a deep breath and followed him. We stood by a window and he spread out my file.

"It looks like you owe $2,983.71. Do you have the full amount?"

"Yes sir I do. I have that amount plus an additional $900 for next months rent."

He took the seven money orders from my hands and started writing down the check numbers for each of them. I just stood there waiting. When he finished he looked at me and said, "OK! Sign here—this document just says that you have paid the amounts owed. There's a balance of $.15 cents owed. But we are satisfied with your payment. We're going back into the court room now and you'll wait for the judge to call your name and give you a copy of this motion."

My attorney friend would kill me if she knew that I didn't read *that* document that I signed either. I looked at the attorney and said, "Does this mean that it's over? Do we really get to stay in our apartment?"

"Yes you have complied. You're good. This case is closed. Just take a seat."

I sat in the courtroom quietly allowing the tears to flow from my eyes. I was still praying. I certainly was not going to believe it until I saw it. Then my name was called... Alicia Santos, please step up to the counter. Your motion has been granted. You are dismissed. CASE CLOSED!

✳

CHAPTER THIRTY-EIGHT

I wore a mask for my daughter that we were ok. But we were one step away from homeless.

You were the one wearing a mask this time. You pretended to not be scared. You really believed that I was going to get us out of this one. This time even *my faith* was shaken. I was worried. We were almost going to be put out onto the street. We were two days away from that experience. My poor decision-making landed us in that mess. Things needed to change. I needed to get my shit in order. I understood that I was supposed to feel *all* of that. I was supposed go through all of it. That was my lesson to learned and after that moment I have never been the same. I am so grateful that we were able to save our apartment. I am so grateful to Kelly and my boss for lending us the money. I am grateful that my prayers were answered.

Prayer: Creador, thank you. Gracias a mis orishas, mis guías y protectores a mi derecha, mis angeles de la guardia. Thank you. For a while I didn't know if I'd make it. I doubted that I would really get through it. So much was thrown at me at the same time. There were moments I didn't believe I could get up and you creator, my force showed me the way. You showed me that I could. You showed me that I would get up. That I would not crumble. My force showed me that I would keep moving even with all the blows. I've been here before and will keep moving. I am so grateful for all the strength... for all the hard lessons... for all the pain... for all the love. I am grateful for your guidance and protection. I know that there is nothing I can't get through. I know that for certain now. So I thank you. I am so full. I feel like life is changing for me. Thank you.

Like Love~
we are 22 wonders of the world
living inside of 133 days
we are countdown
eyes wide open
and so we are present
we are a melting pot
but most people just can't digest us
we are stories that you tell behind closed doors
about things that have nothing to do with you
but for some reason
we are the most interesting part of your day
and so get a life
because if you do we will love you
because we are all of this
every last drop
in the end there will be nothing left of us
we'll be straws sucking air
that was so fucking good
we'll leave you wanting more
we are legacy
she is Susan B Anthony
she is Wyoming
Colorado in 1893
and I will vote for her
She is outer space
like Ellen Ochoa
She is Julia Alvarez

the most beautiful butterfly
She is Latina
unapologetically beautiful
but you can't objectify her
because she is the point
She is Margaret Sanger
and I am positive that she birthed me
she is John Kennedy
except that she is perfect
she is the status of all womyn
and she is a mother
they are Thelma and Louise
living in Harlem
they are white water rafting
they are climbing Mt Everest
but they also know desert
a quiet moment
She is HOME
and that's where her daughter's heart is
She is Picasso
Mona Lisa
She is Nefertiti
I am the Metropolitan Museum of Art
I am lunch in Paris
I am The Louvre
and so I am showing you how beautiful she is
she is sitting on a bench
on the promenade in Brooklyn Heights
she is lower Manhattan
she is brilliant
I hold this torch
she is the Statue of Liberty
at night
she is roses
petals floating in a bathtub
she is candles
she is eucalyptus
I want to inhale her
She is Gershwin
the saddest melody that makes you feel beautiful

FINDING YOUR FORCE

because she is off the richter scale
she knows how to move you

I'm the mothafuckin' transporter
and so we make the perfect couple
like hands traveling together over the Brooklyn Bridge at 1 o'clock in
the morning
we are strolling
through Central Park
The sun is rising
we're your perception
now you can change it
we're your epiphany
we march like penguins
we are walking home now
you can't come with us
so get a life
and if you do we will love you
this poem is not really about you
I'm using you so I don't have to deal with her leaving
and so this poem is about us
like 127 days from today
when a young girl is waving goodbye to herself
like that exact moment
she is 18
and now it's time for you
you have become the ring that I will never take off
I have become your wings
you already know how to fly
and so we are the perfect couple
like sometimes you just have to breathe
Just like that
like we don't owe anybody an explanation
like love
like that's it.
~by Rock WILK

354

We were at dinner when something happened. After weeks of him proposing to me everyday, something changed between us. There was a shift. Things got serious. Over Indian food and a game of hangman I said yes. The car ride was like being in church, as he drove down Sunset Avenue; we talked about marriage and what we both found to be the foundation of that lasting love. We were sent to each other. We were good for one another. We made a promise to each other.

Journal entry~ I was on the train on my way to him and in that moment I got incredibly sad. I miss her. I miss Mariposa. I miss her voice. I miss her laughter. I miss our dreams. I miss us lying together. I've given up on her. I have lost her. I want to return to the fantasy of us. Where everything was perfect... satisfying... progressing... slowly... but moving in the only way she knew how. The first time I smelled her hair I knew she was the one. It wasn't just her hair. It was her neck. Her scent. It was the ocean. It was the breeze off the Atlantic. She is the Caribe on the hottest day of July. It was heaven... purity... perfection... like that newborn baby scent... fresh... safe. I was safe. My heart was safe. It was virgin like. How her tongue tasted... the perfect kiss...it was a bolero... beautiful, a classic. We were the most beautiful love story. It was like she was the first person to have ever touched me. I knew she was perfect for me. I miss her so much. Last night I was surrounded by so many women... I miss a woman's touch. Where do I see myself... where do I see myself—feeling myself? I'm feeling myself pulling away from him. He gives me so many wonderful things but he isn't a woman. See the thing is... I see him in my present... but I am not dreaming a future with him as my husband. Although there are moments I want to say yes. There are moments I want to ask him to marry me. I miss the touch of a woman. I miss her. I miss being with a woman. My body craves it. It's who I am!

I began thinking about what I need for me and what I need to do. *Will he be ok with me not being completely ME? Will I be ok with giving up a piece of ME? Can I give up who I'm meant to be? Is this the kind of partnership I want to be in? Will I be happy?*

Rock and I were on the phone one night when he noted my hesitation in using the word FOREVER. I may not have been able to say forever but I knew that I wanted him in my life in a very real way — forever. I wanted to stay open to the love that we shared.

Yesterday, I felt incredibly heavy so much so, that I felt emotionally drained. I was feeling the death of some part of me. I felt like even in this most beautiful LOVE that he and I shared, it didn't matter how often I said *I am a lesbian* or how often he acknowledged it. I am still with a man... a wonderfully beautiful man. *Were we kidding ourselves? Are we living in denial?*

The truth is that THIS love feels more real than anything I've ever experienced. It's a mature love! It makes sense. It aligns with what I need. On most days he has everything I need in someone who could be my companion. *What is it that I want from Rock? What do I want for me? What am I willing to give up? What can't I give up?*

I wasn't being honest with him or myself. I wanted so much to stay here with him believing that my search was over. I was convinced that finally, I met the person who was my equal. I believed that *he* could give me everything I needed. He was every-thing that I've been looking for in a partner. He is perfect.

I stayed with him despite all the confusing moments we shared and he stayed with me through all of my pain. We stood together in love and confusion. I was standing in faith. But it wasn't the truth of who I am. I was pushing so much of me away that it was hurting me. Such an important part of me felt like it was dying. I started to feel like something was missing in my life. It was like I was searching for something. *Is it meaning? Is it purpose? Is it love? Is it money? Is it sense of self?* I was thinking about the person I once was. I was searching for me. Alicia was missing.

When I get like this Rock starts to worry about what it is I'm thinking. I needed to get quiet and decided to go sit in Grand Central. I was thinking about my relationship with this beautiful man. I was wishing us into existence. I was hoping that we would be something that we're not. Yes it's... comfortable... Yes we're home! We are holding on to each other for dear life.

What we gave each other was beautiful. Our love PURE! But it isn't everything that I need. We weren't giving each other eve-rything we deserve. We ARE worthy of love. We do love each other. I'm thinking about what brought us together... truth, purpose, strength, love, inspiration, passion, past pains, grief and understanding. We believe in things!!! I met someone who actually sees ME and I see HIM! As I sit here alone thinking about ALL that I could have... all that I deserve... it leaves me filled with promise.

He is the Brooklyn Bridge... the moon... magnificent... London Fog...
a love letter and a poem that will last forever. He lives inside of my soul
and keeps a permanent key. He is MY PERSON. This love was the
most beautiful sunset. He is the brightest sunflower. We are the best
burgers in town. I was finally HOME. We were at the end of dreaming
our future together. Forever would mean something different to us
now. MY SOULMATE... and I will love him forever.

you are so beautiful and so you shine,
you glow,
you illuminate everything around you
you are photosynthesis,
everything around you begins to grow,
you feed them,
you fertilize things,
they turn into flowers,
majestic, tall sunflowers,
they drop seeds,
and so it continues,
you started this,
you are light,
you are warmth,
you are the sun,
and thankfully,
every morning you rise.
~by Rock WILK

Prayer: Creator, today I write you a very special letter of love in gratitude for all you have given me... and for the life I know that awaits me. I am so grateful for the gifts of LOVE that you have shown me. I am grateful for the love you have allowed me to experience. Thank you for the ability to give my love and my self fully. Thank you for my ability to be vulnerable and allow my pains to be revealed in love. I am grateful for all the healing that has come from all the LOVE I feel... a healing that truly has been from the inside out.

Today I ask you to continue teaching me about love. I ask you to continue guiding me towards the mastery of love... to fill me with the kind of love that just pours out of me. I ask you to replace every lonely thought with all the LOVE promised to me... keep readying me... continue to prepare me for the greatest LOVE I have ever known. Bring me the love reserved for me... the mirror image of me. Una persona que me ame locamente... que todos los dias le da gracias a dios que yo naci.

Bring me a love like ALICIA LOVE... complete... from every part of me... when she's tired... when she's sick... when she's mad... when she doesn't always know the answers... when it's hard... when it hurts... when she's angry... let it be LOVE. I want to feel the fullness of that love experience... not a passing moment. I want to feel it flowing through me like the blood in my veins.

Thank you for every blessing in my life. In this moment I am renewed and filled with love, peace and tranquility. I am patient. I don't need to worry. I can continue to walk this journey knowing that love will find me. I don't need to search for it... its right where I stand... and so it is~

CHAPTER THIRTY-NINE

"I move in time according to Divine order" ~ Iyanla Vanzant

Letter: for My Destiny~ My Legacy~ My Daughter~

To the most beautiful daughter in the WHOLE wide world: TRUTH! I am really insecure about my success and my ability as a writer and when I am feeling insecure… well you know…you live with me.

"Whenever I am confronted with something I have done wrong, I usually don't lie. If we really want to understand why our children behave the way they do, we must take a hard, honest look at ourselves." – Iyanla Vanzant

There's a RIGHT way and a WRONG way to do things… and I know you would be the first to say, "My mother swears her way is the only way." Forgive me for passing this on to you. Be true to you.

"Some kids do what you say. Some kids do what you say do not do. But all kids do what you do." –Author Unknown

Baby girl, take from me all that is good, all that is great, all that is peace, all that is understanding, all that is patient, all that is accepting and all that is LOVE. Everything else that doesn't serve you… release it! Do the work to get rid of it. The words that I have said that have built you, served you, loved you, encouraged you, supported you – KEEP THOSE WORDS- - THOSE WORDS ARE MY TRUTH. I ask you to release every painful thing I have ever said to you. Don't carry it with you into your future. Please forgive me and let it go. I am so sorry baby girl for the ways I have hurt you and taken my anger out on you. I love you so much sweetheart. Thank you for always forgiving me. You truly are the reason I work so hard at being better, at loving deeper, at working harder, at striving further. YOU are the reason I will NEVER stop moving! Thank you for being my number 1. I adore you.

It's ok to be vulnerable. You don't have to be afraid. You can give of yourself. You are the most amazing person I have ever known. It's beautiful when we can find people to share our private parts with. For relationships to work it musts work both ways. The people we choose to grow with must be vulnerable also. Your VULNERABILITIES for me translate into truth. Don't be afraid to be vulnerable. Let the world see your heart. Don't shelter it. It's wonderful to find people we can share those things that make us hurt, to share our strengths and weaknesses. Don't hide who you are because you were born to stand out!

My daughter you will go through much on YOUR journey… all I ask is that you learn to filter out and remove the dead weeds (including people and situations) that I (or) you have planted in your garden and find YOUR OWN truth. In this letter I don't have to tell you what you mean to me because you already know. I see ME in YOU and you in me. I see how you walk with what I have instilled in you. I see all the gifts that you bring on your own.

You are my legacy. You are my destiny and nothing can change that! With love always, Tu madre

January 8, 2011

I am sitting at the salon under a hair dryer thinking about what today means to me. Tonight is a special dinner in your honor. All the people who love you will be stopping by to bless you as you head for college in just a few days. There are so many Courtney moments flashing through my head right now. The day you were hanging on my leg as I was washing dishes in Florida, sucking your fingers, twirling your hair, in your panties, as you smiled at the camera like my leg was the safest place on earth.

What am I feeling today? What's going on in my mind? What did I dream about last night? My dreams were filled with action. I remember jumping up—something frightened me. I'm sitting in this chair and the heat is singeing my eyebrows—LMAO.

I have so much to do today to prepare for tonight but I am surprisingly calm. Nothing is bothering me. I have a lot to do, but I'm not thinking about to-do lists or cleaning the house. I feel a little numb. I'm not happy or sad. I'm not overly excited. I feel emotionless... calm, quiet. I just flashed to an image of you as a little girl. Just for tonight I do not want to fight with you. I am not going to yell at you. You will do your thing. I will do mine. And we will get ready like we always do. I was just imagining you laying on top of me like you do... so peaceful and it calmed me. *What do I think about you leaving me? What do I think about you starting your new chapter?*

362

My beautiful Courtney, as you turn nineteen this year. I'm thinking, *man! I was around your age when I got pregnant.* During that time I thought my life was over. I was scared—terrified. I felt alone. I was unsure of what to do. I didn't know where to turn or who to tell. *Who could I trust?* My relationship with my dad and mom never felt safe. My home never felt like a safe place for me to confide my deepest secrets, wishes and dreams. And my boyfriend at the time was more afraid of your birth than me. A teenager, barely a woman, standing in that bathroom, him pacing, me saying, "I'm pregnant!!!"

Que hago? They are going to kill me. I hate kids. I never wanted to be a mother. I don't want to fuck my child up the way I was fucked up. Do I keep it? If I have this baby my life will be over. If I have this baby I will never treat her the way I was treated. She chose me to be her mother. She is the reason I was born. I was chosen.

The moment I accepted my calling as your mother, was the moment my life began. Tuesday, May 27, 1992 at 4:35pm, seven pounds, thirteen ounces, twenty-one inches long. My baby was born... and so was a mother.

I will never really know what *this* moment in *your* life feels like for *you*. There may be moments you will feel alone. Moments you won't know where to turn or what to do. Moments your faith will be tested. Moments you will question who you are and where you're headed. Keep questioning... keep moving... its all part of your journey. But never question this... I will always be here for you. Even when I'm gone... when I transition from this place... I will always be with you. I will always lift you when you're hurting. You can trust that I will be here. I love you.

Where there's the truth~ You know I'll be there~ Amongst the lies~ You know I'll be there~ I'll go anywhere~ So I'll see you there~ I'll go anywhere~ So I'll see you there~ I'll be there for you~ Green Day

January 12, 2011

I'm riding the train feeling like shit. I am one day away from taking you to Syracuse. All that I have ever wanted was for you to be happy. So only read this letter when you're feeling lonely when you're sad. Read this letter when you want your mommy near you. *My baby this is it... did you think it would be easy? Did you think it would be smooth – this adulthood thing? As you leave me this is what I want you to know:*

"The voices we need are so utterly absent, totally and completely missing... anybody who writes anything is writing a fucking revolution."
~ Junot Diaz

Start a fucking revolution! Those words have always stayed with me after I attended a discussion that Junot Diaz held in NYC for the release of *The Wondrous Life of Oscar Wao*. The Pulitzer Prize winning writer spent two hours talking about the stories that haven't been written and that are so very necessary. It made me look at what this silence means to me and how it has shown up in my life. Junot really inspired me to change how I see myself as a writer. His talk moved me into a new way of seeing myself as a writer and the words I put onto the page. He talked about the many reasons people are silenced and about the NEED to have our stories told. Junot talked about the dire necessity to tell stories that truly represent who *we are*. He stressed that the only people who can tell *our* stories are us. He talked about his frustration with libraries. That there were few books that represent us. I would say that the large part of this generation is permitting the world around us to dictate who we are.

This generation is filled with a bunch of cowards and I'm being nice here with my language—the word I'm thinking about starts with the letter "P". No one stands up for anything. Most people are hiding behind laptops and social networking sites. Where are the demonstrations? Where are the great speakers and leaders? Where are the groups of people coming together working towards having their voices heard? Where is our generation of Freedom Riders, Mirabal Sisters, Suffragist Movements, LGBT Movements, Black Panthers, Martin Luther Kings, Harriet Tubman's, more Oprah's, Malcolm X's, Young Lords, Dahli Lama's and Mandela's? Where is the Feminist Movement, Civil Rights Movement, Chicano Movement and Afrolatinos movement of OUR time?

"The voices we need are so utterly absent and completely missing..."

At all the schools I visit I end with a talk on the "Responsibility to Serve." I like to remind college students that they owe our countries, our people, society, and the world something for the education they receive. I remind them of the sacrifices that our families made to get here. You are part of this group now. As you begin this journey know that you have a responsibility to serve. I have spent the majority of my life thinking about the ways my voice has been silenced? All the ways I have kept myself quiet. I think you have a great opportunity over the next few years to FIND YOUR FORCE... to FIND YOUR VOICE.

I remembered an argument you and I had several years ago about integration. We had quite the debate in our home. You were on the verge of tears. I was making you so angry. It got to a point where I actually said, "you know what I'm against integration! Fuck integration!"

"Mom, tell me you're not really against integration?"

Our argument was about a blog post I read about the TV network BET. The writer believed that BET should not have a separate channel. That it was sending messages of being all for ONE race and not inclusive of other races. That having there own network was perpetuating segregation. So I brought up Univision. I asked you what you thought of Latino's having our own channels. You told me you were ok with it. My response was, "so if you're not ok with BET then you must be against the Spanish speaking networks?"

"It's different." you said.

"How is it different?" You talked about catering to a community who didn't understand the language... my rebuttal: "aaaaah but what's good for one is good for all." I had to explain to you why I was absolutely ALL FOR Univision and BET having their OWN networks. We continued this long conversation about integration. "Lets look at the major networks (and not the token Latina, Black or Asian correspondent). Let's look at how *we* people of color... are represented in the media (and please let's leave out Ugly Betty for a moment that just happened yesterday).

When you put people in a box separate from the majority... the people who are in the box are going to protect their own. We've always been in a box. On the outside, yeah a few of us have gotten out of the box and grabbed some crumbs on the way up the ladder, "passing for" whatever it is a person needs to pass for...to get ahead. I understand why it is we have had to create our own larger boxes on Univision & BET when we see that ABC, NBC and CBS aren't true representations of the people who live here in this country. Those of us in our little boxes have to create our own outlets, our own labels, start our own companies.

Lets be serious... turn on the TV not much has changed. Yes there's progress and yes I hope we get there in my lifetime. I am thrilled that Oprah started the OWN network. I completely support us and by us yes I AM talking about people of color... we must DO US... because waiting around for someone to give us crumbs will keep us hungry. IF YOU CAN'T FIND IT – BUILD IT!

You then asked me, "Mom lets pretend you're Jewish, you live in Israel, you read the torah. And in your bible you are told that the holy land is YOUR land. You are the chosen. What would you do?" Of course you were asking me how I would resolve the conflict between the Israeli and Palestinian people. You continued, "And the Palestinian's feel that it's *their* land because *they* were living there first. What's the peaceful solution to this problem?"

I must say you left me with my mouth open. I didn't know how to respond to that. You stumped me. All my thoughts were going to come from the place of survivor mode. I wanted to stand in my fighter's stance. My initial thoughts were to protect my own. My response was going to come from the mind of a broken/wounded girl, who's a lion protecting her cub, from a community who has been stripped from those who would like to keep us stripped of our culture, our music, our history and on and on... but I needed to get back to your example and question.

"Ok! I'm a Jewish woman raised with the belief that the holy land is MY LAND. And I will do EVERYTHING including murder to take it... and I'm getting this from a bible. OK I have to say baby girl you pose a REALLY GREAT question. How do I resolve this conflict?" After thinking about a response that would satisfy you I finally said, "I wouldn't have gone in and taken the land. I wouldn't murder the people who were already there. I would have wanted to live there amongst them. I would have respected their space, their land, their customs, their community, their traditions and their religion. I would have welcomed what they bring. I would have understood that I am COMING TO THEIR HOUSE... I would have come in PEACE! I would have shared the land." And of course we got into it – the religious issue and the years of war.

Finally after feeling defeated you said, "We will never be a whole people - - unless we integrate!"

I tried to bring you back to the topic at hand, which was BET and the only thing I could say to you was, "I know you don't like it. I know you wish things were different. Think about it... if Blacks and Latino's aren't being represented and are being kept from have their messages heard, their movies out, their books published then we MUST do it for ourselves."

You wanted to explode...and finally you just said, "we must get off our ASSES and do something to change it... it's not right!!!"

I was never more proud of you than in that moment. You stood up to me. You stood your ground. You held firm to your position. I was quite impressed. I had to give it to you... you didn't back down for a moment. You held on. Nothing could sway you. The fact that you choose, "Unity & Integration" to be your personal mission makes me proud. In that moment I knew I was raising a leader. I saw something in your eyes... a fire, strength and healthy rage. You have found your purpose, or one of your purposes... keep that fire burning little girl... you have found your mission. Give it your all and know that I got your back!

Where do I stand on integration? I feel that it's idealistic – NOT impossible – idealistic. I think it's very necessary. We have been living a way that doesn't work for too long. At the same time, I know what I'm here to do. I know what *my* purpose is. The issue of integration is not at the forefront of my issues to fight... not today anyway.

For as long as I can remember I *wanted* so badly to be "integrated" into the white community. Because to be white was to be accepted in society because anything dark skinned was not acceptable. That's just MY REALITY.

I will not integrate if is for the purposes of continuing to strip me of my culture, traditions and beliefs. At the same time, I don't support segregation because we know what the affects of this have been. If integration means that I can come as I AM... and BE ACCEPTED and RESPECTED for all that I bring...then I am ALL for it—sign me up. If you're telling me that to be integrated I'm not allowed in unless, "I can pass for..." then you can have it! Keep fighting to be heard my beautiful girl...

Finally, you just looked at me exhausted after over an hour of conversation and you surrendered saying, "Mommy you're not really against integration? That's just one more person I need TO convince." My reply, "no sweetie – I'm not against integration its just that right now I'm embracing who I AM, where I COME FROM and the beautiful history that's interweaved in my veins. I am discovering and honoring my Latino/Black roots. That's just where I am at - - but I'll get there. I believe that we will get there – with patience, understanding and love. In the meantime, get off your ass!"

January 17, 2011

It's my first day alone in our apartment. You are off. You are fly-ing. You are away at college. All morning all I've been thinking about is how my life has revolved around you. You have raised me.

My identity has been formed completely around being your mother. I keep thinking about how so many of the choices I've made has centered on how it would affect you. Today I wake up and see that this has all changed. It has been an emotional few days for me. I have tried so hard to just be excited and happy for you. But I can't lie. There is such a big hole in my heart and this is not a bad thing. The hole just means that I need to fill it with new things. I was put on this earth to be your mother. I have al-ways known that you are the reason I was born and that the reason you were born was to save my life. I understand that I was given a gift. It is a very special gift to be someone's mother.

It has been my job to protect you, love you, provide for you, guide you, teach you and learn from you. I understand that I was to answer *that* call and be the best possible mother I could be. I believe that I have given you the very best parts of me. I have given you all of me.

You truly are the most amazing human being I have ever met. And if I had anything to do with the person you are today, for that I am grateful. I am grateful to be your mother. I am grateful to have you as my daughter. I am not going to lie – I'm afraid. Now I have no excuses about why I don't do a certain thing. I don't have to be home for anyone at a specific time. I don't have to run errands for you. I don't know what I'm going to do with myself now.

I sat in a chair for ten minutes just staring into space thinking now what? What do I do with myself? I called you twice today, sent you three text messages… you haven't texted me back once. I miss you. I am not trying to take it personal. After all, I did raise you. You are a strong, confident and beautiful independent woman. I need to chill. This is your time to shine. I will adjust. I will let you go slowly but never completely. I will give you your space. Creator, thank you so much for getting us here… today is the first day of my life~

When I came home from dropping you off, something was left on my pillow. It was *Cielo's* box. It was open. There was nothing inside of it. As I put it near my ear it got louder and louder. She left me a letter…

Dear Alicia, someone I love died last night. I am incredibly sad and scared. What will I do now without my true friend? My box has been with me since the day I was born~ it has kept me from harms way so many times~ now I must to learn to live without it~

You've been here for me through thick and thin~ It's extremely sad to leave you~ You were the one constant in my life~ You were the one I could rely on~ You were the one who never failed me~ You were the one who never disappointed me~ You were the one who had my back… ride or die~

I never thought you would leave me~ But you have left me~ you're gone~ When those girls jumped me and had my hair wrapped around that pole you and my brother were there~ When men broke my heart you were there~ When women broke my heart you were there~ When I was hurting you made me smile and you were always there~ When I was hit you healed my wounds and you were there~ When I cried you wiped away my tears and you were there~ For every happy moment you were there~ For every sad moment you were there~ For everything you were there~

In my most scary moments you were there~ During the worst of my "learned errors" you were there~ When life seemed difficult you were there~ When I didn't believe in me you were there~ When my 4th grade teacher made fun of me you were there~ When I was lonely you were there~ When I was scared you were there~ When I was in pain you were there~ A part of me wants to hold onto you but I know I can't~ I must let you go~ You will always be apart of me I will never forget you~ I thank you for all you have brought me – goodbye dear friend – may you rest in peace~ May "the force be with you!"

Cielo finally shared with me the story about the moment she lost her voice.

I didn't speak because I was afraid that no one would love me... that no one would listen. I was afraid to be in this place alone. I wanted to feel valued, valuable and worthy. I wanted to feel worthy of love. What would it feel like if I was in this place alone? There was something I was resisting. I was afraid of speaking up and speaking out. I am ready to fight for what I believe in now. I am prepared to fight for all the injustices. Why did I lock my voice in that box? I didn't like the sound of my voice. What would happen if I let my voice in? It would be deafening? My voice would be beautifilled. My voice is full of love, truth and honor. What does my voice sound like? What does it feel like? It's moving. It inspires. It is a great force. It is hope, strength and power. My voice speaks for those who are silent, full of pain and invisible. Allowing my voice in has made me unstoppable. My life is transformed. Voice is my FORCE and we are invincible.

373

A few years ago you were in the shower so I had some quiet time alone with my thoughts. I noticed that I had something in my hand as I was going to sleep. It was a pen. I found it interesting that I was gripping a pen. When I noticed the pen I wrote something on the palm of my hand, "inner circle." You got out of the shower and got in bed with me. I slept with the pen under my pillow.

The pen is significant for me. It symbolizes truth, trust, faith and acceptance. It's my tool, it's my weapon and it's my armor. IT IS ME. The pen protects and defends my words, it consoles me when I am hurting, and it helps me to find the answers to the questions that plague me. The pen gives me strength. The pen is how I share my love. The pen is how I serve others. The pen is the vessel for my greatest gift.

CHAPTER FORTY ~ *July 26, 2011*

"Everyone comes into our life to mirror back to us some part of ourselves we cannot or will not see. They show us the parts we need to work on or let go of. They reveal to us the things we do and the effect we have on others. They say to us openly the things we say to ourselves silently. They reveal to us the fears, doubts, weaknesses and character flaws we know we have but refuse to address or acknowledge." Acts of Faith, Iyanla Vanzant

I heard about Iyanla Vanzant about 10 years ago when a friend gave me her book, *In The Meantime*. I read it on two different occasions, but you know how when you read something the first few times... sometimes you just don't get it until you're *ready* to get it. You don't get the messages until you are *ready* to listen and actually *hear* them. Well that's how I felt about Iyanla's work. You are either ready for what she's serving or NOT ready. I was so *not* ready twice.

Then I saw her on Oprah. I felt like I needed to meet this woman. She was an inspiration. I heard that Iyanla had a show on NBC called, *Starting Over*. On the show she was a life coach. The show was about six women who were selected to be on this reality TV show to help them make significant changes in their lives. For a long time I wanted to be on that show. I desperately wanted to START OVER. I would watch the show every single day and take notes. I tried to apply the teachings to my life. But I was never consistent. You told me on more than one occasion that I didn't need *Starting Over* to start over because

I was already doing it. I was already living it. I guess I didn't even realize it.

When I started writing the *letter series* I wanted to hold people accountable for what they had done to me. But that *changed* during the process of *really* looking at the words that I wrote. There were new words calling forth the things I wanted for my life. *The letters* were really about LOVE and FORGIVENESS. The letters were not only about a love of others but they were mostly and profoundly about a deep love of self. I no longer held anyone accountable for the things that have happened in my life. I love them all for what they brought me and take full responsibility for my part in all that I have endured.

What do I want to happen NOW... now that the letters are all out and this memoir is written? I want to keep digging. I want to keep exploring. I intend to take what I have learned and keep moving. I want to keep growing and loving. I will not stop. I am shedding the old and making room for the new.

What have I learned? I read once that all my relationships at any given moment are a true reflection of who I am. And if I take the time to really look at these relationships they can tell me who I was in that particular moment. There are so many things I repeated. There was a pattern. These relationships always taught me where I was headed. Some of these relationships became like the bags I used to carry to work. Do you remember all my bags? For such a long time I carried two bags to work. I carried my novel and hundreds of pages of notes, my laptop, journals and all the things that I *wanted* to do. I carried all of that and never got shit done. I was carrying so much weight. I was carrying my dreams. I did not want to let my dreams go. Then I started to carry only what I needed. I started to carry the dreams one by one. The bags are now gone.

I am staying for a while. I can and have left the past behind me. I no longer carry my luggage on my shoulder. I have no fear of seeing myself, knowing myself and being my self. I finally SEE ME. I am no longer searching for that thing outside of me to fill me. I know how to fill myself. I am finally HOME. These letters have been my suitcases. My journals and this memoir are the maps to my soul. What I have learned about me is that I am not in a rush. There is no one who has anything I need or want. No matter where I am and what I think I know about me and *this* process is that I must always keep getting ready. The only person I need to work on is Alicia. I don't need to worry about what anyone else is doing. I don't worry about getting there first. None of that is important to me. Nothing is more important than arriving when I am meant to. EVERYTHING HAPPENS RIGHT ON TIME.

I ACCEPT ME AS I AM! I love that this is my affirmation this morning. It's about taking what I have and doing as much as I can with it. These letters, this love letter to you and my entire life story is about acknowledging and accepting who I am and where I come from. The greatest gift I have received from this process is ACCEPTANCE. Acceptance of self... Acceptance of others... Acceptance of my TRUTH... Acceptance of the TRUTH of others... Acceptance of what IS~

With acceptance comes a tremendous amount of LOVE for me and for all those I encounter. With acceptance I am completely FULL. I am internally FREE. What I have learned is that it's really about maintaining what I have learned about me and making this my way of life. What I have learned is that all the conflicts and all the drama within me took me further away from the place I wanted to be. It took me away from all the beautiful things I want to attract in my life. The truth is I already have everything I need. It's been with me ALL along. *The FORCE is ME!*

What I have done is gone back so that I can move forward. I was ready to heal. I was *destined to heal*. I was ready to release the past. I have released a past that no longer has a hold on me. I am replacing all the lies about me with the truth about who I am. What I want to remember about this process is that I will not break. I am not the mistakes from my past. I have accomplished an incredible amount. I am not going to beat myself up anymore. I no longer feel guilt or shame. I'm done with those emotions. I am ready to live.

And part of that living is allowing our lives to UNFOLD. That's what my unfolding feels like for me. It feels like I am riding the highest wave. I am accepting every experience and every person that comes along on my path (good or bad) as all part of my unfolding. And while I am on this journey to fulfill my personal legend I know that there are things that are sent to me for this learning. Part of that unfolding is NOT overlooking those things that enter my life as blessings, lessons and teachers. We can't plan that shit. Things happen when they're supposed to happen. Things happen when they are meant to happen.

It's About Time!

"Mom, you've done everything you said you were gonna to do in New York. How does that feel?" You've told me many times how proud you are of me for accomplishing everything I said I was going to do. "Momma, I don't doubt you for a moment. I BELIEVE IN YOU!"

Words really can't describe how that feels to hear from your mouth. Knowing that I have you in my corner and having your validation confirming all the sacrifices, all the tears, all the pain – ALL THE PAIN we have been through together. It has ALL been worth it.

When I published my first story in *Urban Latino* you said, "It's about time!" When we had lunch at the Mexican restaurant and I told you that I was finally done with the memoir you looked at me and said, "It's about time mom! The memoir is for you. I fucking know your story. Finish Afrolatinos so you can write the *Daughters of the Revolution*. That's the story I want read. That's MY BOOK!"

The thing is baby God is always on time. Its funny I look at my life today. I'm not rich by society standards. But I am so rich in all the areas of my life. I have everything that I could ever want and I know that so much more is coming. A dear friend asked me how I was feeling about finishing my first book, "You must be on a cloud!" Me on a cloud...

What's interesting is that I am not on a cloud. I am feet firmly planted where I stand! I am not seeing anything grandiose. I am not pretending that I have anything more today than I had yesterday. I am GOOD. I am better than good. I AM FUCKING FANTASTIC! I am happy to be alive. I have everything I need. I have done everything I said I would do. I feel amazing. I have already left behind so much for you and for the world. Yet I know that I still have so much work to do.

FINDING YOUR FORCE

"No birthing of anything new can occur without the dying of the old."
~ *Marianne Williamson.*

After I dropped you off at Syracuse I knew that I needed to do some spirit work. That very weekend we were getting you settled into your dorms there was a spiritual retreat called *Visiones* in New York City that I really wanted to attend. This exact date and time last year I was in an incredible amount of pain after having come back from traveling. With all the blessings I was receiving in my writing career I was still not happy. I was lonely. I was scared. I was empty.

The most painful moment for me was when I believed and said, "I lost my spirit." I believed that someone had taken my spirit from me. I actually said that, "My spirit has abandoned me" and as I said those words it frightened me. It hurt me. I didn't know how to find IT or where to turn. While I was sitting in that spirit circle I wrote, "Why have you left me? Why have you abandoned me?" and the craziest thing happened. As I continued writing my force responded, "I have never left you. I have been waiting for you all along to touch me, to acknowledge me, to LOVE me, to feed me."

She was starving and desperately trying to shake me awake saying, "Where are you going ALICIA? Why are you looking outside when I'm RIGHT HERE? The force is *inside* of you. I am just sitting around waiting for you to come have some tea with me and begin our LOVE WORK again."

That first week of being in our apartment alone I found myself in a familiar place, hurting. I understood that my spirit was calling out for healing. I acknowledged that there was something going on right now that required my tending. I knew what I needed to do. So I reached

380

out to the facilitator of the previous year's VISIONES workshop to see if she would come do a retreat in our home, my spirit sister accepted.

The workshop was called *UNLEASH & RELEASE: Through the Power of Love*. There were eleven women present. It was a day filled with self-exploration and love. One of the things she asked us to do was write down one thing for 2010 that we needed to let go of. She wanted us to think about our greatest fear for 2010. What was the thing that caused us the most pain?

For me it was the notice of eviction. I wrote in my journal: *What caused me the most pain in 2010 was the fear of poverty, homelessness, and feeling that I wasn't good enough. The greatest fear was the possible loss of our apartment and facing eviction, the embarrassment and humiliation of it. I allowed for things to distract me. I was in relationships where I was taking care of them and not spending enough time taking care of me.*

Then she asked us to *see* ourselves at the end of 2011. *What do we envision? What do we want to UNLEASH?* She asked us to visualize an image of ourselves. What I saw was my spiritual circle. The image was of me standing in my freedom! When I stood in freedom my feet were firmly planted. I was standing in my greatness. I was standing in my grace. I lived in the importance of my work. In that vision I know who I am and what I am here to do. I saw that I AM important in this world.

WOW! Just saying those words carries a lot of weight. I AM IMPORTANT IN THIS WORLD! I looked so beautiful. I was dressed in white. My hair was out. My arms were fully extended and I was twirling like Julie Andrews in the *Sound of Music*. I was smiling and I was living in our house in the Dominican Republic. I looked beautiful, radiant, vibrant and strong. And so it is~ MAKTUB

FINDING YOUR FORCE

On a clear day rise and look around you
And you'll see who you are...
On a clear day
how will it astound you...
that the glow of your being outshines every star...
a world you never heard before
and on a clear day
on a clear day
you can see forever and ever and ever and ever..............
by Barbra Streisand

As I write this final chapter I have that song on repeat. Barbra Strei-sand is in the background my favorite singer of all time. Barbra has sung me out of some pretty dark times. Barbra has brightened so many of our days. ON A CLEAR DAY~ I see so much. I feel so full. I am incredibly grateful. I am so close. We have a memory for just about every song on *The Concert* CD. So this feels right to be playing our girl in this moment. Today feels like the end to me. It's the end of something special. We are at the end of this part of my story. This ending is what completion feels like. This is the end of a chapter not the end of our story. This is where I allow a part of me to die so that the new can be born. This is the beginning of a new a story... my *rebirth*. This is how have I've healed and become strong. This is how I have arrived to who I am today with everything that I am. I have allowed for every wound to be poked and prodded. Observed by experts and complete strangers. Allowing physicians to treat me like a lab rat. I've been running on this wheel for far too long. I have been tested to the maximum. I have felt ashamed, guilty and embarrassed for much to long.

For a long time I didn't want to feel any of it. I believed that it would make me weak. I say bring it. Bring it all back. I've allowed myself to feel all the pain again. *My FORCE is bigger than my problems and there is nothing my God can't handle. These words, my writing… this is my gift to you.*

This story isn't about me my love. It's about you. Life is not perfect. Our life has not been perfect but what I want to leave you with is that OUR story comes from a loving place, a place of strength and faith, a place filled with peace. I want to inspire people to reach for their dreams. I want to serve as an instrument of change. I hope this story serves as a way for people to change how they see themselves. This is the end of this life as I know it and the beginning of something new, something greater and something beautiful. And so it is~ HAPPY BIRTHDAY to US~

ACKNOWLEDGEMENTS

There is so much I am grateful for and so many people I must thank: Mis orishas, mis angeles de la guardia, mis guias espiritu-ales a mi derecha. My mother Carmen Alicia Anabel and my father Fabio Antonio Santos, I am grateful not only for the life you've given me, but for the love that only parents can give.

Mis hermanos Fabio Antonio, Yoslaida Mercedes and Fabiana Patricia so much of who I am comes from sharing my life with you.

Thank you to Emma Luz Diaz and Kelly Diaz Walsh for believing in me, for always having my back and for all that you do for us every day. To my cousins, Dolores, Eneida and Elizabeth, who have been there during my many transitions and transformations, for that I am incredibly grateful. To the Santos and Diaz families, my tios, tias, nieces and neph-ews, primos and primas you are too many to mention know that I love you. Jasmine Diaz my second daughter I adore you.

Daurys Esther Geronimo, with you I learned how to love. You are my Fatima. Thank you for your presence in my life. Te amare hasta el fin del tiempo~ Maktub~

Lalita LaMonte, my best friend you are constant light~ I love you~

Ernest John Aucone, thank you for the greatest gift and blessing I have received in this lifetime, our daughter.

Aurora Anaya-Cerda, thank you for being my first reader and editor and Jakira Torres I am so grateful for your friendship, support, encouragement and love always. I love you both.

Renzo Devia, you have been my partner, brother and best friend. Thank you for the opportunity to work side by side with you. I love you. Leo Fuentes, mi padrino. I am grateful we met on this journey we are starting a new chapter in my life together.

The New York City Latina Writers Group (NYCLWG), thank you to all of my sisters for being my sacred space to write and share OUR stories. I love you all. To my spirit sister Elisha Mi-randa thank you for your feedback, counsel and constant love. We are so grateful to know you. Marva Allen and the Hue-Man Bookstore, thank you for allowing Latina Writers to create in your space. Orlando Plaza and Camaradas, thank you for your constant support of the NYCLWG and providing us with a venue for countless readings, poetry events and the opening of my play I WAS BORN.

To my Kickstarter benefactors who are the reason I was able to publish my first novel. I share this book with you and am so grateful you backed me: Adrianna Mena, Alexandra Jones, Ariel Gore, Aurora Anaya-Cerda, Avigail Alvelo, Azarah, Bernice Sosa-Izquierdo, Bobby DeJesus, Carlos Sebastian, Carmen Mo-jica, Celiany Rivera, Cess Oliva, Chermelle Edwards, Christine A. Torres Sanchez, Dee Winter, Diana Noriega, Ebony Brown, Elisha Miranda, Elly Blanco, Elma Plac-eres Dieppa, Emma Diaz, Francina Osoria, Gabrielle Rivera, Groana Melendez, Gus Mar-tinez, Harold Taylor, Jakira Torres, Javier Enri-quez, Jenny Perez, Julian Gallo, Kait Moon, Mardeah Gbotoe, Maria Morales, Mark Anthony Vigo, Melissa Suther, Mohawk Kell-Yeah Greene, Myrna De Jesus, Nancy Arroyo-Ruffin, Natasha Lycia Ora Ban-nan, Nia Andino, Nivea Castro, Renzo Devia, Robert Oriyama'at, Rosemarie Reyes, Sandra Mila, Sofia Quintero, Sophia Tingle, Susana Caceres, Tamara Czyzyk, Vanessa Ross Aquino, Vanessa Vargas, Vilma Escobar, Yahaira Munoz, Ysanet Batista and Zomnia Lissette.

I am grateful for the authors who inspire me, Isabel Allende, Paulo Coelho, Marianne Williamson, Dr. Wayne Dyer, Iyanla Vanzant y Don Miguel Ruiz. The I WAS BORN cast, Meriam Rodriguez, J Skye Ca-brera, Jenny Perez, and Glenys Javier for bringing my words and play to life. I adore you. Kevin Belden and Luis Antonio Diaz Sr. although you are no longer with me you are both my constant sources of inspi-ration, creativity and strength. The circle of women who lift me, Marie Ward, Lindsey Bondlow, Nancy Arroyo-Ruffin, Maria Morales, Maralis Guz-man, Carmen Mojica, Gabrielle Rivera, Glendaliz Camacho, J. Seary, Pilar Rivera, Peggy Robles, Maria Rivas, Jani Rose and Nivea Castro. Thank you to every person I have met in the Afro communities in Latin America. Rock Wilk you are my person, MYROCK, thank you for constantly pushing me and being the air un-der my wings, I love you. Stephen O'Brien, wherever you are in the world I want you to know that you are someone sig-nificant in my life. Thank you for showing me ME! To the Aucone family, thank you for all you have done for Courtney and I - we love you.

To my McGraw-Hill Family, Patricia Hipplewith, I have no words for the unconditional love, friendship and sisterhood you have shown me. Thank you for holding me in prayer always, I love you. Margo Mitchell for you I will always keep it moving. Keith Fox, thank you for being so good to Courtney and me al-ways – we love you. Charlie Vazquez, thank you for being my partner in creating a space where our Latino/a and Queer Writ-ers can be heard. Bukola A. Jejeloye, my dear friend, thank you for keeping me grounded. To Gloria Rodriguez and the Dealmas Women's Collective, being apart of this spirit circle has changed my life thank you for helping me to find that sacred space in me. Enlightenment, thank you for pushing me to write the letters, the healing is ongoing. I love you.

My beloved Courtniana Aucone, you are my daughter and soul mate. Thank you for allowing me to be a writer, for believing in me when I didn't, for patiently waiting for me to finish editing this book to eat breakfast at 6:00pm, for giving me so much space to do this. I love you so so much~ If I have forgotten anyone know that I love you and am so very grateful for you~

ABOUT THE AUTHOR

Alicia Anabel Santos is a Latina Writer, Producer and Playwright. She is a New York-born Dominican who is passionate about writing works that empower and inspire women to find their voices. Currently, she is completing her historical fiction novel titled *The Daughters of the Revolution*. Her one-woman show *I WAS BORN* was recently selected as part of the ONE Festival debuting in NYC. She is the Founder of the New York City Latina Writers Group, of which there are over 200 members. Alicia has worked for renowned magazines *BusinessWeek*, *Glamour* and *Domino*, but it was an article published in *Urban Latino Magazine*, **"Two Cultures Marching to One Drum,"** that would change the direction of her life. In 2008, Alicia joined Creador Pictures as Writer /Co-Producer of its first documentary, **"*AfroLatinos: La Historia Que Nunca Nos Contaron*."** partnering with Renzo Devia, on a project that will change the way the world sees color and race relations in Latin America, Alicia lives in Harlem, NYC with her daughter Courtniana. She works as a freelance writer and activist against sexual and physical abuse towards women and children. She attended New York University and Rhode Island College.

To write or book the author for speaking engagements please email: FINDINGYOURFORCE@gmail.com

Sign-up for her newsletter at:
www.Findingyourforce.blogspot.com

Made in the USA
Charleston, SC
16 August 2011